SEEKING JUSTICE

THE AMERICAN SOUTH SERIES

Elizabeth R. Varon, Orville Vernon Burton,
and Warren E. Milteer Jr., Editors

Seeking Justice

*The Extraordinary Freedom Suits of
an Enslaved Virginia Family*

Daniel B. Thorp

UNIVERSITY OF VIRGINIA PRESS

Charlottesville and London

The University of Virginia Press is situated on the traditional lands of the Monacan Nation, and the Commonwealth of Virginia was and is home to many other Indigenous people. We pay our respect to all of them, past and present. We also honor the enslaved African and African American people who built the University of Virginia, and we recognize their descendants. We commit to fostering voices from these communities through our publications and to deepening our collective understanding of their histories and contributions.

University of Virginia Press
© 2025 by the Rector and Visitors of the University of Virginia
All rights reserved
Printed in the United States of America on acid-free paper

First published 2025

9 8 7 6 5 4 3 2 1

LIBRARY OF CONGRESS CATALOGING-IN-PUBLICATION DATA
Names: Thorp, Daniel B.
Title: Seeking justice : the extraordinary freedom suits of an enslaved
    Virginia family / Daniel B. Thorp.
Description: Charlottesville : University of Virginia Press, 2025. | Series: The
    American South series | Includes bibliographical references and index.
Identifiers: LCCN 2024060660 (print) | LCCN 2024060661 (ebook)
    | ISBN 9780813953441 (hardback) | ISBN 9780813953458 (trade
    paperback) | ISBN 9780813953465 (ebook)
Subjects: LCSH: Slavery—Law and legislation—Virginia—History. | Free
    African Americans—Legal status, laws, etc.—Virginia—History. |
    Enslaved persons—Emancipation—Virginia—History. | Freed persons—
    Legal status, laws, etc.—Virginia—History. | Actions and defenses—
    Virginia—History. | Trials—Virginia—History. | African Americans—
    Legal status, laws, etc.—Virginia—History.
Classification: LCC KFV2801.6.S55 S44 2025 (print) | LCC KFV2801.6.S55
    (ebook) | DDC 342.75508/7—dc23/eng/20250108
LC record available at https://lccn.loc.gov/2024060660
LC ebook record available at https://lccn.loc.gov/2024060661

Cover art: *Miss Fillis and child, and Bill, Sold at publick Sale in May 12th, Christians-burg, Montgomery County,* Lewis Miller. (The Colonial Williamsburg Foundation; gift of Dr. and Mrs. Richard M. Kain in memory of George Hay Kain)
Cover design: Hollis Duncan

For Elizabeth,
my companion in this, and in everything else, for fifty years

❖ CONTENTS ❖

❖ ILLUSTRATIONS ❖

Figures

Table

❖ ACKNOWLEDGMENTS ❖

I have benefited from the help of others at every stage of writing this book. Without their help, writing it would have been much more difficult and the final version much less complete. In researching the story of Flora and her descendants, I received valuable assistance from Tiffany Couch and the staff of the Montgomery County Circuit Court Clerk's Office; Wendy Taylor and Anne Borg at the Kent Memorial Library, in Suffield, Connecticut; Art Sikes at the Suffield Historical Society; Bill Sullivan at the Suffield Academy; Lee Hamberg and Pat Odiorne at the Southwick Historical Society in Massachusetts; Caitlin Jones at the Massachusetts Archives; Mary Johnson at the West Virginia Archives; and Leland Hanchett, who kindly provided me a copy of his book about Oliver Hanchett when interlibrary loan could not find one. In presenting the story in a way that I hope will satisfy both legal historians and general readers, I benefited from the questions and comments of Loren Schweninger; Kirsten Sword; Anna Suranyi; Nadine Zimmerli, my editor at University of Virginia Press; and the two anonymous readers recruited by the press to review the manuscript. I would also like to thank the Department of History, the College of Liberal Arts and Human Sciences, and the Office of the Provost at Virginia Tech for providing financial support for the publication of this book. And as always, many thanks to my wife, Elizabeth, who patiently tolerated my frequent disappearances into the past and always welcomed me back when I finally reemerged.

❖ A NOTE ON NAMES AND LANGUAGE ❖

As was often the case in the past, the names of many of the individuals who figure in this story were spelled in a variety of ways in various documents over the years. I have chosen to be consistent when I can be. Where possible, I have employed what seems to be the spelling employed by the individual him- or herself; otherwise, I have generally gone with the spelling most commonly found among the various documents in which their names appear. I have, however, retained variant spellings of those names when they appear in the official names of legal cases in order to maintain consistency with the indexes of court records.

In recent years scholars have wrestled with the language surrounding slavery. Slavery was a brutal system that traumatized many of those who were trapped in it, and the memory of that trauma still affects many people descended from its victims. In the course of my research on this and earlier books, I have often discussed my work with descendants of the enslaved people about whom I am writing. These conversations have led me to believe that what many descendants object to is using the word "slave" to describe particular individuals because to do so strips those individuals of their humanity and makes their status as property the defining element of their identity. I have, therefore, adopted the practice of using "slave" or "slavery" to describe the institution, generally, and its victims, collectively, but avoiding the term "slave" to describe specific individuals. I have also continued to employ the word "owner" to describe those holding slaves in recognition of the fact that, however inhuman it seems today, in that era those individuals exercised legally sanctioned real rights over the people they held in bondage.

I appreciate the insights of my editors, the reviewers of my manuscript, and the descendants of the families described in this book. Ultimately, however, the language used here is mine, and the choices made were mine.

SEEKING JUSTICE

Introduction

On September 15, 1851, Andrew Lewis came before the Rockbridge County Circuit Superior Court of Law and Chancery, in Lexington, Virginia, to request a delay in the trial of a suit in which he and members of his family were the plaintiffs. Ten witnesses summoned to testify on their behalf had failed to appear, and two of them, Lewis claimed, could prove "very important facts" to support the plaintiffs' case. Five of the ten had provided depositions, but the plaintiffs' attorney had informed them "they were so defectively taken . . . that they are not fit to be used on the trial." Moreover, Lewis had reason to believe that another potential witness, who had not been deposed, could also provide "very important facts." In light of these developments, Lewis argued, "the plaintiffs cannot go safely to trial without the afores^d. witnesses or their depositions." The court listened to Lewis's request and "on the motion of the plaintiffs" granted them a continuation. Such scenes were not unusual in the courts of antebellum Virginia, where cases often dragged on for years. What was unusual was that Andrew Lewis was Black and enslaved when he appeared before the court in Lexington.[1]

The histories of slavery and of race relations in the United States are long and complicated, and since 1619 Virginia has been at their center. It was there that Africans first reached the English colonies that would form the nucleus of the United States, and it was there that the White, English majority first faced the question of how to include Africans in their midst. Most, they decided, should be held in perpetual, heritable slavery. It was not an immediate decision, though. Slavery, as an institution, had vanished

in England, and initially no law existed in Virginia to sanction its resur-
rection. In the decades that followed, however, White Virginians quickly
adopted attitudes that condemned Africans and their descendants to a sub-
ordinate position in society and gradually enacted legislation to institution-
alize those attitudes in a system of race-based, chattel slavery.[2]

Not all of those first Black Virginians, however, were trapped in slavery.
Some seem to have shared an experience similar to that of hundreds of
White settlers arriving at the time. They were bound as servants to masters
who purchased the right to their labor—but not their bodies—for a defined
period of time. When that period had elapsed, the servants regained their
freedom and could begin working for themselves. Many, both White and
Black, remained poor laborers toiling for modest wages on someone else's
farm or plantation, but others, including a handful of Black former servants,
eventually acquired their own tracts of land and a degree of economic independence. Thus, the same decades that saw the emergence of race-based
slavery as an institution in Virginia also saw the emergence there of a small
free Black population.[3]

Similar situations came to prevail elsewhere as slavery spread through
the English colonies and the new United States. As a result, race alone was
not always the defining factor in determining an individual's legal status;
most Africans and their descendants were considered the property of their
owners and enjoyed no legal personhood, but others lived as free people
of color with at least some of the rights enjoyed by their White neighbors.
This, in turn, led some enslaved individuals to challenge their enslavement,
despite their obvious racial identity. Beginning with Virginia in the seventeenth century, colonies and states that codified slavery also established
legal procedures by which men and women held in slavery could challenge
their enslavement on a variety of grounds and, perhaps, gain their freedom.
These began as ad hoc measures brought under a variety of legal theories,
and different jurisdictions continued to employ different procedures in
such cases, but over the course of the eighteenth and nineteenth centuries what came to be known as "freedom suits" became more common and
more regularized.

Today, freedom suits stand as a stark reminder of a moral and intellectual paradox that lay at the heart of chattel slavery and an example of what
Ariela Gross has described as the "double character" of the enslaved.[4] In
order to operate efficiently as an economic institution and to buttress White

supremacy, slavery required laws declaring that enslaved, Black workers were property rather than people. Under such laws, the men and women held as slaves enjoyed no more legal rights or protection than any other form of property. They could be bought, sold, leased, given as gifts, staked as wagers, used to secure debts, and seized by creditors if those debts went unpaid. They could be exploited economically, physically, and sexually by their putative owners and had neither legal protection against such abuse nor any right to resist it themselves. They could establish families only with the consent of those who claimed to own them, and any families they did form had no standing under the law and could be broken up at any time by those with property claims to their members. Enslaved African Americans worked when and how they were ordered to with little control over the use of their own bodies and with no legal right to the fruits of their own labor. Even if they worked on their own during their free time, they had no legally recognized ownership rights to anything they might produce or earn. And if they ever seemed to challenge the safety of White citizens, they could be beaten, whipped, imprisoned, and even killed with no legal consequences for their abusers. Indeed, masters who killed an enslaved worker killer might even be compensated by the state for their financial loss.[5]

Yet in spite of their denying enslaved men and women virtually all the legal attributes of personhood, slave owners knew that this particular form of property was different. They knew that in spite of any alleged racial inferiority, enslaved workers were unquestionably human. Evidence of this fact lay in plain sight throughout the South. Slave owners interacted on a daily basis with the people they enslaved and came to know them as distinct individuals. They knew that enslaved workers could think critically, could speak intelligently, could perform mathematical calculations, could execute complex tasks in the field, shop, or kitchen, and, if given the opportunity, could read and write as well as a White person could. Owners knew that those they enslaved would bleed if they were beaten, would die if beaten too badly, and that they often died of exactly the same diseases that killed their owners and their owners' families. Most cynically, perhaps, male slave owners and their sons knew that they could have sexual relations with enslaved women; they could use enslaved women to satisfy their sexual urges without damaging their own reputations and could even augment their family's wealth by impregnating those women and selling or exploiting the labor of their own children.

In the face of slaves' legal status as property and the undeniable fact that they were also human, slave owners employed a variety of arguments to defend slavery against those who opposed it and against their own doubts about the morality of the institution they had created. They cited biblical and historical precedents to demonstrate that slavery had been sanctioned by God and had been practiced by all of the world's great classical societies. They employed modern science to delineate inherent moral and intellectual differences among humans and to demonstrate that these differences were visible in the shape of an individual's body or the color of his or her skin. Such differences, they maintained, naturally and unquestionably rendered some groups inferior to others, and they deemed slavery an appropriate status for those "lesser" beings. Enslavers even claimed that slavery served to improve the lives of the people they enslaved; it brought Christianity to heathens, learning to the ignorant, and civility to savages.[6]

By this same logic, slave owners' own identity as members of a race with "superior" intelligence and morality required that they enslave only those individuals for whom that condition was deemed truly appropriate. Thus, in communities that made slavery a defining characteristic of their economy and society, the laws that established its legal framework also defined who could or could not be properly confined by that institution and laid out the means by which, in theory, a release from slavery was possible for anyone who could demonstrate that he or she was not among those it was proper to enslave. In the antebellum South, this was the role of freedom suits. They provided a means by which White southerners could seek to demonstrate to the world and to themselves that the law guaranteed only the right people were enslaved.

This view of freedom suits as a corrective measure within a legitimate institution was fundamentally different from the logic behind more celebrated cases such as *Somerset v. Stewart* (1772) and *Commonwealth v. Aves* (1836). *Somerset* arose in England and *Aves* in Massachusetts; both cases were brought outside of jurisdictions in which slavery was legally established, and neither challenged the legitimacy of slavery itself. In these instances, the plaintiffs argued that freedom was the natural condition for all human beings—Black or White—that it could only be restricted through positive legislation establishing slavery, and that all such restrictions were lifted permanently when an enslaved individual moved, even temporarily, beyond the locale governed by such positive legislation. In the antebellum South, on the other hand, freedom suits started from the assumption that slavery was a divinely and naturally ordained institution but recognized that the humans operating that institution sometimes made mistakes. In isolated cases, an individual whose natural condition was freedom might mistakenly be held in slavery, and a truly just society had to provide a mechanism by which to remedy such mistakes and restore the rights to which that individual was entitled. Antebellum, White southerners believed this was the proper role of freedom suits. To them, freedom suits did not grant enslaved individuals any of the rights or privileges associated with personhood. Rather, they were a means by which to restore rights to those from whom they had been improperly taken.[7]

Enslaved individuals, of course, saw things very differently. They had little interest in the legalistic distinctions between just and unjust slavery. To them, freedom suits represented a potential route out of slavery, but in the antebellum South, it was not an easy route. Southern legal systems embodied White privilege in a multitude of ways and presented a host of what Andrew Fede called "roadblocks to freedom." Procedural rules restricting who could sue for their freedom and on what grounds, limits on Black testimony, and the complete absence of Black jurors, lawyers, and judges all hindered the successful prosecution of freedom suits. Despite these obstacles, though, thousands of enslaved African Americans initiated freedom suits in the decades between the Revolution and the Civil War, and enough of these enslaved plaintiffs won their suits to reinforce repeatedly among enslaved men and women the idea that suing for one's freedom suit remained a viable option.[8]

This was certainly the case for Andrew Lewis and other descendants of a woman known today only as Flora who was enslaved in Montgomery County, Virginia, for almost forty years before her death sometime around 1820. In the annals of the law, their freedom suit appears as Unis v. Charlton's Adm'r, 53 Va. 484, 12 Gratt. 484 (1855), and on rare occasions it continues to show up among the precedents cited in subsequent cases or in discussions surrounding the rules of evidence. It was also known as "the Pauper Case" in 1846, when a lower court verdict in the case briefly made news throughout the United States before rising to Virginia's Supreme Court of Appeals. Neither designation is widely recognized today, though. Few outside a small circle of specialists know anything about the case or the fact that its true significance has little to do with the rules of evidence. It was, however, the largest and most protracted freedom suit in Virginia history, and it offers a fascinating view of the tragedy and complexity of American slavery in the state where American slavery began.[9]

Believing that Flora had been a free woman who was kidnapped and sold illegally into slavery, her children and grandchildren went to court to win their freedom. Together, the plaintiffs brought four separate suits against their enslavers. The suits were eventually decided collectively, and as *Unis v. Charlton* they stand as one of the most extensive and most protracted freedom suits in American history. Ultimately, the four suits involved some forty to fifty plaintiffs suing three named defendants representing more than a dozen individuals with an interest in the case. Legal proceedings continued for thirty years, moving among five county courts in Virginia with evidence from witnesses in four states plus those living in Virginia; the cases came to trial nine times at the district court level and rose twice to Virginia's supreme court of appeals before finally reaching their conclusion in August 1855. In addition, the freedom suits spawned at least three other lawsuits as parties with claims to the enslaved plaintiffs sought to act on those claims before their validity had been legally established.

The suits also left an impressive trail of evidence as they wound their way through the courts. The bulk of this evidence originated in the cases' trial phase, and while the suits moved among courts in five different counties, most of the surviving material exists today in a single file included among the chancery court records of Montgomery County.[10] Their inclusion among the county's chancery records is as mysterious as it is fortunate. The charges in *Unis v. Charlton.* were criminal—trespass, assault and battery, and false imprisonment—and the cases were tried in criminal courts. For some reason, though, records of the cases were eventually filed among chancery materials. This is an enormous boon to historians. Criminal files from antebellum Virginia generally include very little material, often just an indictment and summons directing the sheriff to deliver potential witnesses to the court. Chancery files, on the other hand, often include a wealth of documentation. The file for *Unis v. Charlton*, for example, includes nearly one hundred pages of sworn depositions from thirty-four different witnesses.

Additional evidence from the trial level comes from two common law files, also in Montgomery County, from a record produced in Rockbridge County as part of an appeal to Virginia's supreme court of appeals, and from a variety of order books from courts of law and equity in Montgomery,

Giles, Smyth, Roanoke, and Rockbridge Counties. Letters received by one of the lawyers representing the enslaved plaintiffs have also survived, which provide a window into the legal strategy and the process by which one of the plaintiffs' attorneys assembled evidence with which to argue their case. And records have also survived from the appellate level. The cases rose twice to Virginia's supreme court of appeals, and the opinions issued there focused on broader legal issues that both explain the court's reasoning in these particular cases and set precedents for subsequent cases.

Making sense of this evidence, however, is complicated by a number of factors. First, the surviving evidence is clearly incomplete. There are, for example, no transcripts from any of the nine trials that took place. No one routinely produced trial transcripts in the courts of antebellum Virginia, and none have survived from any of the trials involving Flora's descendants. Sworn depositions have survived from many witnesses who were unable to appear in court personally, but no record has survived of any of the testimony presented orally in court. Nor does it seem that all of the depositions that were taken have survived. Numerous orders exist for the taking of depositions that do not appear among the surviving records, and it is impossible to say if such depositions were never actually taken or were taken but subsequently lost. Other useful documents are also missing. Court order books frequently refer to affidavits or bills of exception (objections raised by the parties' lawyers) presented in court, but in a number of instances the documents described cannot be found in the existing evidence.

A second complication lies in the fact that the surviving evidence is often contradictory or of questionable reliability. This is simply the nature of trial records. Witnesses in the cases often disagreed with one another, and like the jurors 175 years ago, modern readers struggle to decide which witnesses to believe. Moreover, many of the witnesses in these trials were elderly men or women seeking to recall events that had taken place more than fifty years earlier. Bela Spencer, for example, was seventy-nine years old in 1849 when she was asked about events that had occurred between 1781 and 1784. Finally, understanding *Unis v. Charlton* is complicated by the fact that all of the witnesses were White. In cases such as those brought by Flora's descendants, Virginia law declared that African Americans could only testify "where free negroes or mulattoes shall alone be parties." This means that many of the individuals with the most intimate knowledge of the circumstances underlying the suits were barred from sharing what they knew with the court, and historians have no way to recapture it.[11]

These issues have not prevented scholars from exploring parts of the story of Flora and her descendants. Recent studies of slavery and the experiences of Black women in New England by Catherine Adams, Emily Blanck, Elizabeth Pleck, and Kirsten Sword have shed light on Flora's early years in Connecticut and Massachusetts, while two writers in Virginia, Regan Shelton and Douglas Harwood, have offered partial accounts of the freedom suits brought by Flora's descendants. No one, however, has told the full story. This book is an effort to tell as completely as possible the story of Flora and her descendants and of the legal campaign those descendants waged in an effort to win their freedom. Because the story that emerges from the surviving evidence remains shrouded in such uncertainty, though, it is sometimes presented here in multiple, conflicting, versions. Where differing accounts of what happened were presented in court, they will often be presented that way here, and the reader can decide which version to accept.[12]

Despite the confusion and uncertainty surrounding it, the story of Flora's descendants and their legal actions needs to be told in full. Their story provides an important window into Black legal consciousness in the antebellum South and demonstrates the extent to which enslaved actors themselves participated in the legal process. Previous scholars such as Ariela Gross, Anne Twitty, Kelly Kennington, Kimberley Welch, and Dylan Pennington have shown that both free and enslaved African Americans often acquired an understanding of and appreciation for the opportunities available to them to improve their situations and even gain their freedom through antebellum southern legal systems.[13] Few have been able, however, to show the remarkable level of understanding and participation by enslaved plaintiffs that is revealed in the records of *Unis v. Charlton*. Flora herself seems to have understood her legal situation and may have tried unsuccessfully to challenge it in court. Her descendants then took up the effort and demonstrated a remarkable willingness and ability to work for their freedom through a legal system that was designed to frustrate such efforts. They not only understood how to initiate a freedom suit in the proper manner but also identified witnesses who could support their case and suggested to their lawyers strategies for utilizing the evidence those witnesses provided. And while they usually relied on White lawyers to make their case, when necessary, Flora's descendants took matters into their own hands; they appeared in court themselves, made motions before judges themselves, and even deposed witnesses themselves.

An examination of *Unis v. Charlton* also reveals the broad geographic extent of Black legal consciousness. Much of the existing scholarship concerning Black legal consciousness focuses on cases that arose in the Black Belt, where the enslaved population was large and more concentrated, or in the region around St. Louis, which bordered the free state of Illinois. In southwest Virginia, however, the enslaved population was never as large or as dense as it was in the Black Belt. Nor was southwestern Virginia ever part of what Anne Twitty called "the American confluence"—a borderland spanning free and slave states in which both Black and White individuals moved frequently within and between the two legal and economic worlds. *Unis v. Charlton* demonstrates that even in regions where slavery was less widespread, where free people of color were fewer, and where free states were farther away, enslaved people understood and employed the law in surprising ways.[14]

Finally, the story of Flora and her descendants provides further evidence of the critical role played by the oral tradition within enslaved families seeking a legal escape from bondage. Like the Queen family, whose legal battle William Thomas has described so effectively, the enslaved plaintiffs in *Unis v. Charlton* initially based their case on the successful transmission of an ancestor's story through multiple generations. Flora made sure that all of her daughters knew her story. They then passed her story on to their own children, and only the ability of Flora's daughter, Unis, to recall her mother's story and relate it to skeptical White officials in a convincing way enabled her to initiate the freedom suit that grew into *Unis v. Charlton*. Thereafter, family members' knowledge of Flora's story remained an important factor in the ability of their lawyers to argue their case and of historians to tell it.[15]

America today often seems as racially polarized as it was during the antebellum era. Modern Americans continue to debate the nature, significance, and consequences of racism and slavery in their nation's history and may never reach a national consensus on such questions. As it has done in the past, however, Virginia's history can again play a leading role in shaping Americans' perceptions of slavery and of the enslaved. *Unis v. Charlton* left an unusually rich body of evidence through which to follow the journey of an enslaved family as its members pursued their freedom through Virginia's antebellum legal system. They did so in spite of numerous legal obstacles and in the face of widespread racist assumptions about their character and their intellect. Despite these barriers, they battled on. Their story provides a rare window into one of the lesser-known aspects of American slavery and demonstrates the extraordinary determination and the remarkable ingenuity that enslaved African Americans employed in their quest for freedom.

New England Beginnings

September 16, 1825, was a Friday, and Unis Lewis had chores to complete around Seven Mile Farm. As soon as she could, though, she set out for Christiansburg, the seat of Montgomery County, Virginia. Seven Mile Farm took its name from the Seven Mile Tree, a local landmark standing alongside the "Great Road"—originally the Wilderness Road leading to Kentucky. The tree and the farm were, as their names suggest, approximately seven miles west of Christiansburg, and it took Unis a little over two hours to make the walk into town. Christiansburg was a modest village in 1825. At its center lay a public square marking the intersection of Main and Cross Streets. The courthouse, a two-story brick structure, stood in the center of the square, and the streets leading out from it were lined with small houses, shops, and taverns—many of them built of log. Fewer than four hundred people lived in Christiansburg, but as the seat of Montgomery County it was the legal and business center of a region with some ten thousand residents. This, and its location on the Alleghany Turnpike, meant that almost every day saw a significant number of people coming into or passing through town, but their number grew dramatically whenever the county court or the district court met at the courthouse there. Court days brought hundreds of residents from the surrounding region into Christiansburg to attend court, to conduct business, or just to socialize in the courthouse, shops, and taverns.[1]

Unis knew well the road between Seven Mile Farm and Christiansburg. It had been a major east–west thoroughfare in the region since before the American Revolution, and Unis had been walking it since she was a child.

FIGURE 1. Lewis Miller's 1831 painting of the Montgomery County courthouse captures the excitement and crowds of court day in Christiansburg. (Virginia Museum of History & Culture [Mss5:10 M6155:1])

Her mother had often spent court days working in a tavern that John Ditty operated on Christiansburg's East Main Street. She had been a cook there and may have brought Unis or her sisters into town with her to help in the kitchen. September 16, 1825, was also a court day, but Unis was not heading for a tavern and was not going into town to cook. She was bound for the courthouse (see fig. 1), where she planned to bring a lawsuit against Hannah Charlton. Charlton, the widow of James Charlton, was now the owner of Seven Mile Farm and of Unis Lewis, and Unis traveled to Christiansburg that day in order to initiate legal proceedings that she hoped would ultimately free her and members of her extended family from the slavery they had endured for decades.[2]

Unis was in her early forties in 1825 and the mother of at least three children. She had spent most of her life enslaved to James Charlton, Hannah's late husband, who had been a wealthy planter and a prominent figure in Montgomery County's public life. At least a dozen other members of Unis's extended family were also held on Seven Mile Farm: two of her three sons, her two sisters, and seven nieces and nephews. By most accounts James Charlton had not been a particularly harsh master; neighbors recalled that the enslaved people on his farm had been "kindly treated." But James

Charlton had died earlier that year, and his death seems to have been what prompted Unis to head for the courthouse in Christiansburg. Because Charlton had left no will, Virginia law directed that a court-appointed administrator would soon divide his property—including his enslaved property, among his widow, his heirs, and his creditors, and it was almost inevitable that the division of Charlton's estate would scatter members of Unis's family among those entitled to portions of Charlton's estate. In the hope of protecting her family, Unis went to court seeking to initiate a freedom suit.[3]

Freedom suits were a legal process by which Virginia and other slave states sought to balance White residents' fear of African Americans and their desire to exploit Black labor with their professed commitment to the principles of the American Revolution.[4] Enslaved Black labor had long been a central feature in the economy of Virginia. Settlers in what was then the colony of Virginia had begun to purchase captive Africans early in the seventeenth century and by 1705 had established a legal framework for holding Africans and their descendants in perpetual bondage. The American Revolution brought freedom to thousands of individuals who escaped slavery through flight to the British, but the institution of slavery had emerged from the war unchanged, and Virginia joined the new United States with a larger enslaved population than any other state. Virginia had maintained that distinction on every federal census between 1790 and 1820, and by 1820 it was home to 425,000 enslaved Africans or African Americans—more than a quarter of the nation's total enslaved population. Most of these people worked in agriculture, especially raising tobacco, wheat, and a variety of other crops, or in domestic service, but enslaved workers also toiled in the state's shipyards, tobacco factories, iron foundries, and a host of other nonagricultural, nondomestic venues. White Virginians frequently expressed concern about the presence of so many enslaved Black people in their midst and often wished they could be removed from the state entirely, but they seldom acted on those thoughts. They almost unanimously supported the institution of slavery as the most effective means of controlling Black Virginians and were unwilling to give up the profits they obtained from Black labor.

Slavery, however, could be seen as antithetical to the Revolutionary ideal of liberty, and White Virginians' image of themselves as the greatest defenders of that ideal required them to believe that only those with no valid claim to liberty were held in slavery. Thus, they developed a legal system in which freedom was the natural condition of White people, in which only

Black people could be legally enslaved, and in which individual Black people might win their freedom if they could demonstrate a legal basis for it. Enslaved people could do so on a number of grounds: they could show descent from a Native American woman enslaved after Virginia had banned Indian slavery or from a free woman of color; they could show that they had been imported illegally into Virginia after the state banned the importation of slaves for resale; or they could seek to prove that they had been emancipated through a deed or will that had not been honored. To make these claims, state law declared that "any person [who] shall conceive himself or herself illegally detained as a slave in the possession of another" could bring suit "for the recovery of his or her freedom."[5]

Providing enslaved individuals an opportunity to win their freedom did not weaken slavery as an institution. Nor did it suggest that White Virginians harbored any doubts about the legitimacy or morality of slavery. Indeed, as Edlie Wong, Andrew Fede, and Lea VanderVelde have argued, freedom suits actually reinforced the institution of slavery by embedding in the law a view of the world that recognized the existence of both "just or legal slavery, and unjust or illegal slavery." Success prosecuting a freedom suit did not challenge legal slavery as an appropriate institution for most Africans and their descendants; it simply recognized that a particular individual had been enslaved illegally and should be restored to his or her proper status. As VanderVelde noted, "Correcting the status of an individual mistakenly categorized has little impact on other master-slave relations." To White Virginians, freedom suits were not about protecting slaves, and they offered no recognition of any legal or civil rights held by enslaved individuals. Rather, they were a means of restoring to a free person rights that had been taken from him or her illegally. Moreover, as Wong pointed out, anyone who brought a freedom suit "had first to acquiesce to the idea of *just* subjection under slave law before petitioning courts for emancipation based on *wrongful* enslavement." Every plaintiff in a freedom suit, therefore, "risked affirming the legitimacy of the institution that oppressed them."[6]

In Virginia, freedom suits had arisen almost as soon as slavery had. Indeed, a successful suit brought by Elizabeth Key, in 1656, may have led to the passage of Virginia's first laws defining who was or was not a slave. Elizabeth was the mixed-race daughter of Thomas Key, a White planter, and an African woman he held as a slave or an indentured servant. After initially denying his paternity, Key acknowledged that Elizabeth was his daughter, and when he and his wife prepared to return to England, he left the six-year-old Elizabeth to serve a neighboring planter until the age of fifteen, at which time she was to gain her freedom. Thomas Key died shortly after assigning Elizabeth to his neighbor, and in the years that followed she passed to a new master who may or may not have known her history. When that master died, the inventory of his estate named Elizabeth among his "Negroes" rather than his servants, which suggests that she was considered enslaved for life. Elizabeth then sued for her freedom, arguing that, as the daughter of an Englishman and as a Christian, she could not be legally enslaved. After a series of trials and appeals, Elizabeth Key won her freedom, but in the decade that followed the House of Burgesses passed laws declaring that in Virginia a child's status would now follow that of its mother and that conversion to Christianity would not confer freedom on an enslaved individual.[7]

For more than a century afterward, legislation passed in the wake of Elizabeth Key's case helped to ensure that relatively few freedom suits arose in Virginia. No statute regulated the procedure to be followed in such cases, and those who brought them did so on a variety of grounds under common law. Then the American Revolution ignited a passion for "liberty" among many Americans and made opposition to slavery more common and more visible. A number of northern states enacted gradual emancipation laws, and throughout the nation antislavery societies appeared and expanded as never before. In Virginia both manumissions and freedom suits became more common after the Revolution. As they did, White Virginians grew alarmed at the growing number of free Black people and mulattoes in the state and by claims that antislavery activists were using freedom suits to undermine slavery in the state. This increased anxiety eventually led the General Assembly to take action. In 1795, Virginia lawmakers passed legislation to counter the "great and alarming mischiefs" brought about by "individuals, who under cover of effecting . . . justice toward persons unwarrantably held in slavery . . . have in many instances been the means of depriving masters of their property in slaves." The new law codified the procedure to be followed in freedom suits and imposed fines on anyone aiding or abetting the prosecution of frivolous suits. This was followed by additional legislation and judicial decisions that over the next thirty years made freedom suits ever more difficult to launch or to win. Despite these efforts, though, enslaved Virginians filed at least 174 freedom suits between the Revolution and the

Civil War and won many of them. Thus, while the legal hurdles facing enslaved individuals such as Unis Lewis were significant, gaining one's freedom through the courts remained a real possibility, and Unis was determined to do everything in her power to realize that possibility.[8]

Unis's story does not begin when she left Seven Mile Farm, though. It really begins with her mother because in the Virginia of their day freedom and slavery descended through the mother's line. Slavery, as a legal institution, had not existed in England when the kingdom established its first colonies in America. Thus, as enslaved Africans began to arrive in those colonies and as White settlers living there chose to keep them enslaved and profit from their labor, they had to develop new laws to accommodate this new institution. English law, for example, held that one's status and identity followed that of one's father, but as free White settlers and White indentured servants began fathering mixed-race children, such as Elizabeth Key, by enslaved Black women, English precedent threatened to create a population of free, non-White people. Colonial officials responded to this disturbing possibility with legislation declaring that any child of an enslaved woman, regardless of the father's race or status, was also a slave. This reinforced White control over non-White Virginians and provided a mechanism by which White men could satisfy their sexual desires without endangering public safety and could enlarge the colony's workforce simultaneously.

This also meant, however, that any child of a free woman, regardless of her race, was also free, and Virginia had had a small population of free Black women since the early seventeenth century. Because enslaved Africans first arrived in Virginia before any law there recognized the institution of slavery, at least some of the first Africans brought to Virginia were apparently treated as indentured servants and released at the end of their terms. They, in turn, had children of their own with other Africans, with European colonists, and with Native Americans, and free people of color gradually became a small but distinct element in Virginia's population. Their existence then provided the legal basis for a number of freedom suits brought by enslaved men and women. Because no child of a free woman could be enslaved, identifying a free, female ancestor—mother, grandmother, great-grandmother—provided grounds for a freedom suit. Anyone who could prove descent from a free woman of color, even if she had been held in slavery illegally, could not be legally enslaved. This, Unis believed, meant that she and her sisters and their children should be free.[9]

Unis's mother was a woman named Flora, who had originally been enslaved in Massachusetts and Connecticut at the close of the colonial period.
New England slavery is much less familiar today than its southern counterpart, but the institution was nearly as old in New England as it was in
Virginia. Scholars continue to debate when enslaved Africans first entered
the region, but it was certainly no later than 1638. That fall, Captain William Pierce sailed to the West Indies with a cargo that included a number
of Native Americans captured by English settlers in Massachusetts and sent
into slavery on the islands. In exchange, Pierce obtained a variety of tropi-
cal products and an unknown number of "Negroes" he unloaded in Boston
that December. Pierce and others quickly recognized the profit to be made
trading slaves, and New Englanders soon established a flourishing business
carrying timber, foodstuffs, tobacco, sugar, molasses, rum, trade goods, and
enslaved workers along a variety of routes linking England, West Africa,
the Caribbean, and the American mainland. Most of the men and women
trafficked by these New Englanders ended up on Caribbean sugar islands
or in tobacco colonies on the southern mainland. A small number, however,
reached New England, and by the close of the seventeenth century slavery
was an established institution throughout the region.[10]

Enslaved labor was certainly never as common in New England as it
was farther south. Slaves were expensive. Few Anglo-Americans purchased
enslaved workers unless those workers could be put to use in some activity
that would cover the cost of their purchase and their upkeep and still yield
a profit, and colonial New England was home to fewer such activities than
were colonies farther south. By the mid-eighteenth century, enslaved Africans or African Americans made up less than 3 percent of New England's
non-Native population, though their number varied considerably from
place to place within the region. The greatest concentration was found on
large commercial farms in eastern Connecticut and southern Rhode Island,
which employed dozens of enslaved men and women raising cattle and
producing dairy products. Some of these operations had enough bound
workers to qualify as "plantations," and some settlements in Rhode Island's
Narragansett Country came close to matching Virginia's racial profile. In
Charlestown, for example, enslaved workers made up more than a third of
the total population in 1755. Coastal towns, such as Newport and Boston,
also included hundreds of enslaved African Americans, though they represented a smaller share of the community's total population than they did

in Narragansett Country. Colonial Boston, for example, was home to more slaves than any other New England town, but Black people and mulattoes never made up more than 10 percent of its total population. Some of these urban slaves served as domestic servants, but many toiled at a variety of artisanal and industrial occupations. Others labored in the region's maritime economy—building, maintaining, and crewing ships in the carrying trade and in the fishing fleet. Farther inland, in western Massachusetts and northern Connecticut, slavery was less widespread, but it was certainly present. This was a region dominated by small-scale, mixed farming—including tobacco in the Connecticut River valley, and enslaved workers here performed a wide range of agricultural and nonagricultural tasks.[11]

As a legal and social institution, slavery in colonial New England also differed considerably from the systems found in plantation colonies such as Virginia. With fewer enslaved Africans in their midst, New Englanders felt less need for the full range of legislation that defined and regulated slavery in the southern colonies. What Jared Hardesty found for Boston applied throughout New England: "Slavery as an institution was legally ambiguous and ill defined. Legislation regarding slavery was sparse or, in the case of determining the status of slaves' children, nonexistent. Nevertheless, by 1700, slavery was firmly entrenched in Boston and was a customary institution." In many ways, however, this customary institution was just as brutal as the more legalistic version found farther south. Slaves in New England were still chattel. Like other forms of property, they could be bought and sold, passed through inheritance, and seized to satisfy debt. They could still be abused physically and sexually. And while they were often permitted to form unions that resembled marriage, such unions had no legal standing and offered those who entered them no protection from separation through sale, inheritance, or seizure. Africans and their descendants also faced the racism that was almost universal in English and Anglo-American society. Color alone dictated that any person of African descent, slave or free, was considered an alien in New England's White society. They lived in that society but could never really belong to it. At the same time, however, individuals enslaved in New England often retained elements of personhood that their southern counterparts did not. Most fundamentally, they had a right to life and could not be killed by their owners without the killer facing criminal charges. New England slaves could also own and transfer property legally and, apparently, will it to their heirs; they could sue and be sued, make binding contracts, and testify in court—even against White people. Moreover, on a daily basis they lived under a regime that may have been much milder than that found farther south. Because most slaveholdings in New England were quite small and because regional custom treated White servants as members of their masters' families, what evolved in New England is what William Piersen described as "family slavery." "Most Yankee masters and their slaves shared a common residence and daily activities," Piersen wrote. "This led to a necessary intimacy, fostering both a relatively mild form of servitude and a kind of household kinship." In some ways then, New England slavery was distinctly different from the plantation variety. It was still slavery, though, and as Flora's story makes clear, it still denied the enslaved the freedom to shape their lives as they saw fit.[12]

Flora was born sometime between 1747 and 1758, almost certainly in southwestern Massachusetts or northern Connecticut, and by 1774 was living in West Suffield, a precinct of Suffield, Connecticut. Suffield was a prosperous community in the valley of the Connecticut River (see fig. 2). It had been established in 1670, when Major John Pynchon and a number of associates received permission from the Massachusetts General Court to settle a new township in what was then thought to be southern Massachusetts. The town itself was incorporated four years later with thirty-eight grantees, but its development was almost immediately interrupted by the outbreak of King Philip's War (1675–78). With the return of peace, Suffield began to grow steadily as a farming and industrial community. By the mid-eighteenth century, adjustments to the border had brought Suffield under Connecticut's jurisdiction (though the border between Connecticut and Massachusetts remained a matter of dispute for another half century), and the township had grown into a prosperous settlement. Much of Suffield and the surrounding region consisted of rich farmland, the result of sediment deposited in a massive glacial lake some fifteen thousand years ago. On this land farmers produced grain and tobacco on a commercial scale, while other residents operated taverns, sawmills, gristmills, ironworks, tanneries, distilleries, and a copper mine. The town's population also grew, reaching some 2,200 by the eve of the Revolution—including thirty-seven enslaved residents.[13]

People who knew Flora during her years in Suffield later provided depositions in which they identified her as a "servant" of Benjamin Scott, which is also how she appeared in Suffield town records. The term was undoubtedly a euphemism, though, because Scott himself described Flora

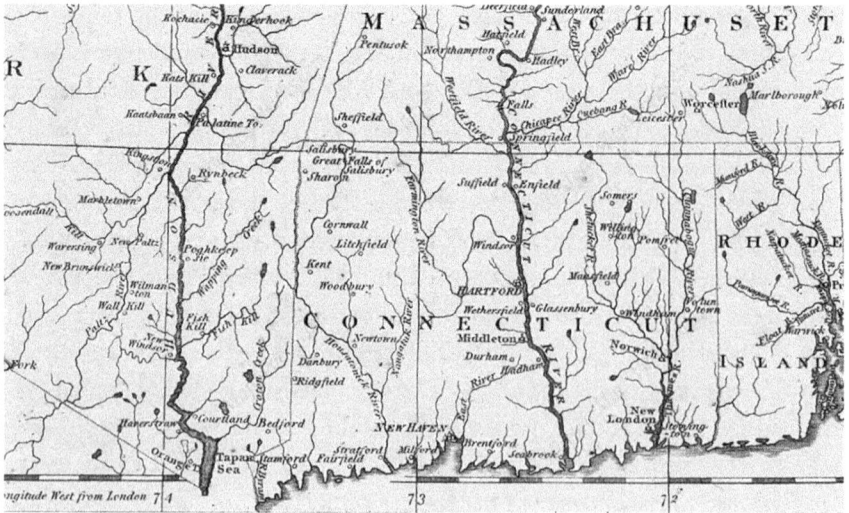

FIGURE 2. Suffield lay just south of Massachusetts in the valley of the Connecticut River. (John Russell, *Map of the northern, or, New England states of America,* 1795)

as a "slave for life" when he sold her in 1781. Scott lived in West Suffield, a precinct lying some two miles west of the town center, though exactly what he did there or how he employed Flora remains unknown. Language the witnesses used to describe Flora's time at Scott's suggest that her situation may have been quite similar to the "family slavery" described by William Piersen. Gustavus Austin, Hannah King, and Susan Sheldon, each of whom knew Benjamin Scott and lived near him in West Suffield at the time he owned Flora, all testified that Flora lived "in the family of said Scott" or "had been living with said Scott," and King recalled that Flora "attended church at West Suffield with his (Scotts) family."[14]

While working for the Scotts, Flora initiated or maintained a relationship with a Black man named Exeter, who lived in Southwick, Massachusetts, some seven miles northwest of Suffield. Exeter, or Ex, was then in his forties and working as a "servant" for a "Mr. Hare" in the Longyard precinct of Southwick. He too may actually have been enslaved, though witnesses disagreed about his exact legal status. Sarah Nelson and Bela Spencer later claimed that Ex had been enslaved until slavery ended in Massachusetts during the early 1780s, though Abraham Rising declared that Ex "was always a free man." Rising and another former neighbor, Silence Remington, also testified that Flora and Ex had a son together, and records in Suffield state that "Prince, son of Flora, servant of Benjamin Scott was born Feb. 21, 1774," but according to Rising and Remington, Benjamin Scott put the child out with a neighbor within months of his birth, and no record of his life after that has survived. Flora and Ex were able to deepen their relationship in 1780, when Benjamin Scott hired Flora out to someone living in South-wick. This brought her closer to Ex, and when her term in Southwick came to an end, Flora refused to leave. Instead, she ran to Mr. Hare's to be with Ex. The men Benjamin Scott sent to bring Flora back to Suffield eventu-ally found her hiding with Ex. When asked why he had hidden Flora, Ex explained that the couple wanted to marry, and Scott's men promised to convey the request to their employer.[15]

Massachusetts was unusual in its treatment of marriage between enslaved men and women. Slave societies often permitted enslaved couples to form unions that resembled marriage, and many slave owners encouraged such unions in the hope they would make the enslaved more contented with their lot and would lead to the births of more workers. Few such societies, how-ever, made any legal provision for such unions, and in this regard Massa-chusetts was different. There, morality took precedence over economics. In order to promote what White officials regarded as proper moral behavior among enslaved African Americans, the colony had enacted and the state retained legislation declaring that "no master shall unreasonably deny mar-riage to his negro with one of the same nation, any law, usage, or custom to the contrary notwithstanding." This provided authorities a basis on which to punish fornication and adultery among enslaved residents, but it also cre-ated a right for such residents to form legally sanctioned relationships. These relationships were not protected, though. While the law employed the word "marriage" to describe these unions, it did not negate the property rights claimed by the owners of the enslaved bride and groom. Owners could still legally separate enslaved couples at will through sale and inheritance.[16]

Because her owner was a resident of Connecticut, Flora could not really claim the Massachusetts law's protection, but she used it as leverage and told the men sent to retrieve her that she would only go back to Suffield willingly if Scott would allow her to marry Ex. Rather than force the issue, Scott's men assured the couple that they would be allowed to marry, and Flora agreed to return to Suffield. There she and Ex were married on April 26, 1781. Benjamin Scott agreed to the marriage with the explicit condition

that Flora "should still continue in his Service," and the minister who performed the ceremony told the couple that "they were not discharged from
Servitude or in any Manner freed from their obligations to their respective
Masters." Scott also seems to have agreed that Flora could spend time in
Southwick, where Ex continued to work at Mr. Hare's. Witnesses later disagreed, however, about how much time Flora actually spent with Ex. Some
reported that she lived in Southwick full-time after her marriage, whereas
others recalled that she went "back and forth frequently" but never spent
more than week at a time in Southwick.[17]

Whatever the exact nature of their situation, Flora and Ex made the best
of it. Following their marriage, the couple had at least one child, a daughter
named Cena, and did their best to establish some semblance of family life.
Flora, however, passed to a new owner in May 1781, when Benjamin Scott
sold her to Oliver Hanchett, and five months later she ran away. She may
have done so because Hanchett tried to prevent her from visiting Ex as frequently as she had been or wanted to. According to Joseph Carvalho III,
slave owners in Massachusetts were often reluctant to permit marriages between enslaved individuals with different owners. Such unions, Carvalho
wrote, "presented either a monetary commitment—i.e., a loss of 'property'—
or an inconvenience to the slave holder. Furthermore, if the two married
slaves were owned by two different masters, the owners may have been con-
cerned as to the ownership of, and responsibility for, the resultant children."
Benjamin Scott had permitted Flora to marry Ex and may have been more
tolerant of her spending time with her husband than her new owner was. If
that was the case, Flora's running away may have been a response to Hanchett trying to limit the time she spent in Southwick.[18]

It also possible, however, that Flora was responding to reports spreading
in the neighborhood about the status and future of slavery in the region.
Throughout Massachusetts and Connecticut, the years of the American
Revolution brought increasing uncertainty about the legal status of slavery.
The Massachusetts constitution adopted in 1780 declared that "all men are
born free and equal," and almost immediately lawsuits began that would
eventually lead the state's supreme court to declare there was no legal basis
for slavery in Massachusetts. In Connecticut, the legislature considered
emancipation bills in 1777, 1779, and 1780, and while none of these became
law, discussions around them showed that the legal ground under slavery
was beginning to shift there as well. Confusion may have been particularly

acute around Suffield and Southwick because of their particular geographic location and history. Both villages lay in a disputed border region of Massachusetts and Connecticut. As colonies, the two had been engaged in a dispute over the border between them since the mid-seventeenth century; their disagreement continued after the Revolution, and the issue was not finally resolved until 1804. While it lasted, both Connecticut and Massachusetts claimed sovereignty over all or part of the disputed territory, and residents of the region often tried to take advantage of the situation by claiming citizenship in whichever jurisdiction seemed to suit their interests best.[19]

Determined to spend more time with her husband, or hoping to secure her freedom in Massachusetts, or for some other reason, Flora fled to Southwick. Hanchett immediately took steps to reclaim her but not, apparently, as a runaway slave. Rather, he swore out a warrant charging her with the theft of her clothing and other property. She was quickly captured, tried for theft before a justice of the peace in Suffield, and found guilty. For her crime, Flora was sentenced to be whipped—"on the naked body eight stripes"—and to pay a fine of triple the cost of goods she had stolen, plus court costs. Unable to pay the fine and costs, Flora was ordered to serve Hanchett for two years. The court's order makes little obvious sense. When Hanchett purchased Flora, the bill of sale described her as a "slave for life," in which case a further sentence of "service to the said Oliver Hanchett for the term of two years" was pointless. Kirsten Sword, however, has suggested that it might have been a precaution taken in the face of growing uncertainty about the future of slavery. Even if Connecticut abolished slavery, Hanchett would still be able to claim two years of Flora's labor by virtue of the sentence imposed by the court.[20]

Undeterred, Flora ran away again early in 1782. This time she was away long enough to rejoin Ex and for them to resume life as a married couple. Hanchett was just as determined, though. He followed Flora to Southwick and brazenly asserted his right to her person—or at least to her labor. Bursting into the room where Flora and Ex were sleeping, Hanchett and an accomplice reportedly "knocked old Ex down" and dragged Flora out of bed. Submit King, who knew Ex in the mid-1790s, later testified that she had often heard him describe what happened that night. "He used to often tell about how they came and stole his wife Flora out of bed in the dead of night," King recalled. "He would weep and appear to feel very bad, and said that he clung to her until they got to the [illegible], and then they put her into the waggon and drove off with her, and he said as far as he could hear her she was hallowing and begging of him to come and help her."[21]

Hanchett then fled the state, taking Flora and Cena with him. Circumstances in Massachusetts were changing, though, and by the time Hanchett seized Flora, the status of slavery there was in the midst of a historic transformation. The Massachusetts state constitution, adopted in 1780, declared that "all men are born free and equal," and the early 1780s saw a series of legal actions seeking to determine precisely what that declaration meant. Perhaps the most significant of these cases were those surrounding the status of a man named Quok Walker. Walker had originally been enslaved by James Caldwell and had then passed to Nathaniel Jennison when Caldwell died and his widow married Jennison. Claiming that he been promised his freedom by the Caldwells, Walker ran away from Jennison and began working for himself. When Jennison then sought to recapture the man he considered his property, Walker charged him with assault. This led to series of suits and countersuits decided between 1781 and 1783. In the last of these cases, *Commonwealth v. Jennison* (1783), William Cushing, chief justice of the Massachusetts Supreme Judicial Court, left little room for deliberation in his instructions to the jury: "The idea of slavery is inconsistent with our own conduct & Constitution & there can be no such thing as perpetual servitude of a rational Creature unless his Liberty is forfeited by Some Criminal Conduct or given up by personal Consent." The jury did not address that larger issue and simply found Jennison guilty of assault, but Cushing later declared that as a result of this case, "slavery in Massachusetts was forever abolished."[22]

A judicial decision, however, did not provide the sort of definitive statement that legislation abolishing slavery might have, and years passed before slavery vanished entirely in Massachusetts. Still, as news of the verdict spread, it challenged long-held practices and conventions regarding the legality of chattel slavery and led many residents of Massachusetts, both Black and White, to conclude that slavery in Massachusetts was dead. Sixty years later, several residents and former residents of Suffield and Southwick declared in depositions filed in Unis's case that Ex and Flora had both been free when Hanchett seized Flora, although they disagreed about how the couple might have gained their freedom. Some believed that Ex and Flora had been individually manumitted by their owners at the time of their marriage or soon after. Others, however, projected back on 1783 the eventual result of the Walker cases and simply declared: "the blacks were all free in Massachusetts at that time." Either way, it seems clear that at least some of Ex and Flora's neighbors believed Flora was free when she was taken and that Hanchett was guilty of kidnapping.[23]

Ex and the attorney assisting him were unwilling to go that far. Ex's attorney, Caleb Strong, had been one of the lawyers pleading the Quok Walker cases, but in this instance he does not seem to have argued that Flora was free. Rather, in response to Hanchett's seizure of Flora, Ex sought damages for the loss of his wife's shoes and clothing and of her "company and assistance." Thus, the legal issue in the case seems to have been one of Ex's right to control his wife's body and property rather than Flora's own right to her freedom. On that basis jurors in Massachusetts found for Ex and awarded him damages. When Hanchett appealed to the state supreme court, however, the lower court's verdict was overturned. Although Chief Justice Cushing had already indicated that slavery violated the Massachusetts state constitution, Oliver Hanchett was a citizen of Connecticut, where slavery was still legal, and Cushing had ruled in another recent case that the owners of stolen "property" had a right to recover it, even if that "property" happened to be a person of color living in Massachusetts.[24]

That decision came in *Affa Hall et al. v. Commonwealth*, the origins of which lay in South Carolina during the American Revolution. In 1779, an English privateer had seized several dozen slaves from plantations along the coast of South Carolina. The privateer, however, was itself captured by a Spanish ship, the *Victoria*, which destroyed the English vessel after taking on board its human cargo. The *Victoria* was then captured by two other English privateers, which set out to take their prize to the British-held city of New York, but on their way north encountered two Massachusetts warships and fled to safety—abandoning the *Victoria* and its cargo. The New Englanders then brought the ship to Boston, where the slaves were held pending their owners' arrival to reclaim their property and pay the cost of their maintenance. Most of the enslaved were reclaimed within weeks and taken back to South Carolina, but two owners, Percival and Anthony Pawley, chose to nominate an agent in Massachusetts to take charge of their property and did not seek to reclaim it until August 1783. By then, word of the decision in *Commonwealth v. Jennison* had been circulating for several months, and the Pawleys' slaves had been released and were living as free men and women in Massachusetts. Eight of the ten individuals claimed by the Pawleys were recaptured, but the supreme judicial court ordered their release on the grounds that they had committed no crime in Massachusetts and could not be held against their will.

In response, the Pawleys' lawyer contacted officials in South Carolina, and that state's governor wrote his Massachusetts counterpart, John Hancock, demanding that Massachusetts respect the sovereignty of South Carolina and return the Pawleys' property. Hancock, in turn, asked Chief Justice Cushing to explain the court's decision to the outraged South Carolinians. In a carefully worded response, Cushing explained that the supreme judicial court had rendered no opinion concerning the individuals' status in South Carolina. "If a man has a right to the Service of another who deserts his service," Cushing wrote, "undoubtedly he has a right to take him up and carry him home to Service." No law in Massachusetts, however, authorized the state to hold the individuals in question against their will. They, like every other "person" in Massachusetts, enjoyed the right of habeas corpus, and the supreme judicial court had simply acted to protect that right. If the Pawleys wished to reclaim their "property," they were certainly entitled to do so, and nothing in the *Hall* decision challenged their right to do so. But the Commonwealth of Massachusetts had no legal basis on which to do it for them.[25]

This same principle governed the circumstances found in *Exeter v. Hanchett,* and the supreme judicial court ruled that Oliver Hanchett had every right to reclaim "property" he held under Connecticut law, even if that "property" was sleeping peacefully with her husband in his Massachusetts home. This decision made legal the forced separation of Flora and Ex; Oliver Hanchett, meanwhile, had already acted to make it permanent. By the time the court rendered its verdict he had disposed of his troublesome "property." Hanchett was said to have taken Flora and Cena to New York immediately after seizing them. In the aftermath of the Quok Walker cases, the owners of enslaved people in Massachusetts were often unsure of the status of their "property," and some acted to preserve their investments by selling enslaved workers out of Massachusetts while the legal confusion still gave them leeway to do so. Taking Flora and Cena to New York may have been Hanchett's way of avoiding the risk that a Massachusetts court would declare them free. Whatever his precise motivation, soon after taking Flora and Cena to New York, Hanchett sold them, and by 1784 they were in the possession of Jacob Lawrence in Dutchess County, some seventy miles west of Southwick. In the months that followed his family's disappearance,

Ex made several attempts to find his wife and daughter, but, as he had no information about their fate or their whereabouts, his efforts failed. He died in 1801, almost twenty years after Flora and Cena were taken, without ever seeing them again.[26]

Flora's new home, Dutchess County, lay on the eastern side of the Hudson River valley, midway between Albany and New York City, and her new owner, Jacob Lawrence, lived in the county's Clinton Township, some twenty-five miles northeast of Poughkeepsie. The middle Hudson valley had attracted relatively little attention from the original settlers of New Netherland. Their focus on furs and international trade led the Dutch to concentrate settlement farther north, around the trading post at Fort Orange, and farther south, around the port of New Amsterdam. They largely bypassed much of the region between the two. Following the English conquest of New Netherland, provincial governors tried to increase the colony's English population through generous grants of land and manorial privileges to a small number of families. Much of the land in the mid–Hudson valley was granted to large landlords who hoped to attract rent-paying tenants to settle their estates. Few settlers proved willing, though, until the second quarter of the eighteenth century, when grain production began to expand dramatically in New York. Dutchess County had fertile soil in which to grow wheat, water to power gristmills, and ready access to urban and international markets for wheat and flour. As a result, its population exploded from less than 2,000 in 1731 to more than 22,000 in 1771 and to 45,276 by 1790.[27]

Among the county's new residents were a significant number of enslaved Africans and African Americans. It was often difficult to attract immigrants to the Hudson valley because the region's large manorial holdings reduced the opportunity for newcomers to establish themselves as freeholders or to achieve that status after working as laborers or tenants. Without enough free immigrants to meet their labor needs, both large and small farmers in the region often purchased enslaved workers, and slavery was well-established throughout the Hudson valley by the middle of the eighteenth century. In Dutchess County, the enslaved population grew almost as rapidly as the free population during this era, nearly tripling between 1756 and 1790. By the latter year, the county's enslaved population had reached 1,856 and made up just over 4 percent of its total population. Slavery was certainly not the dominant labor system in Dutchess County, but it was an important element of the local economy, and enslaved workers there carried out a range of duties. Most of the men served as general farmhands, engaging in a variety of different tasks involved in the region's mixed agriculture. Others worked processing or transporting the grain and flour that provided the county's most important market products. Enslaved women generally performed domestic chores, though they might also work in the fields during the busy harvest season.[28]

In some ways, slavery in the Hudson River valley was similar to the institution Flora had known in Connecticut and Massachusetts. Slaveholdings in Dutchess County were generally small. Enslaved workers rarely lived or worked with many, if any, other Africans or African Americans. Instead, most worked and lived in close proximity to their White owners. According to Michael Groth, this pattern may have led to closer supervision of enslaved workers and to reduced opportunities for the enslaved to establish families or communities of their own, but it also fostered greater intimacy between enslaved workers and their owners and may have lent what Groth calls a "familial nature" to slavery in the region. This, in turn, may have made slavery in the Hudson River valley somewhat less brutal than plantation slavery. It was still chattel slavery, though, and it was still enforced with harsh discipline whenever an owner considered it necessary. Moreover, enslaved New Yorkers enjoyed none of the limited rights that some of their New England counterparts did. Enslaved men and women in New York had no legal right to own or transfer property, make binding contacts, bring suits, or testify in court against White people. Nor were challenges to the institution of slavery as evident in New York as they were in parts of New England. There was no Quok Walker or William Cushing to raise doubts about the legality of enslavement, and efforts in New York to pass a gradual emancipation act, which both Connecticut and Rhode Island did in 1784, failed in 1785.[29]

Little is known of Flora's experience in New York. Jacob Lawrence, on whose farm she was living in 1784, was not a large slaveholder; the federal census of 1790 found just two slaves in his household. This suggests that Flora lived in the sort environment that Groth identified as typical for individuals enslaved in the mid–Hudson valley: having extensive contact with White people and relatively little with others of African descent. In later years, Flora was described as a cook, and if that was her role in New York, she would have spent much of her time in the Lawrences' kitchen. She did have another child while she was living in Dutchess County. In the spring of 1784 Flora gave birth to a daughter who was initially named Rose but later renamed Unis. Unfortunately, it is impossible to say who the girl's father was or what his relationship with Flora may have been. Whatever the nature of Flora's experience in New York, it ended in September 1784, when she was sold to a young man from Virginia.[30]

James Stephens (or Stevens) was from Dutchess County originally but had recently fled New York to escape his creditors and in 1784 was in the process of settling in southwestern Virginia. He traveled back to New York that summer to gather his family and move them to their new home. To cover the expense of the move, he hoped to raise some money in New York by selling a wagonload of deerskins he brought from Virginia, but because he had left Dutchess County to escape debt, he wanted to maintain a low profile on his return and enlisted James Simpkins to act as his agent in selling the skins. Stephens had met Simpkins on the road in Virginia as the latter drove a small herd of cattle from Montgomery County to market in Martinsburg. Simpkins had been living in Virginia for at least a decade but still had a brother in Dutchess County. When Stephens explained his situation and asked Simpkins for help, Simpkins decided it would provide him an opportunity to visit his brother, whom he had not seen "for some time," and he agreed to go with Stephens to New York. Together, the two men traveled north and, arriving in Dutchess County, stayed with Stephens's father-in-law, a Baptist minister known as Elder John Lawrence, who was the brother of Flora's current owner, Jacob Lawrence. Stephens then remained inconspicuously at his father-in-law's house while Simpkins and Elder John Lawrence's son Thomas moved about the neighborhood trying to sell Stephens's deerskins and "buy for him some young negroes." In the course of their travels, Simpkins and Lawrence stopped at the farm of Jacob Lawrence, Thomas's uncle. There they found Flora, Cena, and Unis and inquired about buying them.[31]

Jacob Lawrence initially refused to sell Flora and her daughters because his wife objected to his doing so. Several days later, though, his wife relented, and Lawrence agreed to sell Flora and her daughters. Here the story becomes more complicated, and those complications later became central to the question of whether or not Unis and other descendants of Flora were entitled to their freedom. The first complication is determining who bought Flora. Fifty years later, John and Thomas Lawrence, who were sons of Elder John Lawrence and nephews of Jacob Lawrence, stated in depositions that

James Simpkins bought Flora, Cena, and Unis. Simpkins himself, however, and two sons of James Stephens maintained that Stephens had bought them. It might seem proper to grant that James Simpkins was the witness best qualified to describe his own actions in the purchase of Flora and her daughters, but as explained more fully in subsequent chapters, Virginia law in 1784 made it illegal for Simpkins to import enslaved workers into Virginia. Thus, Simpkins might have faced legal consequences if Flora and her daughters had been his property when they entered Virginia, and it would have been in his own best interest to identify Stephens as their owner. A second complication involves Flora's status when Simpkins or Stephens bought her. John Lawrence, Jacob Lawrence's nephew, also declared in his deposition that his uncle had learned after buying Flora and Cena that they were free. According to John Lawrence, his uncle told him "they were free negroes but he did not know it when he bought them and that I wanted my money back again, and I have sold my negroes to James Simpkins . . . so you take these negroes to James Simpkins and deliver them up to him as his property."[32]

Fifty years later courts in Virginia would wrestle for years with the questions of whether it was James Simpkins or James Stephens who bought Flora and her daughters and what that trio's legal status was at the time they were purchased. For now, though, it is enough to say that in September 1784 John Lawrence did as his uncle directed. He delivered Flora, Cena, and Unis to their new "owner," and several days later, Simpkins, Stephens, and the latter's family left for Virginia, taking Flora and her daughters with them.

❖ 2 ❖

Bound for Virginia

When James Simpkins and James Stephens left Dutchess County with Flora and her daughters, they headed southwest back to Montgomery County, Virginia. Established in 1776, Montgomery County was no longer on the state's frontier—that lay farther west, in Kentucky, but the county did lie astride the main route leading to that frontier and was one of the fastest-growing regions in Anglo-America during the decades immediately before and after the American Revolution. The county lay at the southern end of the Roanoke River valley, in southwestern Virginia, and extended southwest into the valley of the New River. Both of these valleys are part of the Great Appalachian Valley, which is actually a chain of valleys running from northeast to southwest in the midst of the Appalachian Mountains. Individual valleys in the chain are generally bounded on the east and west by higher, steeper slopes of the Appalachian system, through which occasional river gaps provide access to and from the coastal plain farther east. Each valley in the chain, however, is separated from the next valley by a lower and gentler divide between two adjacent watersheds. As a result, moving from one valley to the next involves relatively easy climbs, and following the chain of valleys provides an easily traversed route stretching more than a thousand miles from what is now southern Quebec to northern Alabama. Native Americans had employed this natural highway for millennia before the arrival of European settlers, and when Europeans did arrive, they quickly took advantage of the trails blazed by generations of indigenous travelers.

Among the Europeans following these native routes during the eighteenth century were thousands of families moving south from Pennsylvania. Between 1720 and 1770 a great wave of immigrants, especially Germans and Ulster-Scots, fled their homelands in search of peace or opportunity in the New World. Many entered through the port of Philadelphia and quickly moved inland, looking for land on which to establish farms for themselves. As immigrants continued to arrive, available land in southeastern Pennsylvania became scarcer and more expensive, and later arrivals gradually moved north and west into the Lebanon and Cumberland valleys. These valleys are also segments in the Appalachian valley chain, and as continued immigration brought yet more would-be settlers to the region, the search for available land took many of them southwest via the Great Appalachian Valley into western Virginia. There they met another stream of migrants moving west from more densely settled parts of Maryland and Virginia along the Potomac and James Rivers, and both groups continued south up the valleys of the Shenandoah and Roanoke Rivers. As they did so, they widened what had originally been a narrow footpath into the slightly wider, slightly smoother Great Road (or Great Philadelphia Wagon Road) and its less improved branches: the Carolina Road, which led south into the back-country of North and South Carolina, and the Wilderness Road to Kentucky and Tennessee.[1]

The leading edge of European settlement reached what would become Montgomery County during the early 1740s. The number of settlers in the region remained relatively small, however, because southwestern Virginia was still a contested borderland in which British, French, and Native American interests often collided. France had no physical presence that far south and east, but the New River valley lay in the watershed of the Ohio River, and French officials were seeking to prevent any British expansion into the Ohio valley. One of the ways in which they did so was by cultivating economic and diplomatic relationships with Native Americans throughout the Ohio valley and by acknowledging Native American rights to land claimed by the British. Native Americans no longer lived in the Roanoke or New River valleys, but several tribes claimed land there as tribal territory, hunted there frequently, and occasionally clashed with Europeans trying to settle there. These conflicting interests led to escalating hostilities between French and British forces around the Forks of the Ohio River and, eventually, to a full-blown war between Britain, France, and Native

American allies of the two imperial powers. Britain's victory in the French and Indian War (1754–63) eliminated French influence in the Appalachian region and reduced Native Americans' ability to resist British settlement there. This, in turn, opened the way for English, Germans, and Ulster-Scots to resume their advance into southwestern Virginia. The British government tried to restrict this advance and reduce conflict between settlers and Native Americans by issuing the Proclamation of 1763, which barred British settlement west of the eastern continental divide. On paper at least, this closed the New River valley to further settlement. The proclamation was widely ignored, though, and within five years even this paper barrier had been lifted when the Treaties of Hard Labor and Fort Stanwix moved the line limiting British settlement much farther west.

Before the French and Indian War, politically connected men in eastern Virginia had organized land companies that secured enormous grants from the colonial government on the condition that they attract settlers to occupy the land. Following the war, with Native American resistance almost eliminated and officials in London unable to enforce restrictions on migration into the region, these companies finally enjoyed an opportunity to profit from the grants they had received. They resumed aggressive campaigns to recruit settlers that brought in many immigrants eager to take up company land. As a result, European settlement in the New River valley expanded rapidly in the decade preceding the American Revolution. Thousands of new immigrants came to the region: clearing land and beginning to establish farms, gristmills, taverns, and churches in steadily growing numbers. And as the region's population grew, so did the political structures needed to govern it; older, larger counties were repeatedly divided in order to create new counties and keep government close to the governed as they moved farther and farther west.

Among the counties formed in this way was Montgomery, which the newly independent government of Virginia established in 1776. The county was originally much larger than its modern counterpart and included all or parts of what are now nine other Virginia counties plus a significant portion of what is now southern West Virginia. Its first seat was also much farther west, at Fort Chiswell, but as settlers continued to arrive, Montgomery County itself was divided, in 1790, and Fort Chiswell fell in the newly created Wythe County. Left without a place to meet, the Montgomery County Court selected a spot on the Great Road for a new seat and established the town of Christiansburg, which has remained the county's seat to this day even as its borders shrank with the creation of new daughter counties between 1790 and 1861.[2]

Early residents of the county included a handful of large landowners, but the great majority held between one hundred and five hundred acres, and early in the settlement process, many of those acres were still wooded. Nevertheless, on cleared land in the county's river and creek bottoms, hundreds of small farms began to emerge. Many of Montgomery County's founders had come from eastern Virginia, where tobacco dominated the economy, but tobacco barely figured in the new county's agriculture. Without the broad, navigable waterways found in eastern Virginia, farmers in the New River valley found it nearly impossible to move bulky products such as tobacco to market profitably. Instead, early settlers in Montgomery County raised corn, wheat, hemp, and a variety of other crops for home use and for the market. Much of what went to market was sold locally to new settlers or to migrants traveling the Great Road on their way west. Hemp was different, though. Demand for hemp grew significantly during the War for Independence, and most of what was grown in the county was sent east for use on naval or commercial vessels. In addition, thousands of head of cattle grazed on uncleared bottomland or on mountain slopes too rough or steep for cultivation. Some of the milk and meat they produced was consumed locally, but butter could be shipped and cattle could be driven to larger markets north or east of the county.[3]

Even without tobacco, slavery appeared immediately in Montgomery County; indeed, enslaved workers had begun arriving in the region before the county was even established as a separate entity. Some of the county's early settlers had come from places where slavery was less widespread or completely nonexistent and were unfamiliar with Africans and the institution of slavery. Others had moral objections to enslaving human beings or simply lacked the capital or credit necessary to acquire enslaved workers. A significant number of the county's earliest settlers, however, brought enslaved workers with them when they migrated to southwestern Virginia or acquired them soon after their arrival. By the time Flora and her daughters reached Montgomery County, enslaved Africans or African Americans represented a significant portion of the population there. The county's earliest-surviving tax list, compiled in 1782, reveals that two years before Flora and her daughters arrived, there were already at least 556 enslaved men and women in Montgomery County. For some of these individuals, slavery in Montgomery County may have resembled the institution that Flora had known in Massachusetts, Connecticut, and New York. More than half of Montgomery County's slave owners in 1782 held just one or two individuals. These enslaved men and women probably lived in close proximity to their owners and had relatively little contact with others of African descent. Their days were most likely spent working alongside their owners—clearing land, constructing houses and barns, and performing a variety of agricultural and domestic chores essential to the establishment and operation of family farms. Their experience may have closely resembled the "family slavery" that William Piersen described as common in much of rural Massachusetts.[4]

The institution of slavery and the experience of enslaved people in Montgomery County were fundamentally different, though, than they were in rural New England or in Dutchess County, New York, at that time. While Montgomery County was a much newer community than either of those in which Flora had lived previously, slavery was already more widely established in southwest Virginia than it had been in any of Flora's previous homes. In 1782, enslaved workers made up approximately 9 percent of Montgomery County's total population and were present in nearly 12 percent of households in the county—rates that were higher than those found in rural New England or in Dutchess County, New York, at the time. Moreover, while the growth of slavery had slowed in Dutchess County, and its abolition was already underway in Massachusetts and Connecticut, slavery was growing rapidly in Montgomery County during the 1780s. Between 1782 and 1790 the number of enslaved persons in the county increased by almost 50 percent, and this rapid growth would continue for decades thereafter. By the late eighteenth century, many planters in eastern Virginia had more enslaved workers than they could use profitably. A century of natural increase had caused the region's enslaved population to grow dramatically. Meanwhile, many of the region's farmers had begun shifting their efforts from growing tobacco to raising wheat and other grains that required much less labor than tobacco. As a result, by the final quarter of the eighteenth century, farmers in eastern Virginia were selling large numbers of enslaved workers to those establishing new farms farther west. In Montgomery County, this contributed to the enslaved population growing in number from 828 to 2,026 between 1790 and 1830 and from 6 percent of the total population to more than 16 percent.[5]

As a social and legal institution, slavery in Montgomery County was also very different. As noted above, most early slaveholdings in the county included just one or two individuals, but most of those who were enslaved in Montgomery County lived on larger holdings. In 1782 a majority of enslaved workers in the county lived on holdings with at least five such workers; more than a third lived on holdings with at least ten; and 12 percent of those enslaved in the county lived on just two plantations—thirty-four at William Preston's Smithfield and thirty-three at William Christian's Mahanaim. On these larger holdings, the enslaved had less contact with their enslavers and were more likely to associate more often and more closely with others of African descent than was the case in New England or in Dutchess County. Nor did law or tradition temper Virginia's version of chattel slavery. As described in chapter 1, legislation or tradition in Massachusetts, and to a lesser extent Connecticut, provided certain limited rights to men and women enslaved there. Virginia's slave code offered no such comfort; nor did most of the state's slave owners. In Virginia, enslaved individuals were chattel. They held no rights under state law, and in their day-to-day lives, most enjoyed even less recognition of their humanity than their counterparts in New England did.[6]

Like their purchase and departure from New York, the arrival and disposition of Flora and her daughters in Virginia remains clouded in conflicting memories and eventually became a point of contention in the freedom suits of Flora's descendants. Both William and Thomas Stevens testified that Flora, Cena, and Unis came to Virginia as their father's property, and Thomas "understood" that his father then sold all three to a man named Samuel Langdon. Francis Charlton, James's brother, also testified that he "understood" James Charlton had purchased Flora from Samuel Langdon, but, he declared, his brother "told me" he bought Unis and Cena from James Simpkins. Finally, Henry Carty testified that he "understood from James Charlton the late owner of the negroes that he purchased them from James Simpkins." All that is certain is that soon after they arrived in Virginia, Flora, Cena, and Unis all became the property of James Charlton.[7]

At the time, James Charlton was just beginning his rise among the county's political and economic elite. Born about 1752 in Lancaster County, Pennsylvania, Charlton had come to Virginia about 1763, when his parents brought the family south and settled in what is now Roanoke County. Within a decade the family had relocated to what would soon become

Montgomery County, where James married Abigail Bowles, in 1776, and served in the militia during the American Revolution. After the war, Charlton impressed his neighbors enough that in 1786 members of the county court recommended him to the governor as "a proper person to serve as a Magistrate for this county." He was not actually sworn in until 1793, but Charlton then remained on the county court until his death in 1825. In that era, county courts were the most important institution in Virginia's local government and filled both judicial and executive functions. In Montgomery County about thirty men served as magistrates at any given time, though usually just four presided over the court's monthly sessions. As a judicial body, county courts were authorized to hear criminal cases involving White defendants that did not involve death, all criminal cases involving Black defendants, and civil cases involving sums of less than twenty-five shillings (twenty dollars). As the county's executive body, the court levied local taxes, licensed taverns, authorized the construction of roads and dams, proved deeds and wills, appointed or recommended for appointment most other local officials, and served as the local arm of state government. In addition to his role as a magistrate, Charlton also served as trustee for the town of Christiansburg, following its establishment in 1792, and served as the county sheriff in 1814.[8]

As he rose among Montgomery County's political leaders, Charlton also joined its planter class. In the early 1780s, he was living on sixty-seven acres along Meadow Creek, some seven miles west of the land on which Christiansburg would later be established. According to the county tax list, he owned no enslaved workers in 1782; so Flora and her daughters may have been the first such workers he acquired. In the years that followed, though, Charlton expanded his holdings of land and workers considerably. In 1809 he built a large, two-story log house on 247 acres he purchased just north of Meadow Creek. There he established Seven Mile Farm, named for a large tree marking the distance from Christiansburg along the Great Road (see fig. 3). At his death, in 1825, Charlton owned more than 1,500 acres of land on which twenty-one enslaved workers raised corn, wheat, rye, and flax while tending sheep, hogs and cattle.[9]

Flora's role in the Charlton household was that of a cook. Witnesses in her daughters' freedom suits recalled Flora cooking at communal corn huskings in the neighborhood and in the Christiansburg tavern of John Ditty on court days, but most of her time was probably spent in the Charlton

FIGURE 3. Seven Mile Farm was James Charlton's home at the time of his death, in 1825, and the home of many of Flora's children and grandchildren. (Virginia Department of Historic Resources)

family's kitchen—first on Meadow Creek and later in a detached structure that stood behind the main house on Seven Mile Farm. The large stone hearth of that detached kitchen still stands (see fig. 4) and represents the only surviving physical link to Flora and her years spent working for James Charlton. Flora also had at least one more child after moving to Virginia, a daughter named Phillis born in 1792. Flora may have had other children as well, who died or were sold out of the region, but it is impossible to be certain. Nor is it possible to identify the father or fathers of these children or to say what their relationship with Flora might have been. When James Charlton died, his estate included four enslaved men, one of whose lower appraised value suggests that he might have been older than a prime hand. He or one of the other men on Seven Mile Farm might have been Flora's husband, but it is impossible to say.[10]

Beyond the work she did and the daughter she bore, little else is known for sure about Flora's life at Seven Mile Farm. Long after James Charlton died, a neighbor, Jane Burke, testified that he had been good to his enslaved workers. "Flora was kindly treated by Squire Charlton and his family more

FIGURE 4. This stone chimney is all that remains of the kitchen at Seven Mile Farm. Flora must have spent hours working around this hearth in the decade before her death. (Photograph by the author)

like a mother than a slave," Burke recalled. She also declared that Flora "had as much liberty as any slave I ever knew . . . and did pretty much as she pleased." Another witness, John Gardner, declared, "I never knew her treated otherwise than other negroes are treated." Others who had known Charlton, however, painted a different picture. Henry Carty described him as "a man of severe temper and likely to keep his slaves in subjection," while Elijah Meacham claimed to have seen Flora "tied to the bed posts" when her behavior angered Charlton. The accuracy of all of these assessments is debatable, of course; all of them come from depositions filed in *Unis v. Charlton* long after Charlton's death and from individuals whose precise connections to him remain a mystery.[11]

Flora and Charlton's other enslaved workers no doubt lived in simple quarters near their owner's house. None of the original outbuildings remain at Seven Mile Farm, but at one time a large kitchen and at least two "negro house[s]" stood behind the main house. Like the main house, these were probably built of log but in a much simpler style and probably lacked both wooden floors and glass windows. As a cook, Flora may have lived in the kitchen, or she may have lived with her children in a "negro house." Clothing and food for the enslaved were undoubtedly simple as well, but they did have the ability to make their lives somewhat more comfortable. According to Elijah Meacham, a neighbor, Charlton "allowed the said Flora . . . to go at large and hire herself out." He must have allowed others to do so as well because after his death three of Charlton's enslaved workers had money with which to buy tools and a sorrel colt from his estate when his personal property was sold at auction. Like many slave owners in antebellum Virginia, James Charlton apparently allowed those he enslaved to work for themselves on their own time and to keep at least some of the money they earned to spend as they wished.[12]

The Charltons may also have permitted, encouraged, or required Flora and their other enslaved workers to attend religious services. Independent Black churches were illegal in Virginia until after the Civil War, but many enslaved Virginians, either willingly or unwillingly, attended White churches. White southerners saw religion as a useful tool in justifying and maintaining the institution of slavery and used it to serve their own interests by emphasizing to slaves those parts of the Gospel that called on servants to remain obedient. Methodists, for example, operated a "plantation mission" that targeted slaves in the southern United States. Church leaders adapted a catechism originally written for children, modified it "to inculcate the duties of servants to their masters," and presented to slaves what one history of the church called "a strange Methodism of law and obedience, not grace and love." Baptists and Presbyterians also encouraged masters to bring their slaves to services and in some cases encouraged slaves not just to attend but to become members of the church.[13] In antebellum Montgomery County, enslaved African Americans were members of at least nine congregations in three different denominations. The largest number were Methodists, which was also the largest White denomination in the county, and African Americans made up more than a third of the church's membership in the county by the 1850s. The county's Presbyterian and Baptist churches also included enslaved members, though they were fewer in number than among the Methodists. To whatever denomination they belonged, however, Black members were certainly not equal. Most of the Methodist and Presbyterian churches in the county are reported to have had separate galleries for enslaved worshippers, and surviving church records suggest that Black access to the sacraments of baptism, communion, and marriage was limited.[14]

Members of the Charlton family were prominent among Presbyterians in early Montgomery County. Elizabeth Charlton, James's mother, was reportedly the daughter of a Presbyterian minister, and, according to local tradition, the first Presbyterian preaching in the county occurred at the home of James Charlton in 1791, when two ministers stopped there on their way to visit settlers along the Holston River. Both Charlton and his wife died before the Presbyterians organized a church in Christiansburg, but his daughter Matilda was an early member of the congregation, as were at least three of her children and two daughters of her sister, Rhoda Charlton Currin. Either by example or coercion, the Charltons may have contributed to at least three of Flora's grandchildren also joining Christiansburg Presbyterian Church. Phillis's daughters Matilda, Flora, and Mary were all received into the congregation by examination or profession of faith between 1851 and 1857. Presumably they had attended services before their admission to membership, and some of their siblings may also have attended without ever seeking or qualifying to join.[15]

At least two more of Flora's family members joined the Methodist Church. Her daughter Phillis and Phillis's son Tarlton both belonged to the Methodist congregation in Christiansburg. It is impossible to say, however, when they joined the church because no list of members before 1861 has survived. During the antebellum era, more African Americans in Montgomery County belonged to the Methodist Church than to any other denomination. This may simply be because Methodism was the largest denomination in the county, but it may also have been a result of the fact that the treatment of Black members by their White counterparts may have been slightly better among Methodists than other denominations. White southerners generally referred to African Americans by their first names only, though they sometimes added a modifier such as "Old" or "Aunt." They rarely employed a surname, though, even when it seems clear that most enslaved people had surnames. Few records from Presbyterian or Baptist congregations in Montgomery County include the surnames of enslaved members. Methodist records, on the other hand, routinely accorded enslaved African American this level of dignity. Lists of Black members invariably identify them by their full names, and they identify married women by their married names. Methodism also provided an opportunity for enslaved members to meet openly and regularly in a group of their own. Members of Methodist congregations were generally divided into "classes" that met separately to study and worship in smaller groups, and separate Black classes appeared in Montgomery County at least as early as 1844. Black classes generally had White leaders, but class meetings still represented an opportunity for enslaved Methodists to enjoy fellowship together and demonstrate their commitment to their faith and to one another.[16]

Flora lived in Virginia for at least thirty years before her death, but she never forgot her earlier life in New England and New York. Among the hundreds of immigrants settling in Montgomery County during the late eighteenth and early nineteenth centuries were a handful with whom Flora could reminisce about her former life. Samuel Pearce's family, for example, had moved to Virginia from Dutchess County, New York, in the late 1780s and settled along Meadow Creek. Pearce later stated in a deposition that "Flora frequently came to my father's house and I have frequently heard her and my mother talk about acquaintances in New York."[17] And she never stopped believing that she had once been free. Years after Flora died, Henry Carty recalled in two different depositions that Flora had claimed she had been free before Oliver Hanchett dragged her out of bed and took her to New York. According to Carty, Flora had told him this repeatedly over the years: "she told me at different times that if she had her just rights she would be a free woman."[18]

This may have been an effort on Flora's part to lay the groundwork for a successful freedom suit. In her study of freedom suits filed in St. Louis, Anne Twitty noted that it seems plaintiffs in such cases sometimes prepared the way for their suits by discussing publicly the basis for those suits. According to Twitty, such discussions may have served enslaved individuals in two ways. First, doing so may have been part of "cultivating reputations as individuals who were entitled to their freedom." Such conversations might help potential plaintiffs by planting in the minds of White neighbors, and potential jurors, that they had a legitimate basis on which to claim their freedom. Second, such discussions may have given the enslaved an opportunity to gauge their chances of winning a freedom suit. "By repeatedly asserting their status as free people," wrote Twitty, "slaves also may have been testing the waters, determining whether such a claim would be backed by the white community."[19]

It is unclear, though, whether Flora ever made any legal effort to challenge her enslavement. As in so many other regards, depositions offered in *Unis v. Charlton* provide contradictory evidence. Several witnesses declared that Flora had never made any effort to assert her freedom. Other neighbors, however, offered different accounts. Henry Carty, for example, was quite explicit in declaring that Flora had tried to regain her freedom. In one of his depositions, he declared that just two years after James Charlton bought Flora, "she stated that she had been made a slave in this country, and requested me to write back to her former place of residence and ascertain whether she was not entitled to her freedom." In the other, he recalled that the late Ezekiel Howard, who had been a magistrate in Montgomery County, had told him that Flora had applied to Howard to commence a freedom suit. Carty also stated that James Charlton had said to him, "If she ever went there again on that account he would correct her for it." Another witness, Elijah Meacham, also claimed that Charlton had told him Flora had asked Howard "to get a warrant for her freedom" but that Howard had refused to grant it. A third witness, Henry Wysor, may never have actually testified, but in seeking an order to depose him, Flora's grandson, Andrew Lewis, stated that he expected Wysor to testify that he had been at the house of James Charlton when Charlton discovered that Flora had gone off to Ezekial Howard's in order to make a claim for her freedom. According to Andrew, "the said Charlton took the said Wyson [*sic*] & others and went to said Howards in pursuit of said woman Flora and found her at said Howards and took her back to said Charltons and abused her & threatened to whip her if she ever went to Howards again."[20]

Any effort Flora might have made to gain her freedom, however, failed before reaching the courthouse, and she remained enslaved at Seven Mile Farm until her death, sometime between 1813 and 1825.[21] If nothing else, though, Flora made sure that members of her growing family (see fig. 5) knew her history. Flora's daughters—Cena, Unis, and Phillis—each had children of their own, though their marital status remains unknown. In 1825, Cena had an adult son named Julius; Unis had three grown sons—Reuben, Andrew, and Randall, at least two of whom bore the surname Lewis; and Phillis was the mother of seven children: Bill, Mary, Matilda, Flora, Helen, Tarlton, and James. Each of Phillis's children was described as a "boy" or "girl" on the inventory of Charlton's estate except for James—"a child." Two of Phillis's older children bore the surname Johnson, though another went by Jackson, and her youngest was identified as James Parks, suggesting that Phillis may have had children by several different men. Most of the family still lived on James Charlton's plantation when he died, although Unis's son Randall had passed to a local carpenter named John Swope sometime before 1825. In addition, one of Flora's granddaughters, Rhoda Ann, seems to have been given to Charlton's daughter, also named Rhoda, and to have moved with her to the farm of William Currin when Rhoda Charlton married Currin in 1804. But wherever they lived, all of Flora's daughters, as well as her older grandchildren, knew the story of her life and her claim to freedom.[22]

Prior to 1825 they made no effort to act on their knowledge. They knew they were not free, as their mother or grandmother had been, and life at Seven Mile Farm was far from ideal, but it could certainly have been worse. Most members of their immediate family remained together on Charlton's farm, and he seems to have been no worse a master than most others in the neighborhood. But the situation of Flora's descendants became much more precarious when James Charlton died. The death of a slave owner inevitably triggered concern among his or her enslaved property because the death of any individual owning property led to the distribution of that property among new owners. Under the best of circumstances, individual descendants of Flora would be apportioned among Charlton's widow and children, all of whom still lived in Montgomery County at the time. If that happened, Flora's descendants might still be able to maintain relationships with one another through occasional visits. But the children of James Charlton might well decide to move west, as some of their neighbors already had. Moreover, the appraised values of Flora's descendants ranged from $475 to $95, and dividing them among Charlton's heirs in a way that seemed fair to all of them might prove impossible. If that happened, the heirs might decide it would be easier to sell the enslaved and divide the proceeds of the sale. They might also have to sell some of the enslaved in order to settle debts owed by Charlton at his death. And once they went up for sale, some or all of Flora's descendants might pass to interstate slave traders and end up on distant cotton or sugar plantations with no hope of ever seeing their families again.

Sale to a distant plantation was not just an abstract concept in Montgomery County at that time; it was regularly made real in the form of coffles of enslaved workers making their way south through the county. As described

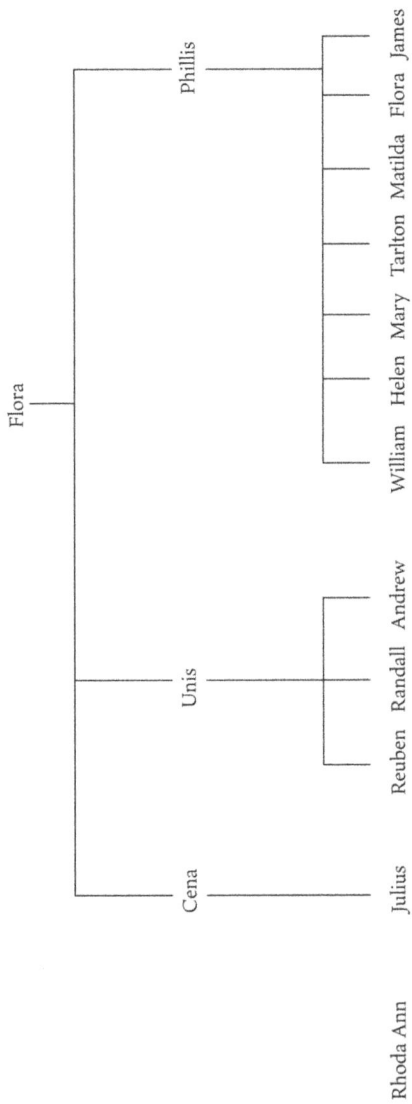

FIGURE 5. Descendants of Flora in 1825

earlier in this chapter, by the third quarter of the eighteenth century, many Virginia planters had more enslaved workers than they could employ profitably and had begun selling their surplus to settlers establishing new farms farther west. That market was relatively limited, though, until the invention of the cotton gin and the forced removal of Native Americans from the Old Southwest created the Cotton Kingdom. New cotton plantations in what became Alabama, Mississippi, and Louisiana created an insatiable demand for workers during the first half of the nineteenth century, and many of those workers came from Virginia. Interstate slave traders advertised throughout Virginia, buying enslaved men, women, and children for export and shipping them south for sale in markets throughout the Southwest. Some traveled by ship to New Orleans, but thousands made the journey overland to Natchez, Memphis, and other slave-trading centers, and James Charlton's Seven Mile Farm actually lay on the route by which many of these coffles of enslaved Virginians made their way south.[23]

The same Great Road that Flora, Cena, and Unis had followed to Virginia in 1784 was in the early nineteenth century one of the main routes connecting the mid-Atlantic region to the expanding Cotton Kingdom. It was, therefore, one of the main arteries of a booming interstate slave trade. One modern scholar, Phillip Troutman, has calculated that in the years after 1810 at least one or two slave traders' coffles, and perhaps as many as four, passed through Montgomery County every week during the peak travel season between September and April. All of these passed Seven Mile Farm in plain sight and some stayed in the neighborhood overnight. George Featherstonaugh, an Englishman traveling through the American South in 1834–35, came upon "a camp of negro slave-drivers" preparing to cross the New River five miles west of Seven Mile Farm. This party consisted of some three hundred men, women, and children who had spent the night camped along the river and were just setting out for the day when Featherstonaugh encountered them. It is unlikely that these bound captives had much, if any, direct contact with enslaved workers living in the area, but their story and their fate would have been obvious to anyone who saw them. When James Charlton died, Flora's daughters and their children knew exactly what the future might hold for them.

Triggering events that suddenly threatened to change the situation of an enslaved person were common among those who initiated freedom suits. Polly Crocket, for example, had been free before she was kidnapped and sold into slavery in Missouri. She eventually married an enslaved man with whom she had two daughters and seemed reconciled to a life in slavery. Everything changed, though, when her husband was sold south. Polly's daughter, Lucy Delaney, described the change in her own autobiography: "When my father was sold South, my mother registered a solemn vow that her children should not continue in slavery all their lives, and she never spared an opportunity to impress it upon us, that we must get our freedom whenever the chance offered." Unis had already lost at least one of her children. Her son Randall had been sold, given, or in some other way transferred to John Swope, who lived west of Seven Mile Farm in what would later become Pulaski County. As a mother, and a grandmother by now, she must have been terrified by the prospect of seeing her family further divided through the death of James Charlton. This risk of seeing their family separated seems to have been the trigger that led Flora's descendants to initiate their freedom suits.[24]

But filing such suits was dangerous. Unis and the others had no doubt heard Flora describe what happened to her when she tried to initiate the process. Henry Carty later declared in a deposition that he heard James Charlton threaten to "correct" Flora if she ever tried to contact a magistrate about her claim to freedom. Another witness, Elijah Meacham, testified that he had seen Flora "tied to the bedposts," and when he asked why, Charlton replied, "the damn old bitch had been to Ezekiel Howard Esq. to get a warrant for her freedom." James Charlton, of course, was dead now, but his widow or sons might be just as vengeful, and as Kelly Kennington has detailed, owners possessed a variety of weapons they could employ to punish any of their enslaved workers seeking to sue for their freedom. They might seek to protect their investment by selling it or hiding it by taking it out of the jurisdiction in which the suit was filed. They might punish the plaintiff by selling his or her family members or, if they preserved the family intact, by subjecting its members to physical punishment. Slave owners had near total control over the food supplies and work schedules of their workers and a free hand to punish them for any violation of the owner's rules—either real or imagined. Owners, in other words, had multiple ways in which to take vengeance against any enslaved worker with the temerity to file a freedom suit.[25]

As a result, enslaved individuals thought very carefully before bringing suit, but Flora's descendants must have felt that they had no other realistic option. Running away might have seemed an alternative for adults without family attachments. The Ohio River, and freedom, were just two hundred miles away, and one of that river's tributaries, the New River, was within five miles of Seven Mile Farm. Healthy adults, traveling alone or in a small party, might have thought the journey possible. But Phillis had young children, who would have slowed any party traveling with them, and their cries might have revealed the entire party to slave hunters. Flight by a group as large and diverse as Flora's descendants would have been very risky. But leaving Phillis or her children behind would break the family up just as permanently as the auction block might. Faced with the near certainty of separation if they did nothing, and with flight looking just as dangerous, Flora's descendants decided it was worth the risk of suing to gain their freedom.

❖ 3 ❖

Virginia Courts and Enslaved Plaintiffs

Unis went first. On September 16, 1825, she made her way to the courthouse in Christiansburg and submitted a petition to Montgomery County's Superior Court of Law. In it she claimed that she was being "illegally held in slavery" by Hannah Charlton, James's widow, and sought to initiate the legal process to gain her freedom.[1] Unis seems to have done so without the assistance of a lawyer, yet she followed precisely the mechanism that state law called for in such cases. This raises the question of how Unis knew what she needed to do to initiate a freedom suit or even knew that such suits were a remedy available to her.

Historians of slavery have long recognized the existence of what Booker T. Washington called "the 'grapevine' telegraph"—the web of connections by which information traveled among and within enslaved communities. Church services, sanctioned family visits, and work-related travel all brought enslaved men and women together with the consent of their owners. Unsanctioned meetings were also common, though. Enslaved people often organized illegal religious gatherings, secret social gatherings, and countless surreptitious rendezvous at which they could speak freely about their hopes, their fears, and their plans for the future. They also passed on news they had picked up going about their work. Enslaved workers could easily listen to the conversations of people for whom they worked, and the small number who learned to read could steal glimpses at books or newspapers in homes, shops, or taverns. All of this information was carried back to the enslaved community for its members to share and discuss among themselves.[2]

More recently, scholars of Black legal consciousness have looked more specifically at how the grapevine telegraph spread legal knowledge among the enslaved.[3] Free and enslaved African Americans regularly talked among themselves, sharing stories of their own experiences with the law and information they had picked up from conversations they had with White people or overheard White people having among themselves. This was especially true in southern cities, where free people of color were more common, and in towns along the Ohio and Mississippi Rivers, where a constant stream of Black and White workers and travelers brought news from far and wide. It was also true throughout the rural South, and enslaved residents of Montgomery County could have acquired legal knowledge in a number of ways. In Unis's case, it seems that the likeliest source was her own home. James Charlton served for more than thirty years on the Montgomery County Court. Two of his sons, James Jr. and William, were also members of the court during the first quarter of the nineteenth century, as was one of his sons-in-law, William Currin, who also owned Flora's granddaughter, Rhoda Ann.[4] All of these men were, no doubt, frequently at Seven Mile Farm. They must have brought with them news of what was happening in the courthouse and shared it with other members of their households—including some of the enslaved members. Flora, Unis, Cena, and Phillis were, no doubt, frequently in the Charlton house, cleaning or serving meals, as James and others discussed courthouse happenings. White members of the household and their guests probably took no notice of the enslaved people working around them, but what White residents talked about in the big house was quickly shared in the quarters of the enslaved.

Freedom suits were relatively rare across the history of antebellum Montgomery County; other than those brought by Flora's descendants, only eight are known to have arisen in the county between its creation, in 1776, and the abolition of slavery there in 1865 (table 1). All eight of these cases, however, opened between 1803 and 1825—the decades immediately before Unis initiated her suit, and they included successful examples of each of the main arguments commonly employed by plaintiffs in Virginia freedom suits: descent from a free woman; importation in violation of the state's nonimportation act; and enforcement of a prior act of emancipation. Legal motions filed in the cases brought by Flora's descendants show that their suits sparked great interest among the county's White residents. Thus, it seems likely that the earlier suits had as well, and if White residents talked

TABLE 1. Montgomery County freedom suits

DATE	CASE	GROUNDS	OUTCOME
1803–11	*Nanny Pegee* *v.* *John Hook*	Violation of the nonimportation act	Freed by jury; verdict annulled; freed by jury; upheld on appeal
1806–15	*Rachel Viney* *v.* *Henry Patton*	Born to a free woman	Freed by jury
ca. 1807–14	*Ann & Roderick* *v.* *Henry Edmundson*	Freed by previous deed	Jury found for defendant; new trial ordered on appeal; superior court found for plaintiffs on "matters of law" and ordered them freed.
1811	*Rhoda, James, and Bob* *v.* *Edward Rutledge*	Freed by previous deed	Superior court freed Rhoda
1812–20	*Polly* *v.* *Henry Patton*	Not specified	Freed by jury
1815	*Rachel Viney, for Jupiter* *v.* *Andrew Johnston*	Born to a free woman	Freed by jury
1815–26	*Ruth* *v.* *James Sallust*	Violation of the nonimportation act	Jury found for plaintiff; verdict annulled by supreme court
1825–26	*Esther & Peter* *v.* *Conrad Wall*	Not specified	Suit dismissed at direction of plaintiffs' counsel

about the cases, news of them must have spread among the enslaved via the grapevine telegraph. Unis and her siblings undoubtedly followed as closely as their situation permitted the progress of freedom suits filed in the county, and it is clear from their actions that they acquired a clear understanding of what was needed to initiate and to maintain such a suit.

Descent from a free woman was the grounds on which members of the Viney (or Veney) family won their freedom. When Rachel Viney launched her freedom suit against Henry Patton, in 1806, she was enslaved despite having been freed years before through a suit brought by her mother, Sarah, in Northumberland County. Early in the 1780s, Sarah and five relatives had sued for their freedom on the grounds that they were descended from a Native American woman named Mary, who had been brought to Virginia after the House of Burgesses banned the enslavement of indigenous people. Sarah won her suit in 1791, but by then Rachel's owner had ignored the requirement that he not sell any individual involved in a freedom suit. While the case was still pending, he sold Rachel to a man who took her to Montgomery County and sold her to Henry Patton. Years later, Rachel learned of the verdict in her mother's case and brought her own suit against Patton. She also brought a separate suit on behalf of her son Jupiter, who had been leased or sold to Andrew and David Johnston in adjacent Giles County. With the county court's permission, Rachel then traveled with her lawyer to Richmond County to locate and depose witnesses who could recall her mother's case and confirm Rachel's identify as Sarah's daughter. With the evidence they gathered, her lawyer was able to convince jurors that Rachel and her seven children were the descendants of a free woman and had been enslaved illegally. All were awarded their freedom in 1815.[5]

Nanny Pegee and Ruth sought their freedom on different grounds. They maintained that they had been brought to Virginia in violation of a state law banning the importation of slaves except in certain limited cases. Virginians had tried since before the American Revolution to restrict the importation of enslaved workers. By the mid-eighteenth century, many of Virginia's large planters already had as many workers as they could employ profitably on their own and had begun selling their surplus hands to people still seeking additional labor. Planters selling enslaved workers had no desire to see prices depressed through the importation of additional workers, and their class had the political power to protect its economic interests. As a result, colonial Virginia's House of Burgesses had tried to restrict the importation of additional slaves by taxing them heavily. Those efforts had been overruled by British authorities, but after claiming its independence Virginia wasted no time in restricting the slave trade. In 1778 the House of Delegates passed "An act for preventing the farther importation of Slaves," which was then incorporated into a 1785 "act concerning slaves." Both laws barred the importation of slaves for sale, though each provided an exemption for free immigrants who wished to bring their enslaved workers into Virginia and settle there. In those cases, though, the owner had to appear before a justice of the peace within ten days and swear an oath that he or she had brought no slaves into the commonwealth "with an intention of selling them." Both laws also declared that any slaves imported in violation of the act would be freed automatically. The 1778 law declared that "every slave imported into this commonwealth contrary to the true intent and meaning of this act, shall upon such importation become free," while the later statute provided that "Slaves which shall hereafter be brought into this commonwealth, and kept therein one whole year together, or so long at different times as shall amount to one year, shall be free."[6]

Nanny Pegee had been born in North Carolina about 1772 and was probably the child of a Black man and a White woman. As a child, she had been bound out for a term of service to a man named Thomas Jones, who took her with him when he moved to Virginia in 1781. In Virginia, Jones described Nanny Pegee as a slave, and she and her son, David, were part of the "sundry property" attached by one of Jones's creditors in 1787. That creditor, John Hook, kept Pegee enslaved on his plantations in Franklin and Montgomery Counties for more than a decade, and during that time she had six more children, all of whom were also held in slavery. Finally, in 1803, Nanny Pegee brought suit against Hook in Montgomery County for "assault battery & false imprisonment" and sought freedom for herself and her children. Because the original complaint has not survived, it is impossible to say on what grounds Nanny Pegee based her claim of freedom, but in part, at least, she did so on the grounds that Thomas Jones had brought her to Virginia as a slave in violation of a state law barring the importation of slaves into the commonwealth for sale.[7]

In 1804, the jury in Nanny Pegee's case found that Thomas Jones had brought her into Virginia as if she had been enslaved but had never taken the oath required under the 1778 nonimportation act in order to bring enslaved workers into the state with him when he settled in Virginia. Jurors in the case also found that Nanny was the child of a white women, which meant that she should never have been enslaved in the first place. Thus, it declared, "We find the pltffs are free persons." A year later, however, the court of appeals annulled the jury's verdict and ordered a new trial. In 1807 the district court in Staunton ordered that the new trial be held before the district court in Franklin County, and in 1808 jurors in Nanny Pegee's second trial also found that she and her children were free. In 1811, Hook appealed again to the state's court of appeals, but this time the high court affirmed the jury's verdict. Nanny Pegee and her children were free.[8]

Ruth, the plaintiff in *Ruth v. Sallust*, also sought her freedom on the basis of illegal importation to Virginia. Ruth had originally been enslaved in North or South Carolina and "was taken by the British during the invasion of those states in the course of the Revolutionary war." She was subsequently recaptured by Americans and sold to a man named Zecharia Pig in Pittsylvania County, Virginia. When Pig died, Ruth passed to Adam Gray, when he married Pig's widow. Gray then took Ruth to Montgomery County and sold her to James Sallust in 1792 or 1793. Soon after Ruth was sold to Sallust, however, a man named Lowry appeared claiming to hold "the right of the person from whom she had been taken by the British." Lowry brought suit against Sallust, recovered Ruth in 1795, and immediately sold her back to Sallust. Twenty years later, in 1815, Ruth brought suit seeking freedom for herself and her children on the grounds that Zecharia Pig had never sworn the oath required to make her original importation into Virginia legal under the 1778 statute. Thus, her lawyer argued, she should have been freed automatically and was now being held illegally by James Sallust. The case took seven years to make its way to trial, but in September 1822 a jury found for Ruth and declared that she and her children were "free persons and not slaves." Sallust appealed, and in February 1826, five months after Unis sought permission to sue for her freedom, the state court of appeals overturned the jury's verdict in Ruth's case. The higher court declared that while Zecharia Pig may have imported Ruth illegally, he had not then been her legal owner, and his failure to obey the law should not deprive her rightful owner (Lowry and then Sallust) of his property. Therefore, the supreme court determined that the lower court's verdict had been "erroneous" and declared it "annulled." That seems to have ended Ruth's case, and she and her children remained enslaved.[9]

Enslaved individuals in Montgomery County also brought suit on the grounds that they were being held in slavery despite having been freed by an earlier will or deed of emancipation. Sometime between 1807 and 1814, for example, Ann and Roderick brought suit against Henry Edmundson for illegally holding them in slavery. The plaintiffs maintained that their previous owner, Alexander Baine, had freed them in his will, but the jury found for Edmundson. Ann and Roderick then appealed to the Montgomery County Superior Court of Law, which in August of 1814 upheld their appeal and ordered a new trial. But no new trial ever took place. Two months after ordering it, the superior court held another hearing at which it considered "the matters of law arising upon the case." This time it also found for the plaintiffs and ordered them "to recover their freedom" immediately.[10]

The superior court was less generous in the matter of Rhoda, James, and Bob. The three were children of Sarah, a woman who had been enslaved by Robert Shanklin. In 1806, Shanklin had provided a deed of emancipation by which Sarah and her daughter, Rhoda, were to be freed upon his death, but neither James nor Bob had been born when the deed was written, and the document made no provision for additional children born to Sarah. It is unclear what happened to James and Bob when Shanklin died, in late 1807, but Sarah and Rhoda presumably gained their freedom. Under Virginia law they were then supposed to leave the commonwealth within twelve months or face reenslavement. Sarah must have remained, perhaps because her sons had not been freed, and in 1811, Rhoda, James, and Bob were all taken into custody by Montgomery County's overseers of the poor, who under Virginia law could apprehend and sell into slavery any emancipated individuals who stayed beyond the permitted twelve months. Rhoda, James, and Bob then sought a writ of habeas corpus, and the superior court ordered one of the overseers of the poor, Edward Rutledge, to appear and explain the situation. After hearing from Rutledge, the court declared with little explanation that Sarah and Rhoda had gained their freedom effective the date of Shanklin's deed of emancipation. It said nothing, however, about Bob or James, who presumably remained enslaved and in custody.[11]

Freedom suits filed in Montgomery County prior to Unis's case demonstrate that the plaintiffs in such actions enjoyed a remarkable degree of success and suggest that Unis had good reason to be optimistic when she set off for the courthouse in 1825. In the six freedom suits concluded in the county before 1825, nearly all of the enslaved plaintiffs had prevailed. Only in the case of Rhoda, James, and Bob does it seem that any of the enslaved plaintiffs failed to win their freedom. Equally remarkable is the fact that most of these victories came through jury verdicts rather than court orders. The six suits concluded before Unis brought hers included verdicts from a total of six juries. Five of the six found for the plaintiffs. And, of course, all of the jurors in these cases were White men, and many of them were slave owners. That notwithstanding, they seem to have been willing to consider the merits of the particular case before them rather than simply voting to uphold White privilege.

These earlier freedom suits also demonstrate the extent and limits of the means by which the legal system in Montgomery County acted to provide illegally enslaved plaintiffs with the tools they needed to have a reasonable chance of winning a freedom suit. Since 1711, if not before, at least some enslaved Virginians suing for their freedom had received public assistance in prosecuting their suits, though it is unclear how many received such aid or under what circumstances. In 1795, access to such assistance was finally codified and, in principle, extended to "any person who shall conceive himself or herself illegally detained as a slave in the possession of another." Under this law, anyone believing themselves to be held in slavery illegally could petition a district, county, or corporation court for the privilege of suing *in forma pauperis* (that is, in the manner of a pauper) and would enjoy that privilege if his or her complaint seemed credible "to the satisfaction of said court." Parts of this law were subsequently included in an 1818 statute "providing a method to help and speed poor persons in their suits," and this was the legislation governing freedom suits at the time Unis initiated hers.[12]

The most immediate benefit of securing pauper status lay in the fact that the county was then required to provide the plaintiff with "counsel learned in the laws" to assist him or her pursue a cause of action. Such assistance was essential. Then as now, the law was a forum in which every word was critical and in which arcane forms and procedures had to be followed properly. Even a literate White person often found find it difficult to navigate properly the maze of antebellum legal procedures, and even small mistakes could result in delays or the complete failure of a legal proceeding. For an illiterate person, Black or White, it was virtually impossible to proceed successfully, so having a trained lawyer's help was a critical first step in filing a freedom suit. It did not, however, guarantee how motivated or effective that lawyer would be, and a number of factors might have influenced how aggressively individual lawyers prosecuted freedom suits.

The statute governing freedom suits in Virginia failed to explain how counsel assisting an enslaved plaintiff should be identified. Anne Twitty, Kelly Kennington, and Loren Schweninger, who have studied freedom suits elsewhere in the antebellum South, found that lawyers often volunteered to represent enslaved clients after learning of their situations through contact with the plaintiffs or courthouse gossip. Some did so because they were intrigued by the legal issues, some from a sense of duty, and others simply because they needed the fee. In Virginia the last of these possible motivations seems not to have applied since state stipulated that any attorney appointed to represent the plaintiff in a freedom suit was to serve "without fee or reward." In some cases, attorneys seem to have been appointed by the court without having previously expressed any wish to serve and with little prior knowledge of the case. This did not make it impossible for lawyers to give freedom suits their undivided attention, but it certainly might have reduced their incentive to do so.[13]

There is also the fundamental fact that attorneys representing enslaved plaintiffs were all White and were often slave owners themselves. This might seem an obvious barrier to a lawyer's effectiveness in such a suit, and in some cases it might have been. However, modern scholars such as Andrew Fede, Lea VanderVelde, and Loren Schweninger have concluded that southern lawyers representing enslaved plaintiffs suing for their freedom generally undertook their role as the client's advocate as professionally and effectively as possible. These lawyers probably did not believe that their efforts threatened the institution of slavery. As VanderVelde noted, "correcting the status of an individual mistakenly categorized has little impact on other master-slave relations." In fact, the attorneys prosecuting freedom suits often saw their actions as necessary steps to correct the occasional mistake made in an essential southern institution. In the words of Loren Schweninger: "[They] believed that by enforcing the laws regulating slavery they were protecting, not undermining, the institution. And the courts, by granting freedom to slaves who were being unlawfully detained, were enabling the southern states to preserve their slave-based economy and class-structured society." Despite these practical and intellectual issues, Schweninger concluded that "the great majority of solicitors who agreed to prosecute freedom suits were industrious, effective, [and] dedicated," and the success rate of plaintiffs in Montgomery County certainly supports that view.[14]

In addition to providing counsel, pauper status also ensured that "[the plaintiff] shall not be compelled to pay any costs." This eliminated another huge obstacle to enslaved plaintiffs winning their freedom through the courts. Slaves often had money of their own. Some earned money working on their own time—Sundays or holidays; others sold produce from gardens they kept or fish they caught. Few, however, had enough to cover the cost of a lawsuit, especially one as protracted as those involving Flora's descendants. Robert Craig, one of the attorneys appointed to assist Unis, frequently represented White clients "unable to employ counsel" and received five dollars each time he did so. Lawyers' fees, however, were only part of the expense involved in a legal action such as a freedom suit. Courts charged for issuing writs or subpoenas or for providing copies of records, witnesses had to be compensated for their time and travel, and such costs quickly mounted. The cases brought by Flora's descendants spent seven years in Smyth County, for example, and the plaintiffs' costs there amounted to $62.82—exclusive of attorneys' fees.[15]

It did no good, however, to establish and fund such resources if eligible individuals had no opportunity to employ them. If necessary, therefore, judges in the county also took steps to protect the ability of enslaved individuals to utilize the help provided under the law. When, for example, Ruth decided to bring a suit against James Sallust, she had traveled to Christiansburg to petition the superior court for permission to sue *in forma pauperis*. Sallust, however, tried to stop her from doing so by physically preventing her from appearing before the court. The presiding judge not only accepted Ruth's petition and granted her permission to sue Sallust but also fined him eight dollars "for a contempt offer'd the Court in attempting to force out of the Courthouse Ruth a woman of color who was waiting on the Court for the purpose of presenting her petition for leave to sue the said Sallust." Court officers sometimes also took steps to help enslaved plaintiffs understand the legal process. In April 1828, for example, William B. Charlton, a defendant, served notice to Cena, a plaintiff, of the time and place that he would be taking a deposition from a witness. Cena not only had little experience with the legal system at that point but was almost certainly unable to read the document delivered to her. The official who served it, however, reported to the court that "he delivered to the within named Seine a true copy of the within notice and read and explained the same to her."[16]

Enslaved plaintiffs still remained enslaved, though, and until their suits were settled, they remained vulnerable to their owners, who might retaliate for their bringing suit against them. Owners might, for example, seek to protect their assets by selling enslaved plaintiffs out of the county or state. To reduce the chances of this happening, the law required defendants in freedom suits to post bonds equivalent to the value of the plaintiffs in order to guarantee that the plaintiffs would be available "to answer the judgment of the court," and judges in Montgomery County took this requirement seriously. Henry Patton's bond specifically required that he "not remove the s^d. Rachel Viney beyond the jurisdiction of the court," and when the superior court learned that James Sallust had sent four of the plaintiffs in Ruth's case out of the county, the presiding judge ordered him "[to] produce here in court . . . the four plaintiffs who have been removed as well as all the other plaintiffs" and show why he should not forfeit his three-thousand-dollar bond. Judges in the county also tried to protect plaintiffs from other forms of retaliation. James Sallust's bond, for example, required that he not "beat or misuse" any of the plaintiffs in Ruth's case, and Conrad Wall was ordered to appear in court to answer an accusation that he had "beaten and illtreated" an enslaved man named Peter, who was suing Wall for his freedom.[17]

Some judges in Montgomery County also went beyond what state law required in order to provide enslaved plaintiffs a fairer opportunity to make their cases. Because they remained enslaved, plaintiffs in freedom suits had no right to expend either their time or their energy meeting with lawyers and preparing for trial without their owner's consent. Nor were they allowed to travel without their owner's permission. In some cases, however, judges ordered defendants to allow enslaved plaintiffs adequate opportunity to develop their cases. Henry Patton, for example, was initially commanded only to allow Rachel Viney "to attend at the court to be held in & for Montgomery County" but was later ordered to permit Rachel and her son Santy to travel to Richmond and Culpepper Counties to take depositions from witnesses in their case. Similarly, James Sallust was first required to allow Ruth "to come to the clerks office for subpoenas for their witnesses, and to attend their examination and the trial" and later required to grant her "leave to go to Pittsylvania County and to the states of North and South Carolina in search of testimony if in the opinion of her counsel such a measure be necessary." Such orders were not required by the legislation governing freedom suits, but they seem to have been common in Montgomery County.[18]

It is impossible even to be certain how many different lawyers represented Flora's descendants during the three decades it took to resolve their cases. Surviving records identify at least ten: David McComas, Robert Craig, Archibald Stuart, William Ballard Preston, Daniel H. Hoge, John T. Anderson, Francis T. Anderson, James L. Woodville, James Garland, and James G. Paxton.[19] All ten came from locally prominent families and several from families with state or national reputations. Most were already well-established in their legal careers when they became involved in the cases, though Paxton and Preston were only in their twenties and new to the profession. All of them had or went on to very successful careers in law and politics. William Ballard Preston, the son of Virginia's twentieth governor, entered the House of Delegates soon after joining Unis's legal team and went on to serve in the House of Representatives and as secretary of the navy under Presidents Zachary Taylor and Millard Fillmore. Archibald Stuart and James Garland also held positions in both state and national government; James G. Paxton served in both the House of Delegates and the state senate; David McComas and James Garland became respected judges; and Francis Anderson served on the state's supreme court of appeals. Most of these men also combined their legal and political careers with that of a large planter, and the Anderson brothers operated an ironworks in addition to farming and practicing law. And all of these men had links to slavery. They all came from families with enslaved workers, and most of them owned slaves themselves at the time they were working to win the freedom of Flora's descendants. Indeed, several of the plaintiffs' attorneys held significant numbers of people in bondage. Daniel Hoge, for example, owned more than thirty enslaved workers while he was involved in the cases, and between them John and Francis Anderson owned forty-three enslaved workers and rented dozens more for the family's ironworks.

None of the lawyers known to have represented Flora's descendants left any evidence of opinions regarding slavery or African Americans that deviated from those of White southerners in general. William Ballard Preston is sometimes described as an opponent of slavery, but his opposition was limited in its scope and duration. In 1832, shortly after the bloodiest slave rebellion in the state's history, Virginia's House of Delegates debated the gradual emancipation of enslaved Virginians. During this debate, Preston did say that "the slave has a *natural* right to regain his liberty" and that Black Virginians had been made property not by natural law but by an act of the assembly. Therefore, he declared, "when the public necessity demanding their emancipation is greater than the public necessity for their retention as slaves . . . it is in the power of any subsequent Legislature to repeal the statute." Preston's views, however, were not motivated by any concern for the plight of Black Virginians; they were, he admitted, motivated by "self-preservation"—by his desire to avoid the sort of massive slave rebellion that had overthrown Haiti's "deluded planters." And when the assembly chose not to upset the status quo, Preston quickly made his peace with the institution of slavery. Like so many of his peers, he could neither imagine a peaceful, multiracial Virginia nor formulate a realistic plan for removing Black people from the state if slavery was ever abolished there. His view of African Americans' inferiority, his fear of racial mixing, and his willingness to profit from the labor of enslaved workers overrode his concern about the dangers of slavery. In 1833, a year after the House of Delegates' debate, Preston bought Fanny, Henry, and Tom at the sale of a neighbor's estate, and by 1836 he owned at least six enslaved people. He continued expanding his workforce for the rest of his life, and by the time he died, in 1862, he was one of the largest slave owners in southwestern Virginia, holding more than two hundred African Americans in bondage on multiple plantations in Montgomery and Henry Counties.[20]

The cases of Unis and her fellow plaintiffs were not entirely in the hands of White, slave-owning lawyers, though. Indeed, one of the most remarkable points to emerge from a close analysis of *Unis v. Charlton* is the role that the enslaved plaintiffs themselves played in the legal process. While evidence of Black legal consciousness sometimes appears in appellate court records, it is most evident in the mundane material generated at the level of the trial court. Order books, motions before the court, subpoenas, depositions, and the marginal comments written on some of these documents provide fascinating glimpses of the roles that enslaved men and women sometimes played in antebellum legal proceedings. Documents from the various files related to *Unis v. Charlton,* for example, clearly reveal that Flora's descendants were not just passive objects about which White lawyers and slave owners argued among themselves. Unis and her sisters and at least some of their children understood fully what their cases were about and what the outcome of those cases would mean to them. They not only initiated their suits but participated in them as actively and as frequently as they could, in spite of the numerous hurdles they faced.

The greatest obstacle, perhaps, was the fact that they remained enslaved. As African Americans in Virginia, they were assumed to be slaves until they could prove otherwise. Thus, until their suits were finally resolved, the plaintiffs belonged to their presumptive owners and had no right to expend either their time or their energy meeting with lawyers and preparing for trial without those owners' consent. As described above, judges in Montgomery County did sometimes order defendants in freedom suits to provide enslaved plaintiffs adequate opportunity to meet with counsel, but no evidence has survived of such an official order in any of the cases involving Flora's descendants. Nor could the plaintiffs easily communicate with their lawyers through letters because it seems unlikely that any of the plaintiffs could read or write. They might be able to find White allies willing to do so on their behalf, but that required finding a person they could trust. And once the plaintiffs' trials actually began, their roles were equally restricted. The statute governing freedom suits required a plaintiff's owner "to have him or her forthcoming to answer the judgement of the court" but did not specifically require that plaintiffs be allowed to attend their own trials. Judges could order a plaintiff's owner to allow it, but even if a plaintiff did attend, he or she could participate only indirectly through an attorney. Because they were Black and the defendants were White, none of the plaintiffs could actually testify in their cases.[21]

In spite of these obstacles, Flora's descendants played important roles in advancing their cases. Most critically, they could relate Flora's history to their lawyers and enable those lawyers to shape a legal strategy. Flora herself was dead by the time her descendants brought their suits, and it is unclear how much of her history any White witness understood. Flora had clearly passed her story on to her children and grandchildren, though, and their statements were critical to initiating legal proceedings. Initially, Unis appeared alone and told her story to judges and magistrates; she convinced them that her complaint deserved a hearing. Then, as the proceedings unfolded, family members continued sharing details of their history with the lawyers arguing their cases, details the lawyers used to find White witnesses who could then tell Flora's story in court. But family members did more than tell their own stories; they also collected information from the neighborhood around them. They may have spoken directly to White neighbors, they may have overheard White people's conversations, or they may have spoken to other enslaved workers who passed on information they had gathered, but somehow they obtained valuable information about their cases that they passed on to the lawyers arguing those cases.

Much of this activity remains invisible today because it probably took place in conversations between the lawyers and their clients that generated no written record. On occasion, however, the plaintiffs did leave paper trails documenting their actions. A single letter from Andrew Lewis, for example, has survived among the papers of Francis T. Anderson, one of the plaintiffs' lawyers. It clearly demonstrates Lewis's role in identifying Susanna Clark as a potential witness. In the letter, Lewis told Anderson, "I have found out there is an old lady here from the North who was well acquainted with my Grandmother and who knew her well. She gives the same account that old Mr. Metchem gave only it is stronger if anything. . . . Her testimony settles the whole matter at once so you will see how important it is to us." He then went on to share his own take on the best strategy for using Clark's testimony as effectively as possible. "We are trying to keep all this from the other side until you can have the subpoena issued for her attendance at the trial which I wish you to have done as soon as you get this letter. . . . You will please get the necessary subpoena as soon as possible."[22]

It is impossible to say for sure whether or not Lewis wrote the letter himself. Enslaved Virginians did sometimes learn to read and write, despite the opposition of most White Virginians to Black literacy. In this case, however, evidence suggests that someone else may have written the letter on Lewis's behalf. In the inventory of James Charlton's estate, Lewis is identified as Andrew; in all of the surviving court papers, he is identified as Andrew; and an endorsement on the letter itself identifies the author as Andrew. The letter, however, is signed "Andy Lewis," and the letter and signature seem to be in the same hand. The letter also includes a postscript to Anderson: "Please direct your letter to Mr. Joseph Page Christiansburg," which may indicate that Page was serving as Lewis's amanuensis. The only Joseph Page known to have lived in Montgomery County during this era was William Joseph R. Page, the son of David Page, a carpenter living in Christiansburg in 1850. According to the 1850 census, David Page held one enslaved man, age forty-five—the approximate age of Andrew Lewis that year. Moreover, because this particular census enumerator did not distinguish between hired slaves and those owned by the householder, and because when David Page died, in 1854, neither his will nor the inventory of his estate mention any enslaved workers, it seems that the man identified in 1850 was probably hired, as Andrew was until his case was resolved. Joseph Page was just sixteen years old in 1850, which would have made him fifteen when Andrew's letter to Francis Anderson was written. A teenager certainly could have written the letter and like many White Virginians may have been in the habit of calling an African American man by a diminutive—"Andy" rather than Andrew. For his part, Lewis may have felt safer asking Joseph for help sending a letter rather than asking his father, David Page, especially if the elder Page was his temporary master.[23]

Flora's descendants also participated in deposing some of the witnesses in their cases. Many witnesses in legal proceedings testified in court, but if age, poor health, or distance made it unreasonable to expect a witness to appear in person, sworn depositions could be taken before court officials

and read as evidence when a trial was held. Because no trial transcripts
have come to light in any of the suits filed by Flora's descendants, depositions constitute a significant part of the surviving evidence from the cases,
and in several instances they show that enslaved plaintiffs actively participated in their creation. Most of the depositions in these cases identify the
questioner as "counsel for plaintiffs" or "counsel for defendant," but four
specify "question by Plaintiff." In two of those instances, it is possible that
whoever took down the deposition simply wrote plaintiff rather than counsel for plaintiff, but in the other two it was definitely not a lawyer asking
the question. In these two examples the questioner specifically referred
to Flora as "my grandmother." Other evidence indicates that the enslaved
plaintiffs even tried taking depositions themselves when they found themselves without professional legal assistance. In 1851, depositions were taken
for the plaintiffs from five witnesses who had failed to appear in court.
When the depositions were taken, however, the plaintiffs were "unable to
procure the services of an attorney to attend the taking of said depositions";
so they deposed the witnesses themselves. Unfortunately, when they were
eventually able to share these depositions with their lawyer, he informed
them that the resulting statements were "so defectively taken that they . . .
are not fit to be on the trial."[24]

And while none of the plaintiffs could testify in their cases because they
were Black and the defendants were White, they did sometimes appear in
court to argue on their own behalf and did so under oath. Andrew Lewis,
for example, came before justices at least twice to speak about his family's
case. In September 1849 he appeared before a justice of the peace in Rockbridge County "and made oath" that a witness whose testimony he wished
to have presented in court lived in Pulaski County, "more than one hundred
miles from Rockbridge court house." He therefore asked that the witness
be allowed to provide a deposition instead of testifying in person, and his
request was granted. Two years later, Lewis was back before the court in
Rockbridge to explain the defective depositions described above. With no
lawyer available to take the depositions, the enslaved plaintiffs apparently
set out to depose several witnesses themselves. Then, after being told by
their lawyer that the resulting depositions were defective, Andrew appeared before the judge to explain what had happened. On September 15,
1851, "Andrew one of the plaintiffs appeared in court & made oath" that the
five depositions taken without the assistance of counsel were "not fit to be

used on the trial." He then asserted that the witnesses "can prove very important facts" in the case and argued that "the plaintiffs cannot go safely to trial without the afores^d. witnesses or their depositions." As a result, Lewis sought and obtained a continuation of the cases.[25]

Not only did the plaintiffs participate in the legal proceedings surrounding their cases, but they sometimes traveled beyond their home counties to do so. As described more fully in later chapters, the freedom suits of Flora's descendants moved among five different counties before their final resolution, and though the depositions in which Flora's descendants asked questions were all taken in Montgomery County, Andrew Lewis's two court appearances were both in Rockbridge County, seventy-five miles away. At least one of his cousins may also have traveled to Rockbridge on trial-related business. In 1846 John Logan, a lawyer in Christiansburg, wrote the plaintiffs' attorney, Francis Anderson, that "Phillis says she does not know of any way of sending her daughter to you except by stage. . . . I will make the arrangement for her to go by stage & for you to pay the stage fare at Fincastle." Anderson's office was in Fincastle; he had no other known clients in Christiansburg; and Phillis Johnson, Unis's sister and coplaintiff, had four adult daughters at that time. Thus, it seems likely that Logan was referring to one of those daughters. Members of Unis's extended family also attended at least some court proceedings in Roanoke County. When Francis Anderson agreed to represent the family, he told a Roanoke County magistrate that "at the last term of the Superior Court for Roanoke County, application was made to him by the paupers in these causes to appear as one of their council."[26]

Enslaved Virginians could only travel legally with the permission of their owners, and nothing in the statute laying out the procedures to be followed in freedom suits required that plaintiffs be allowed to travel to prepare their cases. Judges could, however, issue orders requiring that enslaved plaintiffs be permitted to travel. No such order has survived among the records of *Unis v. Charlton*, but there were precedents for them in Montgomery County. Courts there had previously issued orders permitting Rachel Viney and her son to travel to eastern Virginia in order to locate witnesses who could help them make their case and orders permitting Ruth to travel to Pittsylvania County and to North and South Carolina to gather evidence in her suit against James Sallust.[27]

Flora's descendants knew Flora's history and why it mattered, they knew enough about the law governing freedom suits to initiate their cases in ways consistent with the requirements of those laws, and they proved to be persistent and effective advocates of their cause. None of these factors guaranteed that Unis would succeed when she left Seven Mile Farm and headed for the courthouse in Christiansburg. Still, she had reason to be optimistic. During the preceding twenty-five years, judges and juries in Montgomery County had often shown a willingness to give claims such as hers a fair hearing, and to act on the results of those hearings. Now it was up to her.

❖ 4 ❖

The Trials Begin

Like so many other aspects of her story, the beginning of Unis's legal odyssey is obscured by incomplete and confusing evidence. The first known reference to her case appears in the order book of the Montgomery County Superior Court of Law. On September 16, 1825, Unis came before Judge James Allen to present a petition in which she claimed she was "illegally held in slavery by Hannah Charlton" and sought permission to sue for her freedom *in forma pauperis*. As noted earlier, permission to sue as a pauper would bring Unis a court-appointed lawyer to help prepare and argue her case and would relieve her of all costs related to her suit. Judge Allen responded to Unis's petition as the statute governing freedom suits required. He first appointed Robert Craig to serve as Unis's counsel. Craig was thirty-three years old at the time and had been practicing law for more than a decade. He had often been appointed counsel for indigent White litigants and had recently been appointed to assist Esther and Peter in a freedom suit they were bringing against Conrad Wall. Craig was also active and prominent in local politics. In 1825 he was already serving his second term in Virginia's House of Delegates and would go on to serve five terms in the United States House of Representatives between 1829 and 1841.[1]

Having appointed Craig to assist Unis, Judge Allen directed him to "examine her case and make a true statement of the facts of the same, and his opinion thereon, and return the same to this court on tomorrow." The judge also directed Unis "to go this day to procure her evidence" and return to court the next morning. Clearly, it seems that Judge Allen intended to consider Unis's petition as quickly as possible, but in spite of his orders to

Craig and Unis, it was not to be. September 17, the next day, was the last day of the superior court's September term. Judge Allen handled a full day's business that day and then closed the court's term without hearing anything from Unis or Robert Craig. There is no evidence that Unis or Robert Craig provided any evidence to support her claim before the court's term ended or that Judge Allen took any action regarding Unis's petition. Without comment or explanation, the matter simply vanished from the court's docket.[2]

Unis, however, was undeterred, and six months later she tried again. This time she followed an alternate procedure described in the statute governing freedom suits. On March 15, 1826, Unis went before Hamilton Wade, a justice of the peace in the county, and lodged a complaint that she was being "illegally detained in slavery" by Hannah Charlton. Justices of the peace had no authority to grant pauper status to those lodging such complaints, but they were expected to act on them in specific ways. As the law directed, Wade issued a warrant ordering Hannah Charlton to appear before him or another magistrate on March 18 to answer the charge against her. No record of that appearance has survived, but if it took place, Charlton would have been required to post a bond equal to Unis's market value (two hundred dollars, according to the appraisal of James Charlton's estate) that she would allow Unis to appear at the next session of the superior court in order to petition the court for permission to sue *in forma pauperis*. Unis, however, had already entered such a petition the preceding September, so it is unclear what, if anything, happened on March 18. Nor is it clear when Flora's other children and grandchildren joined Unis in filing complaints. No record has survived of their appearing before a justice, as Unis did, but they must have done so at about the same time she did because their petitions to sue as paupers all came before the superior court of law with hers when that court met in April 1826.[3]

When the superior court convened, the presiding judge was still James Allen, who had received Unis's petition the preceding September and had appointed Robert Craig to investigate her case. While no evidence has survived of Judge Allen's having done so, someone had initiated further steps to investigate the claims of Unis and Flora's other descendants. Sometime between September 1825 and April 1826, a second lawyer, David McComas, had been assigned to join Craig as counsel for the plaintiffs. McComas, a native of Wythe County, was also an established lawyer with prior experience handling freedom suits; in 1819 he had been "assigned as additional counsel for the plaintiffs" in *Ruth v. Sallust*. He would later go on to serve as a distinguished judge in western Virginia. The lawyers' charge had also been expanded to include investigating the circumstances surrounding all of Flora's descendants, and the attorneys had already begun to identify witnesses to support their clients' claims of freedom. Unfortunately, the only evidence provided by those witnesses that has survived is a single affidavit dated April 11, 1826, the day before Judge Allen heard the petitions of Unis and Flora's other descendants to sue as paupers. In this affidavit, Hamilton Wade, the justice before whom Unis had appeared in March, declared that Elijah Meacham had testified under oath that he had known Flora in the 1770s, when they both lived in Connecticut, and that he had always understood Unis, Cena, and Phillis to be her children. According to Meacham, Flora had been enslaved by Benjamin Scott but was freed when "the state of Connecticut passed a law giving freedom to all the slaves of the said state." Sometime thereafter, Meacham had been told, Flora had been kidnapped by Oliver Hanchett and sold as a slave. After moving to Virginia in the 1790s, Meacham had seen Flora on James Charlton's farm and claimed "that he well knew her to be the same [woman] he had seen in possession of the said Benjamin Scott."[4]

Meacham's testimony and any other evidence available to Craig and McComas was, presumably, contained in a report provided to Judge Allen, and on the basis of that report the judge authorized four separate suits to proceed *in forma pauperis*. The first was that of Unis against Hannah Charlton. Two months earlier, in February 1826, John McCandless Taylor had been granted letters of administration in order to oversee the division of James Charlton's estate. Unis, however, was among the "dower slaves" who had passed immediately to the widow as part of the one-third of the estate to which she was entitled by law. Apparently, none of Flora's other descendants were included among the dower slaves, so Unis was the sole plaintiff in her suit against Hannah Charlton. Twelve other descendants who were still part James Charlton's estate became coplaintiffs in a second suit brought against the administrator of the estate, John McCandless Taylor, and the heirs of James Charlton, among whom the plaintiffs were to be divided if they lost their case. Judge Allen also authorized a third suit brought by Rhoda Ann against her owner, William Currin, and a fourth brought by Randall against his owner, John Swope. In each of the four suits, the formal complaint was one of "trespass assault & battery and false imprisonment," and in each case the plaintiffs sought monetary of damages of ten thousand dollars plus their freedom.[5]

Trespass, assault and battery, and false imprisonment were torts (wrongful acts that cause harm to an individual), and each of the cases brought by Flora's descendants constituted a civil suit lodged in the county's court of law, rather than a complaint heard in its court of chancery. Until 1875, Virginia maintained two parallel court systems, law and chancery (or equity). Depending on the circumstances of the case, either could provide a route to freedom for enslaved individuals, but the two systems operated under different rules and followed different procedures. Because of these differences, as Loren Schweninger has noted, "the first order of business was to decide which court would offer an appropriate venue for their filing of a freedom suit." Enslaved people seeking their freedom on the basis of a contested will or deed of manumission often chose to go before courts of chancery because these cases involved competing notions of fairness, and chancery courts could seek to reach conclusions that were "fair" to all parties. Flora's descendants, however, alleged that they were the victims of a simple wrongful act; they were being held against their will by specific individuals in violation of specific state laws. Their cases were better suited to the court of law, and that was where they went.[6]

As described more fully below, the identity and grouping of plaintiffs and defendants in the four cases changed several times over the years, but they remained four separate cases. The four were listed separately on court dockets, and on several occasions one of the four came to trial by itself. Everyone involved, however, understood that the four cases were inextricably linked to one another through the plaintiffs' connection to Flora. If Flora had been a free woman, all of her children and any individuals born to her female descendants were entitled to their freedom. Flora's status, therefore, became the central question in each of the four cases, the four raised many identical legal and procedural questions, and they relied on many of the same witnesses. So interwoven were the four cases that when two of their files were temporarily lost, the court clerk responsible for them downplayed the loss when transferring the remaining files to another court. "It will make, perhaps, no real difference to the parties," he wrote, "as the cases now sent you embrace every interest in contest." And for reasons of efficiency and economy it made sense to combine many of the cases' elements during their long legal odyssey. Thus the four cases frequently came to trial together; courts ruled that depositions taken for any one of the cases could be used as evidence in all of them; when the cases came before Virginia's Supreme Court of Appeals they were heard together; and today most of the surviving material from all four cases is contained in a single file.[7]

Once the court had ruled that Unis and Flora's other descendants had grounds to sue, and their suits were properly filed, the plaintiffs entered a sort of legal limbo. There was certainly no presumption that they were free. In Virginia at that time African Americans were presumed to be enslaved unless they could provide absolute proof of their status as free people of color. Thus, until a freedom suit was resolved, the plaintiff remained enslaved. Courts recognized, however, that the plaintiffs in such suits did sometimes win. If that happened, the plaintiff would suddenly become a free person under the law, and the state wanted to be certain it would be able to enforce the court's judgment, which might be impossible if the plaintiff had been sold while his or her case was pending. To avoid such a predicament, the plaintiff in a freedom suit was to remain in the custody of the county sheriff until the individual claiming to own that plaintiff posted bond "to have him or her forthcoming to answer the judgement of the court." Once the bond was posted, though, plaintiffs were returned to the custody of their putative owners to live and work as they had before until their suits were settled.[8]

In the case of Flora's descendants, bonds were set in April 1826: six hundred dollars for Unis, four thousand dollars for the twelve who were part of James Charlton's estate, six hundred dollars for Randall Lewis, and five hundred dollars for Rhoda Ann. No record has survived confirming that the bonds were actually posted, but they apparently were, and the plaintiffs returned to the control of those claiming to own them. For Randall and Rhoda Ann that meant John Swope and William Currin, respectively, and the two probably resumed lives very similar to those they had known before bringing their suits. For the other plaintiffs, however, the picture was more complicated. Initially Unis returned to the custody of Hannah Charlton, and the others to that of John McCandless Taylor, the administrator of Charlton's estate. But Hannah Charlton died in 1827, and her dower slaves, including Unis, passed back to the estate of James Charlton. That estate was supposed to be divided among Charlton's eight surviving children and the heirs of his deceased daughter, Nancy Charlton Thompson, but this proved impossible as long as the freedom suits remained unsettled. No effort to divide the estate was made at all until February 1834, when William B. Charlton petitioned the county court to order its division. In response, the court appointed commissioners to make a "full and fair distribution" of both the real and personal property in the estate of James Charlton, but eight months later, in October 1834, the commissioners reported they had been unable to fulfill their charge. They had accomplished a successful division of Charlton's land, but the unresolved freedom suits made it impossible to divide Charlton's enslaved property. The commissioners reported that "after spending several days trying to make division it was agreed by the representatives of said Charlton that it was not expedient to make division of the personal estate until the decision of said suit." William B. Charlton tried again in 1836. This time the county court appointed commissioners specifically to divide "all the slaves belonging to said estate" but stipulated that "the said slaves after being divided are to remain in the hands of the administrator [of the estate]." In this instance, no report has survived, but no evidence suggests that any of the enslaved individuals were actually assigned to particular heirs. Even if they had been, such an arrangement would have required constant adjustments as some of the enslaved women continued to bear children, children who immediately became new assets to be divided among the heirs and new plaintiffs in the pending suits.[9]

As a result, most of Flora's descendants remained for years under the control of the estate's administrator, who hired them out each year and divided the income this produced among the heirs of James Charlton. Every year from 1826 until at least 1846, the estate's administrator reported the income—a total of more than ten thousand dollars—generated by renting out the enslaved workers belonging to the estate, but he never reported from whom the money came. The workers might have been hired by Charlton's heirs, perhaps in accordance with which individuals the heirs expected to receive in the estate's eventual division; they might have been hired by individuals who, over time, acquired different heirs' rights to shares in the Charlton estate through purchase or debt settlements; or they might have been rented out to third parties with no connection to the estate but a willingness to pay for hired workers. As a result, it is impossible to say where most of Flora's descendants lived while their suits were pending or what tasks they performed. It seems quite likely that they were separated at this time and that many of them no longer lived or worked at Seven Mile Farm, but it is impossible to be certain. Only Phillis and an unknown number of her children can be followed with certainty and in their case for only two years. Phillis was pregnant in 1827, and James Charlton's eldest son, William B. Charlton, contracted with the estate to care for her and her children until March 1829. Otherwise, it remains impossible to say to whom the estate's enslaved workers were leased.[10]

Nor it is clear how long this situation lasted. Surviving records include two reports examining the accounts of John McCandless Taylor, the administrator of James Charlton's estate. They record the receipt of annual payments for "hire of negroes" from March 1826 until March 1846 and the distribution of "shares" of the rental income among Charlton's heirs. No record after March 1846 has been found, though, until a final division of the estate occurred in November 1855. Nor do tax records clarify the situation. Slave owners in Virginia were required to pay annual taxes on their personal property, including enslaved workers over the age of twelve, and the number of such workers fluctuated constantly as individuals aged or died. The number of enslaved individuals on whom John McCandless Taylor owed taxes jumped significantly between 1826 and 1827, as one might expect when he assumed the role of administrator to the estate of James Charlton. That number remained elevated through 1838 but then dropped significantly in 1839 and remained steady thereafter. None of Charlton's heirs, however, showed a significant increase in their taxable human property in 1839. Moreover, by then several of Charlton's heirs had sold their shares of the estate or had transferred them to creditors, and it is impossible to say with any certainty who might have held claims to the personal property of James Charlton—including his enslaved workers. Unis and the other plaintiffs should have remained enslaved throughout the course of their legal odyssey, and all of the surviving evidence indicates that they did. It is impossible, however, to say where they lived or for whom they worked as they awaited the outcome of their suits.[11]

For thirty years, the plaintiffs in these four suits enjoyed or endured a peculiar status. They were largely shielded from one of the greatest threats to their well-being because the defendants' bonds reduced the chance that they would sell the plaintiffs out of the county or state while their cases remained before the courts. The plaintiffs remained enslaved, though, without even the modest rights accorded free people of color in Virginia. Family members were probably leased to different people and forced to live apart from one another. They had little control over their daily lives. They were still obliged to work when, how, and where they were told to, and to work for the benefit of others rather than themselves. They had little control over their family lives. They were still required to live where they were told to live, even if that meant living apart from their parents, spouses, or children. And they lived with the constant, tantalizing knowledge that they might win their freedom but had no guarantee that they would.

Once the suits brought by Flora's descendants were approved to go forward, matters were supposed to move quickly. Legislation outlining the procedure for freedom suits declared that "every petition or suit instituted for the emancipation of a person held as a slave shall be tried at the next quarterly or superior court succeeding such petition or suit, without waiting its regular turn on the docket, unless good cause be shown, by one of the parties, for the continuance thereof."[12] Gaps in the surviving evidence make it impossible to follow each of the four suits through every step of the legal process, but it is clear that none of the suits proceeded quickly or smoothly, and that none came to trial before September 1828, three years after Unis initially appeared in the superior court seeking permission to sue and more than two years after the court granted her and Flora's other descendants leave to sue.

Delays arose in part from the time it took to gather evidence, from tactics employed to deliberately delay the process, and by changing circumstances. The defendants initially failed to appear in court and answer the charges against them and continued this tactic until the court ordered the sheriff to compel their appearance. The plaintiffs then took months to submit their declarations—formal, sworn statements necessary to advance their suits. Then, once the declarations had been submitted, the defendants refused to appear in court and enter pleas until the court entered directed judgments against them by default and ordered juries to assess damages. Only after a year of such delays, in April 1827, did the parties finally enter the trial phase. Both sides, however, immediately sought continuations in order to depose witnesses, and before any trial began further delays arose. In the case of *Randall v. Swope* it is unclear what prompted them; the superior court simply ordered continuations "for reasons appearing to the court." *Rhoda Ann v. Currin* was also continued once "for reasons appearing to the court," but then William Currin died, and the suit against him had to be "revised" when an administrator was named for his estate.[13] Similarly, the death of Hannah Charlton led to a revision of Unis's suit and a new round of delays. Hannah Charlton died in the summer of 1827, and on September 13, 1827, Unis's suit against her was "abated by the death of the defendant." The death of Hannah Charlton also meant that the dower slaves—including Unis—returned to the estate of James Charlton. Unis could then have been added as an additional plaintiff in the suit already in process between other descendants claimed by the estate of James Charlton and the estate's administrator, John McCandless Taylor, and Charlton's heirs. Instead, the court, or the plaintiffs' lawyers, or the plaintiffs themselves decided that Unis should bring a separate suit against Taylor and the heirs. The defendants in that case then refused to appear until the court entered a judgment for the plaintiff and ordered a jury to assess damages. Only then did Taylor and Charlton's heirs respond to Unis's suit, and finally, on September 12, 1828, a trial began.[14]

Ultimately, the four cases brought by Flora's descendants came to trial separately or together nine times between 1828 and 1853. The nine trials fall into two distinct phases, though, based on the lawyers representing the plaintiffs and the grounds on which they based the plaintiffs' claims to freedom. The first phase involved four trials held between 1828 and 1835. In each of these trials, the plaintiffs were represented by some or all of the same four lawyers—Robert Craig, David McComas, Archibald Stuart, and William Ballard Preston. Craig and McComas had been appointed by the time the cases were initially allowed to proceed, in April 1826. Archibald Stuart joined the plaintiffs' legal team sometime before October 1827. He had been practicing law in Campbell County since about 1817 and had been appearing in Montgomery County courts since 1825. He would go on to a successful career as a lawyer and a planter in Patrick County and would serve in both the House of Representatives and the Virginia Senate. William Ballard Preston also joined the plaintiffs' attorneys sometime between April 1828, when he was admitted to practice before the Montgomery County Superior Court, and September 1829. Preston was young and inexperienced, but he came from one of the county's most prominent families. His grandfather, William Preston, had established one of the first plantations west of the Blue Ridge Mountains, and his father, James Patton Preston, had recently served as the state's governor. William Ballard, himself, would go on to a long and distinguished career in the law and would serve in Virginia's House of Delegates and Senate, in the United States House of Representatives, and in the cabinet of Presidents Zachary Taylor and

Millard Fillmore. Unfortunately, it is impossible to say precisely who was involved in which of these four trials. All four attorneys presented a joint statement to the court after the second trial, in September 1829, but this is the only surviving document naming the four together. Indeed, the 1829 statement is the first-known evidence of Preston's participation in the suits and the last-known evidence of McComas's.[15]

These first four trials also employed a common strategy largely based on demonstrating violations of Virginia's 1778 "act for preventing the farther importation of Slaves." No full transcripts have survived for any of the trials held in any of the cases brought by Flora's descendants. Thus, most of the evidence describing what transpired in the courtroom comes from the depositions of witnesses who were allowed to forego appearing in person and from the "bills of exception" filed by the attorneys when they objected to evidence presented at the trial or to a procedural decision by the judge. Fortunately, as described more fully below, the venue in which the cases were tried moved repeatedly. The first two trials took place in Montgomery County, the third in Giles County, and the fourth in Smyth County. Each of these changes of venue increased the distance that witnesses had to travel in order to testify, which led more to do so through depositions. Thus, the evidence available to historians is more complete for the third and fourth trials than for the first two, but from the beginning it is clear that in all four of these first trials the principal argument in the plaintiffs' case revolved around possible violations of Virginia's nonimportation statute.

This approach is certainly not surprising. Arguing that an enslaved individual had been brought into Virginia illegally was a well-established basis for claiming that individual's freedom. Judicial interpretations of the 1778 act placed the burden of proof on the plaintiff; courts assumed that an enslaved plaintiff suing for his or her freedom had been brought to Virginia in accordance with the law's provision unless the plaintiff could provide positive proof of a violation. This made it a more difficult avenue to employ illegal importation as the basis for a freedom suit, but it had been used in two of the freedom suits initiated in Montgomery County before those brought by Flora's descendants, and no jury in the county had ever rejected it. Moreover, at least one of the lawyers representing Flora's descendants in these first cases had already enjoyed success with the nonimportation strategy. David McComas, who was one of the plaintiffs' lawyers from 1826 until at least 1829, had earlier been assigned to serve as "additional counsel for the plaintiffs" in *Ruth v. James Sallust*. A Montgomery County jury had found for Ruth and ordered her freed on the grounds that she had been brought into Virginia in violation of the state's 1778 act to prevent the further importation of slaves. That verdict was subsequently overturned by the supreme court of appeals on the grounds that the man who originally brought Ruth into Virginia and sold her had not been her legal owner, and that James Sallust had purchased Ruth from her legal owner only after that owner had established his title to her. The court's ruling did not challenge the validity of claims of freedom based on illegal importation. It simply found that Sallust should not be made to suffer because the man who originally brought Ruth into Virginia illegally had not been their legal owner: "his importation of them did not forfeit the right of the true owners, or entitle the slaves to their freedom."[16]

The supreme court of appeals' decision in Ruth's case came in February 1826, so McComas and his colleagues had time to consider it and adjust their approach in the suits brought by Flora's descendants. They did so by focusing their attention in these first four trials on establishing that Flora had been imported into Virginia by her true owner and that he had done so illegally. Two men, James Simpkins and James Stephens, had traveled from Virginia to New York, had participated in the purchase of Flora and her daughters, and had accompanied them back to Virginia. Simpkins had been born in Virginia and was living there when he traveled to New York. Under the 1778 nonimportation statute, "citizens of this commonwealth" had no right to purchase slaves outside of Virginia and transport them to Virginia, so any enslaved individuals Simpkins had purchased in New York should have been freed automatically upon their arrival in Virginia. James Stephens, on the other hand, was still in the process of settling his family in Virginia, and the 1778 statute specifically exempted from the ban any enslaved workers imported by "those who may incline to remove from any of the United States, and become citizens of this." Stephens could bring into Virginia any enslaved workers he owned when he left New York, but to do so legally he had to appear before a magistrate within ten days of arriving in Virginia and swear that he had not brought the enslaved workers into Virginia to sell.[17]

To the plaintiffs' first legal team, it seemed that the surest route to their clients' freedom lay in proving that James Simpkins, already a Virginia resident, had purchased Flora, Cena, and Unis in New York in 1784 and imported them illegally into Virginia. If they could establish that fact, then all three should have been freed immediately in 1784, and any children born to them since that time should also be freed as the children of free women. Gaining their freedom was also possible if James Stephens had bought Flora and her daughters, but it would be more difficult. By the time these trials began, Virginia's supreme court of appeals had ruled that "twenty years' possession, by the master, of slaves thus brought into the state, without any claim of freedom on the part of the slaves, justifies the presumption that the master had duly taken the oath required by law." If Stephens had brought Flora and her daughters into Virginia, the plaintiffs would need to rebut the presumption of compliance with positive proof that Stephens had failed to take the oath in 1784 or that one of the enslaved women had claimed her freedom before 1804.[18]

Simultaneously, the plaintiffs' first lawyers also pursued a second strategy to gain their clients' freedom, though not as aggressively as they did the issue of compliance with the nonimportation act. If Flora had actually been a free woman when Jacob Lawrence sold her in New York, then neither Simpkins nor Stephens had any legal right to purchase her in the first place. Testimony from Elijah Meacham, offered in support of Unis's 1826 complaint against Hannah Charlton and her petition to sue *in forma pauperis,* certainly supported this line of argument. Meacham claimed to have known Flora in Connecticut, where she had been enslaved to Benjamin Scott until "Connecticut passed a law giving freedom to all the slaves of the said state." After that, said Meacham, Scott permitted Flora to "enjoy her freedom, and to go at large," but sometime thereafter Flora disappeared from the neighborhood, and "it was generally reported and believed . . . that she was run off by Oliver Hanchett and David Brunson in order to make a slave of her." If that were true and Flora had actually been a free woman when she was sold to either Simpkins or Stephens, then her daughters and all of her daughters' children were also free, but proving in a Virginia court the status of a woman living in Connecticut forty years earlier must have seemed more challenging than proving what happened in Virginia. Attorneys for the plaintiffs did occasionally ask questions or raise objections that indicate they considered Flora's status at the time she was sold in New York to be possible grounds for claiming the freedom of her descendants, but surviving documents from the early trials include relatively few references to Flora's status before her importation to Virginia.[19]

It is impossible to determine much at all about the first trial. According to the superior court's order book, two separate cases came to trial in September 1828: *Unis v. Taylor and the heirs of James Charlton* and *Andrew, Reubin, Cena, Julius, Phillis, William, Helen, Mary, Tarlton, Matilda, Flora, and James v. Taylor and the heirs of James Charlton*. Both trials began and ended on the same days, though, and both were heard by the same twelve jurors. They were recorded separately in the court's order book, but it seems clear that the two trials were actually conducted as one. Reconstructing what happened in that trial, however, is almost impossible. There are no transcripts from any of the trials, and this one seems to have generated no bills of exception. Attorneys for the plaintiffs certainly knew about the testimony that Elijah Meacham had provided to Hamilton Wade in 1826, but it is impossible to say whether or not Meacham testified in 1828. One other witness statement taken before the 1828 trial has survived, a deposition by Massa Simpkins, the sister-in-law of James Simpkins. Only one of the defendants, William B. Charlton, asked Simpkins any questions, though, making it impossible to say with certainty on what grounds the plaintiffs might have based their claims of freedom. The questions Charlton asked, however, suggest that he was preparing to counter claims made on two possible grounds. He first asked Simpkins who purchased Flora and her children and brought them from New York to Virginia. She replied that James Stephens had, which would have been important information if Unis based her claim on a violation of Virginia's nonimportation statute. Charlton also asked Simpkins if before leaving New York she had ever heard that Flora was a free woman or had any claim to freedom. Simpkins's declaration that she had heard no such claim could have been used to counter any effort by Flora's descendants to secure their freedom on the grounds that their ancestor had been a free woman.[20]

Whatever strategies the parties employed in this first trial and whatever evidence they presented, neither party prevailed. After hearing the evidence and deliberating over two days, members of the jury declared "they could not agree." The judge then discharged the jurors, and both suits were continued until the court's next session. At that same session of the court, in September 1828, Randall's case against John Swope was also continued to the next term, and Rhoda Ann's was revised to reflect the names of the administrators of William Currin's estate.[21]

Over the next several months, John Swope, William Currin's administrator, and the heirs of James Charlton seem to have lost confidence in their ability to win their cases under the circumstances then prevailing in Montgomery County. When the court next met, in April 1829, the defendants requested that all four cases be continued until the next meeting of the court. This motion was granted. Then, two days later, on April 17, the defendants returned to court seeking a change of venue to remove the cases from Montgomery County. Defendants in all four cases apparently made the same request, though only the affidavit of William B. Charlton's has survived.[22] In it, Charlton maintained that it was impossible to conduct "a fair and impartial trial" in Montgomery County "in consequence of the excitement of public feeling in the said county in favor of the claim of the slaves to freedom." He went on to assert that "from the length of time the suits have been depending, from the fact that there has been a trial in which the jury did not agree, and from the further fact much property is depending on the decision of the causes . . . the opinion of the citizens of Montgomery is generally made up in relation to the said causes." The request was denied, though, and the defendants moved to strengthen their cases in anticipation of a new trial.[23]

Before that trial could even begin, the identity of the plaintiffs changed yet again. At least through April 1829, Unis had been the sole plaintiff in one of the suits filed by Flora's descendants. Even after Hannah Charlton died and the defendants in Unis's suit became identical to those named in the suit brought by Andrew and eleven other descendants, Unis remained the sole plaintiff in what, in the court's order book at least, was a separate legal proceeding. Sometime between April and September 1829, however, that changed. Unis's sons, Andrew and Reuben, her sister Cena, and Cena's son, Julius, all became coplaintiffs in Unis's case and vanished from the case henceforth identified as *Phillis et al. v. Taylor et al.*, in which the plaintiffs were Phillis and her children: William, Helen, Mary, Tarlton, Matilda, Flora, and James.

The reason for this change remains a mystery. Cena, Unis, and Phillis were all daughters of Flora; all three were seeking freedom for themselves and their children; their suits were all authorized to proceed at the same time, in the same manner, and with the same counsel; and following the death of Hannah Charlton all three were suing the same defendants—the administrator and heirs of James Charlton's estate. The only significant difference between Phillis's situation and that of her sisters seems to be that Phillis had been born in Virginia. As noted above, in these first trials the plaintiffs' lawyers seem to have based their case principally on violations of the 1778 nonimportation statute and to a lesser degree on Flora's status before her importation. Cena and Unis, therefore, had two possible routes to freedom: their own illegal importation or their descent from a freewoman. Phillis, however, had never been imported to Virginia. Thus, her only claim to freedom was descent from a free woman, and this may explain why the cases of Unis and Cena and their children were separated from that of Phillis and hers.

Almost immediately after the plaintiffs were rearranged, Phillis's case came to trial again. This trial opened on September 16, 1829, and continued until September 18. As was true of the earlier trial, little evidence has survived of what happened in court, but it does seem that the plaintiffs' case still revolved around compliance with the nonimportation act. When the defense called James Simpkins to testify, the court initially ruled that he was "an incompetent witness." This was probably because if Phillis won her case, he might face legal or financial consequences for having sold "property" he had no right to sell. Simpkins had a vested interest in the outcome of the trial and might not testify truthfully. In response, the defense submitted documents by which John McCandless Taylor, administrator for the estate of James Charlton, and Charlton's heirs granted Simpkins a release from "all right of recovery" if the plaintiffs gained their freedom. Simpkins accepted the release, and the court then permitted him to testify, despite the objection of the plaintiffs' lawyer. Once again, after hearing and considering the evidence, though, jurors announced "they could not agree," and the case was continued to the next term.[24]

Now it was the plaintiffs' turn to seek a change of venue. Immediately after Phillis's second trial, lawyers representing Flora's descendants asked to move all of the trials out of Montgomery County. Robert Craig, David McComas, Archibald Stuart, and William Ballard Preston submitted a joint affidavit in the days after of Phillis's trial. In it they declared that "a fair trial of the above case may not be obtained in this county from the fact that there has been already two hung juries, from the great interest and conversation which it has produced in the county, and from various other circumstances." And, they added, this did not apply only to Phillis's case; "the same circumstances will operate in the various pauper cases in this court against the administrator and heirs of James Charlton decd." They asked, therefore, that all four cases be moved to another jurisdiction. Having rejected a similar request from the defense six months earlier, the court now granted that of the plaintiffs, and on September 19, 1829, all of the suits filed by Flora's descendants were ordered moved to Giles County.[25]

Giles County is adjacent to Montgomery County, and its seat, Pearisburg, is about thirty-five miles northwest of Christiansburg. The move meant that many parties to the suits, including witnesses, probably had to travel farther to participate in the court proceedings, but no one complained to the court about any inconvenience the move might create. The move also brought the cases into an environment in which slavery was less well-established. Giles County is more mountainous than Montgomery and had less land suitable for commercial agriculture. It was also more distant from the Great Road, which carried much of the human and commercial traffic through southwest Virginia. Thus, there was less incentive to employ slaves in Giles County, and in 1830 they made up just 8.8 percent of the county's population, compared to 16.5 percent in Montgomery. Perhaps the judge in Montgomery County who ordered the move believed that the suits would generate less interest or concern among the residents of Giles County than they would in Montgomery. It might also have reduced the chances that jurymen would be slave owners. No one at the time, however, mentioned these possibilities.[26]

The cases of Flora's descendants remained before the court in Giles County for just over three years, and these were years that saw dramatic changes in Virginia, changes that profoundly affected the institution of slavery and the lives of the people held in its grip. The changes arose from the terror sparked by Nat Turner's Revolt. Turner was an enslaved man and self-ordained preacher living in Southampton County. In the late 1820s he began to receive what he took to be signs that God had chosen him to challenge the White-controlled system holding him, his family, and his community in bondage. On the night of August 21, 1831, he and a handful of enslaved companions set out to kill as many White Virginians as they could in the hope that this would inspire other enslaved people to join them and spark a wider revolt that would overturn Virginia's racial hierarchy. Turner did gain several dozen adherents to his cause, and they did manage to kill at least fifty-five White men, women, and children over the next forty-eight hours, but the slaveholding community responded quickly and with overwhelming force.

Turner himself eluded capture for more than two months, but many of those who had joined him were killed or captured within days. Dozens of other enslaved men who had played no role in the revolt were summarily executed by White militia units and mobs that roamed the county seeking "justice." A week after the revolt began, military leaders finally issued an order calling for White people to stop killing suspected rebels and threatening to punish any who continued to do so. That seems to have ended the extralegal killings, but in the months that followed several dozen enslaved men and women and a smaller number of free people of color were tried for their alleged participation in the revolt. Some of the accused were acquitted, but eighteen enslaved men were hanged (as was one free man of color), and twelve others were sold out of the state after being convicted of participation in Turner's plot. Turner himself was finally captured in late October. He was tried, convicted, and hanged within two weeks.[27]

Less than a month after Turner's execution, Virginia's General Assembly convened in Richmond. In the months leading up to the legislative session, White Virginians had responded to Nat Turner's Revolt in radically different ways. Some called for tighter restrictions on both enslaved and free Black people, especially on Black preachers, and on the distribution of abolitionist literature. Others, however, suggested that the only way to guarantee the security of White Virginians was to remove all Black Virginians from the state. Advocates of the assisted, voluntary removal of free people of color—"colonization," in the language of the day—had been making their case for years, and modest efforts to accomplish their goal had already begun. But now discussion turned to the state unilaterally emancipating and removing enslaved African Americans despite any objection from either the enslaved or their enslavers. All options seemed up for consideration, and throughout the fall of 1831, newspapers carried articles and letters advocating and opposing different approaches to the "problems" presented by slavery and free people of color. Meanwhile, supporters circulated different petitions calling for the increased regulation of Virginia's Black population, for the removal of free Black people from the state, and for the emancipation and removal of enslaved Virginians.

When the assembly convened, however, many of its members seemed disinclined to consider the full range of options offered by the public. Governor John Floyd's message to the assembly only asked its members to silence "negro preachers," strengthen laws intended to preserve "due subordination" of the enslaved population, and provide an annual appropriation to fund the removal of free people of color. Thus, when the House of Delegates responded by creating a "Select Committee on the Colored Population," it does not seem to have expected that committee to consider any plan for emancipation. This expectation was challenged, however, as petitions generated in the aftermath of Nat Turner's Revolt came before the assembly. Proslavery members of the House were happy to refer those calling for greater restrictions on Black Virginians or the removal of free people of color to the select committee but objected to accepting or referring any petitions raising the possibility of emancipation. Many members, however, were uncomfortable rejecting petitions from their constituents, so over the objections of proslavery members, petitions calling for emancipation were also referred to the committee. In the weeks that followed, members of the House offered competing resolutions calling for the select committee to recommend gradual emancipation or to refrain from doing so. Finally, in January 1832, came a resolution calling for the select committee to be discharged from considering any petition calling for emancipation and declaring "that it is not expedient to legislate on the subject." This was met with a rival resolution instructing the committee to inquire into the expediency of holding a public referendum on a proposal calling for the gradual emancipation and removal of enslaved Virginians.

And so began the great debate. For three weeks members of the House spoke at length on every aspect of the issue. Was slavery evil? Who was responsible for its establishment in Virginia? Were the enslaved people or property? Did slavery deprive White men of honest labor and fair wages? Did the federal Constitution bar state action? How could White Virginians best ensure their own security and property? It was during the course of this debate that William Ballard Preston, at the time one of the lawyers representing Flora's descendants in their freedom suits, declared that slavery in Virginia was a creation of the legislature and that the legislature could modify or abolish that institution if doing so served the public good. As described in chapter 3, he did so in the belief that the danger of slave rebellion might outweigh the economic benefits of slavery. Throughout the weeks of debate, the public galleries of the House were open, and many of the speeches were printed in the newspapers. Thus, everyone in Virginia, Black or White, had the opportunity to hear, read, or hear about what was said in the assembly.

In the end, nothing came of the calls for emancipation. When the debates finally ended, members of the House rejected any change in the status quo. They adopted a report of the select committee that declared it would be inexpedient for the House to consider any steps to abolish slavery in the commonwealth. It did, however, amend the report to include a vague statement that could be interpreted as leaving the door open for reconsideration at some indeterminate date in the future. For good measure, the assembly also passed legislation further restricting the activities of free and enslaved Black people in Virginia.[28]

No doubt, all of the parties engaged in the suits of Flora's descendants followed reports of Nat Turner's Revolt and of the debates in Richmond, but it is impossible to say what effect, if any, those events had on the suits' progress. For most of the time that the cases were before the court in Giles County, they were simply continued from one meeting of the court to the next. Eventually, those of Unis and Phillis were set for trial in October 1832, but that of Unis was continued at the last minute on a motion of the defendants. Thus, only *Phillis & others against Charltons adm'. & others* ever came to trial in Pearisburg.[29] As in all of the trials involving Flora's descendants, no transcript has survived from Phillis's trial, and the only evidence of the parties' legal strategies comes from depositions and bills of exception. It seems, however, that Phillis's attorneys still based her claim of freedom on two familiar grounds: that Flora had been free when she was taken to New York and sold or, if she had been legally enslaved there, that she should have been freed immediately when James Simpkins brought her into Virginia in violation of the nonimportation act. Under either scenario, Phillis would be entitled to her freedom as the daughter of a free woman.

Earlier in 1832, as the parties prepared for trial, Henry Carty and Elijah Meacham had been among the witnesses summoned to appear on the plaintiffs' behalf. Instead, both men provided depositions that were read into evidence at Phillis's trial. Carty first declared that he had always understood that James Charlton had purchased Flora and her daughters from James Simpkins—who should not have been permitted under Virginia law to import slaves into the commonwealth. Carty further testified that Flora herself had often claimed that she had been enslaved illegally: "She told me at different times that if she had her just rights she would be a free woman." And, he said, Flora had asked him to write "back where she came from to obtain information from the people there concerning her freedom." Carty also said that Ezekiel Howard, who had been a county magistrate before his death, had told him that Flora applied to him for her freedom. Elijah

Meacham also indicated that Flora may have been freed before she was brought to Virginia. He testified that sometime around 1792 he had spoken to James Charlton about Flora's status and that Charlton had told him, "if she obtained her freedom it would not hurt him so bad, but it would ruin James Simpkins." This was apparently a reference to the fact that if Flora had been free, Charlton would have grounds to recover from Simpkins the money he had paid for her and her children or, if she had been a slave, that both Simpkins and Charlton might be liable to significant fines under the 1778 nonimportation act.[30]

In response, the defendants seem to have concentrated their efforts on showing that Flora and her daughters were actually imported by James Stephens when he brought his family to settle in Virginia, which was allowed under the nonimportation statute, and that Flora had been legally enslaved at the time Stephens bought her. It is impossible to be certain how the defendants planned to address the issue of the oath Stevens should have taken when he imported Flora and her daughters, but they were probably counting on the presumption of compliance by arguing it had gone unchallenged for more than twenty years. To help make their case, they had taken depositions from James Stephens's sons while the cases were still pending in Montgomery County. Thomas and William Stephens were then living in Indiana and had apparently responded under oath to questions the defense submitted in writing. Both men declared that their father, James Stephens, had owned Flora and her daughters when they arrived in Virginia. The depositions had reached Christiansburg too late to be used in Phillis's trial there, in September 1829, but the defense hoped to use them when the trials shifted to Giles County. The plaintiffs, however, objected to any use of the depositions on the grounds that the plaintiffs had not been properly notified the depositions were to be taken, and, in spite of the Charlton heirs' insistence that the depositions included material evidence, the plaintiffs' argument seems to have prevailed. The defense then had the depositions taken again, after first providing the plaintiffs with the required notice, and presumably had them read into evidence at the 1832 trial.[31]

Overshadowing the evidence offered, however, were procedural questions that prompted numerous objections, especially from lawyers representing the plaintiffs. Thomas Lawrence had testified for the plaintiffs on the first day of the trial. The next day, after the defense had begun presenting its case, Lawrence was allowed to testify a second time in order to provide "an important fact" he had omitted during his earlier testimony and "for the purpose of rebutting facts stated by the defendants witnesses." Then, on third day of the trial, as the lawyers were making their closing arguments, a question arose concerning what exactly Lawrence had said during his second round of testimony, and when one of the jurors requested clarification, the judge permitted Lawrence to take the stand a third time. When court reconvened the next morning, defense lawyers sought to introduce new evidence to show that Lawrence's latest testimony differed from that he had provided in one of the earlier trials. The judge granted the request and allowed one of the defendants' lawyers to testify as a witness about Lawrence's earlier testimony and to use his notes and a bill of exception from that earlier trial "for the purpose of refreshing his memory" as he testified. Counsel for the plaintiffs then objected both to the introduction of new evidence after closing arguments had begun and to the witness's use of written notes as an aide-mémoire, but the objections were overruled, and the testimony was allowed.[32]

After all that, the jury failed again to reach a verdict, and the case was continued to the next term. But the trial had also generated seven bills of exception (five from the plaintiffs and two from the defendants), and the presiding judge, James E. Brown, seems to have decided that he had had enough. After the trial concluded, Judge Brown suddenly discovered a potential conflict of interest. He announced: "[T]he judge of the court in consequence of the connection existing between his family and that of William B. Charlton one of the distributees of James Charlton Dec[d]. who has a very large amount of property depending in these suits which involve some important legal questions feels a delicasy in deciding them." As result, he ordered all four suits transferred again, this time to Smyth County.[33]

Smyth County is even farther from Montgomery County than Giles is. Marion, the seat of Smyth County, lies some seventy-five miles southwest of Christiansburg, so travel to the courthouse became more expensive and more time-consuming. This proved a boon to historians, though, because the greater inconvenience involved in traveling to Marion meant that more witnesses testified through sworn depositions than had been the case in earlier trials. And with more depositions available, it is possible to provide greater detail concerning the evidence each party offered to make its case and to understand why earlier juries had been unable to agree on a verdict. As it was in Giles County, slavery was also less common in Smyth County than it was in Montgomery. By 1840, enslaved workers comprised 12.8 percent of the population of Smyth County, compared to just over 20 percent in Montgomery, though what effect, if any, this had on legal proceedings is impossible to gauge.[34]

The move to Smyth County certainly did nothing to expedite the legal process. Records of the suits were received in Marion in April 1833, and officials there immediately placed them on the court's docket. For more than two years, though, each time the court convened all four cases were simply continued until next term. Three of the four never did come to trial, in Smyth County, but *Phillis and her children against John McC. Taylor adm. of James Charlton decd. & others* finally did in August 1835. Surviving depositions indicate that little had changed in the basic strategy employed by the plaintiffs' lawyers. At least two of the original lawyers—Robert Craig and William Ballard Preston—were still representing Flora's descendants, and the central point in their argument remained that Flora and her daughters had been brought to Virginia in violation of the state's nonimportation act. The plaintiffs did continue to raise the question of whether or not Flora had actually been a free woman when she was brought to Virginia, but it remained a secondary issue in their case. The central question, therefore, was still whether Jacob Lawrence sold Flora and her daughters to James Stephens or to James Simpkins and which man imported Flora, Cena, and Unis into Virginia.[35]

Attorneys for the plaintiffs continued to argue that James Simpkins had purchased Flora and her daughters in New York and brought them to Virginia in violation of the Virginia statue barring "citizens of this commonwealth" from importing enslaved workers purchased outside Virginia. At an earlier trial, Henry Carty and Elijah Meacham had provided depositions stating that Simpkins had sold Flora to James Charlton, and now the plaintiffs provided depositions from John and Thomas Lawrence, nephews of Jacob Lawrence, that explained precisely how Simpkins had acquired her. According to the Lawrences, when James Stephens arrived in New York and began selling the deerskins he had brought from Virginia, he employed Simpkins as his agent because Stephens had fled New York to escape his creditors and "being very much in debt, dare not be seen there." When Simpkins bought Flora, Cena, and Unis, however, he reportedly did so on his own behalf. John Lawrence testified that he was present when the sale took place, and when asked, "Did you hear James Simpkins say for whom he purchased the negroes," Lawrence replied, "he told me he purchased them for himself so he could make money by them." Thomas Lawrence confirmed his brother's account and testified that Jacob Lawrence had passed a paper to James Simpkins that Thomas Lawrence took to be "a bill of sale": "It bound Jacob Lawrence and his heirs to support the title of the negroes to James Simpkins and his heirs." The defense objected to any reference to a bill of sale unless it could actually be introduced in evidence, but the court seems to have allowed the deposition to be read during the trial.[36]

For their part, the defendants offered witnesses to rebut the plaintiffs' case and to testify that it was James Stephens who bought Flora and her daughters. Stephens's sons had already provided depositions stating that their father had purchased Flora and her daughters in New York just before moving his family to Virginia. William Stevens had testified that he was present when the sale took place and that "the money was paid by my father." Moreover, both sons claimed that their father owned the wagon in which Flora and her daughters traveled to Virginia and that "their removal was at his expense." James Simpkins himself also provided a deposition in which he declared emphatically that he had "no interest either direct or indirect in the said slaves, before they were removed to Virginia." Cross-examined by lawyers for the plaintiffs, Simpkins confirmed that he had initially acted as Stephens's agent when selling the latter's deerskins because Stephens was "embargoed" in New York as a result of the debts he owed there. He had even participated in the initial, unsuccessful, discussion with Jacob Lawrence about buying Flora. After that, though, Simpkins declared that he stopped trading as Stephens's agent. When Lawrence changed his mind and agreed to sell Flora and her daughters, "Stephens made the bargain himself, and paid the money himself."[37]

The trial continued for three days and ended with yet another hung jury. The case was then continued to the next term, as were the other three, but none of them ever came to trial again in Smyth County. For the next four years each was continued repeatedly "for reasons appearing to the court." Finally, in May 1840, attorneys for both parties appeared in court, and "by their consent, and for good cause shown," the judge ordered the suits transferred to Roanoke County for disposition.[38] No evidence has survived to indicate who initiated this change of venue or on what basis, but it is not difficult to imagine why both the plaintiffs and the defendants would have welcomed the move. Travel from Montgomery County to Smyth County was both time-consuming and expensive, whereas Roanoke County was adjacent to Montgomery, and Salem, the county seat, lay just twenty-five miles from Christiansburg. Holding the proceedings in Roanoke County would still place them beyond the "great interest and conversation" in Montgomery County that had prompted the initial change of venue but would reduce significantly the travel involved for the individuals named in the suits, their attorneys, and the witnesses.

The move to Roanoke County also brought the proceedings into a jurisdiction in which the institution of slavery was more well-established than in any of those in which the cases had been heard previously. Farmers in Roanoke County certainly did not produce tobacco in the quantities grown in Southside Virginia. The county was, however, the second-largest producer of tobacco in the state's western census district, and in antebellum Virginia, tobacco meant slaves. In 1840, enslaved workers made up 28 percent of the population of Roanoke County, compared to 20 percent in Montgomery County and less than 13 percent in both Giles and Smyth. As a result, slave owners were more likely to number among the jurors who heard any freedom suit tried in Roanoke County.[39]

For the plaintiffs, however, the most significant effect of the change in venue was the change in their legal representation that accompanied it.

❖ 5 ❖

A New Legal Strategy

S urviving records from the suits brought by Flora's descendants make
it difficult to reconstruct accurately the changes that took place
among the plaintiffs' lawyers as their suits worked their way through
the legal process. It seems, however, that once the cases moved from Smyth
County to Roanoke County, in May 1840, none of the four lawyers known
to have represented the plaintiffs between 1826 and 1840 continued to do
so. It is impossible to be certain because the surviving records so rarely
name the attorneys for either party in the suits. Depositions occasionally
identify by name the attorneys questioning a witness. It is clear, for example, that William Ballard Preston represented the plaintiffs at the taking
of a deposition in December 1833 and that Robert Craig did so at depositions taken in October 1832 and July 1835. More often, however, both
depositions and court orders simply refer to "counsel" or "attorneys" for
the plaintiffs without providing any names. On May 5, 1840, for example,
when the judge in Smyth County ordered the cases transferred to Roanoke
County, the order book recorded: "This day came the parties by their attorneys." For two years after that, however, even such generic references are
missing, and it is unclear if anyone provided trained legal counsel for the
enslaved plaintiffs. In fact, the surviving evidence suggests that they represented themselves during this period.[1]

By this time, the plaintiffs' cases had been in court for more than a decade and had been to trial four times. Unis and the other plaintiffs had not
yet won their freedom, but they had enjoyed multiple opportunities to see
some of what lawyers did preparing for trial. They had been able to learn

about the theoretical possibility of initiating a freedom suit through the enslaved community's grapevine telegraph and through conversations they may have overheard among the White residents and guests at Seven Mile Farm. Such sources probably did not tell them much, however, about what was actually needed in order to present their story in a courtroom. For the past decade, though, they had, to some extent, interacted with their attorneys and, in the process, had evidently learned more about the practical steps necessary to present their case in court.

In December 1840, for example, the enslaved plaintiffs seem to have taken depositions from two witnesses, Henry Carty and Francis Charlton, without the aid of a lawyer. The notice sent to the defendant, John McCandless Taylor, alerting him to the time and place at which Carty and Charlton would be deposed was signed "Andrew a pauper," and the notification employed the first person—"I shall at the house of John Wade"—suggesting that Andrew would be taking the lead. And when the depositions were actually taken, it seems that it was Andrew who questioned the witnesses. It was certainly one of Flora's descendants. Both of the depositions identify the questioner as "plaintiff," and in each case the questioner referred specifically to "my grandmother" or "my grandmother Flora." Of course, both the notification and the depositions were written, and both employ standard legal language, suggesting that perhaps an attorney or a clerk actually wrote them, but neither suggests that a lawyer initiated or participated in the questioning of these two witnesses.[2]

Surviving records do not reveal why Andrew found himself deposing witnesses in 1840. None of the attorneys originally appointed to assist Flora's descendants had died or left the region by then, and all of them remained active in law and politics for years after disappearing from these cases. Nor has any evidence come to light explaining their departure from the cases. It seems that Messrs. Craig, McComas, Stuart, and Preston may simply have decided that they had done enough. They had spent more than a decade working on cases for which they had received no compensation and had incurred considerable expense for their time and the cost of their travel to Giles and Smyth Counties. They had taken cases to trial four times, and each of those trials had ended in a hung jury. They may simply have felt there was little reason to expect that future trials would end differently and that they had done their fair share to preserve the honor of Virginia's legal system. They could now step aside with a clear conscience.[3]

The plaintiffs seem to have remained without legal representation until early 1842, though their suits continued to wend their way through the legal system. Files for the four cases reached Salem in October 1840 and were placed on the docket for the following March, when the next term of the superior court was scheduled to begin. When the court convened, however, the presiding judge, Edward Johnston, announced that he was recusing himself from participation in these and six other cases in which he worried about the appearance of a conflict of interest. "The judge of the court," Johnston declared, "having been heretofore employed as counsel in the ten causes last above named, & therefore feeling a delicacy in regard to the trial of the same, it is ordered that they be continued until the next term." When that next term opened, in August, the suits were continued again without action or comment, perhaps because the court had not yet found a substitute judge to hear them, but by March 1842 a substitute judge had been identified, witnesses had been summoned to appear, and a trial was set to begin.[4]

When the court convened, the plaintiffs, still without lawyers, discovered that eight witnesses called to appear on their behalf had failed to appear, and they successfully asked for a continuance: "On motion of the plaintiffs & for reasons appearing to the Court, the four causes last named are continued until the next term." The plaintiffs also recognized that they needed professional representation and took steps to secure it, though not through the court directly. Francis T. Anderson, whose office was in Botetourt County, was among the lawyers gathered at the courthouse that day, and five months later he explained in an affidavit what had happened that morning. "At the last term of the Superior Court for Roanoke County," he declared, "application was made to him by the paupers in these causes to appear as one of their council. It being represented to him that none of the council originally assigned or engaged in their causes were in attendance, & that the plaintiffs were in need of professional aid, after looking into the papers to see the grounds of their application he consented to appear for them." Anderson, however, may have taken some time "looking into the papers" and making his decision. He mentioned no specific action he had taken in March, and there is no clear evidence of his acting on the plaintiffs' behalf until that summer. Instead, another attorney, Daniel H. Hoge, seems to have stepped in to provide immediate assistance. In his own affidavit, also provided in August 1842, Hoge explained that at the court's March term he had spoken to Hetty Richardson, one of the witnesses summoned by the plaintiffs, and "had some conversation on the subject of her testimony." He also claimed that he sought a subpoena for this witness "soon after the close of the last term of this court." Thus, it seems that Hoge, rather than Anderson, was the attorney who, according to the court order book, asked in March that eight other witnesses be summoned to appear on the plaintiffs' behalf at the court's next term.[5]

Hoge may have provided legal assistance to Unis, Andrew, and the other plaintiffs for a few more weeks or months, but by July 1842 Francis T. Anderson had assumed the primary responsibility for their suits. Anderson came from a wealthy, slave-owning family in Botetourt County, where his father operated a plantation and an ironworks using enslaved workers. Anderson had graduated from Washington College (now Washington & Lee University) in 1827, began practicing law in 1830, and by 1842 was an experienced and respected member of the bar. Nothing suggests that he had any role in the cases of Flora's descendants before March 1842 or that he was even aware of the suits before encountering the plaintiffs at the courthouse in Salem. Soon after meeting them, though, Anderson took up their cause and began working aggressively on their behalf.[6]

The decision of Francis Anderson to assist Flora's descendants marked an important turning point in their legal odyssey. By the summer of 1842, almost seventeen years had passed since Unis first approached Judge James Allen in Montgomery County. For most of that time, she and her coplaintiffs had been represented by some or all of their original lawyers—David McComas, Robert Craig, Archibald Stuart, and William Ballard Preston. Those lawyers had consistently based their case most heavily on their argument that Flora, Cena, and Unis had been imported to Virginia by James Simpkins in violation of the state's 1778 nonimportation statute and should have been freed immediately upon their arrival. They had gone to trial four times with this strategy, and each of those trials had resulted in a hung jury. Francis Anderson, however, immediately seized on the potential offered by a different approach. As he explained in the affidavit he submitted to the court in August 1842:

> From an examination of the causes this affiant [Anderson] was strongly inclined to believe that Flora the female ancestor of the plaintiffs, had been freed in the state of Connecticut, & afterwards fraudulently conveyed to the state of New York & there sold, and it seemed that no

effort had been made to collect testimony to support that important fact in the cause. He has been informed that the former council relied upon other points in the cause, which they deemed sufficient to establish the plaintiffs right to freedom, & therefore regarded it unnecessary to investigate that branch of the case. But as there had been three or four trials & hung juries this affiant deemed it of very great importance to the plaintiffs & to the justice of the cause that that very important fact should be investigated.[7]

This new approach to the cases would not have been possible without the active participation of Flora's descendants. Anderson himself seems to have known nothing about Flora or the suits brought by her descendants until he met the plaintiffs in March 1842. At that time, he later explained, none of the plaintiffs' original lawyers had been available to familiarize him with the cases, and he had been forced "to rely upon the illiterate paupers" for information. Flora's children and grandchildren may have been poor and illiterate, but they knew the story of her life. They had heard it growing up, and they knew specific details of her experiences in New England and New York. Unis and her sisters were able to tell Anderson that their mother had lived in Hartford County, Connecticut, had once been the property of a man named Benjamin Scott, and had been kidnapped about the year 1782 by Oliver Hanchett and David Brunson. As a lawyer and a slave owner, Anderson would certainly have known that descent from a free woman was grounds for a successful freedom suit, but without the detailed information provided by Flora's descendants, it would have been much more difficult, perhaps impossible, for him to locate witnesses whose testimony would be admissible against White defendants in a Virginia court. That family members had preserved these essential details for sixty years was critical to the next phase of their legal campaign to gain their freedom. As Anderson explained in his affidavit, though, their recollections first had to be "investigated" before they could yield any evidence admissible in a court of law.[8]

He began that investigation almost immediately. Before Anderson had even begun to represent Flora's descendants in court, he "embraced the earliest opportunity to obtain respectable references to gentlemen in Hartford Connecticut from whom he might obtain information." When his first effort failed to elicit a response, Anderson secured references to three more "gentlemen of high standing" in Hartford and wrote to them in late July.

This time he received a reply. It came from the Rev. Joel Hawes, a respected Congregational minister in Hartford. Anderson wrote to Hawes seeking his help on July 27, 1842, and Hawes was well placed to provide it. He had been the minister at First Church, in Hartford, for more than two decades and had extensive connections throughout New England's network of Congregational ministers. He was also a staunch opponent of slavery. Though initially a supporter of colonization and never, in the words of an early biographer, "a political preacher," Hawes had grown steadily more outspoken in his opposition to slavery. In 1838, he had helped to establish the Connecticut Anti-Slavery Society, and in 1843 he would host Frederick Douglass when the Black abolitionist gave his first speech in Hartford. Most critically, perhaps, his Hartford home was just twenty miles from Suffield, where Flora had lived before being taken to New York, and the city hosted several newspapers that circulated throughout northern Connecticut and southwestern Massachusetts.[9]

Anderson's letter to Hawes has not survived, but it is clear from what followed that he asked Hawes for help identifying individuals in Connecticut who might be able to verify the claim that Flora had been a free woman when she was taken to New York and sold as a slave. He also seems to have told Hawes that the case would be heard in late August and must have urged him to act as quickly as possible. Hawes immediately placed announcements in at least two regional newspapers, the *Connecticut Courant* and the *Hartford Courant* (see fig. 6). Readers were informed that "a suit is pending in Virginia for the freedom of several colored persons who claim they are the children of FLORA, once the slave of Benjamin Scott, formerly a resident of this county, but liberated by him, and afterwards, about the year 1782, carried into New York and sold, as is claimed, by Oliver Hanchett and Davis Brunson, and thence transported to Virginia." Anyone with "information on this subject" was asked to contact Hawes or Amos M. Collins, another abolitionist living in Hartford. The response was quick and encouraging. The announcements appeared on August 5 and 6, and by August 12 Hawes had received two letters from Suffield "bearing information on the case." He promptly wrote Anderson that the news from Suffield "leaves no room to doubt that we shall be able to send facts very materially affecting the case committed to your advocacy." He promised to move forward with "all dispatch to get the necessary affidavits," but recognizing that "it may necessarily require some time to have the business done thoroughly, I thought it best to

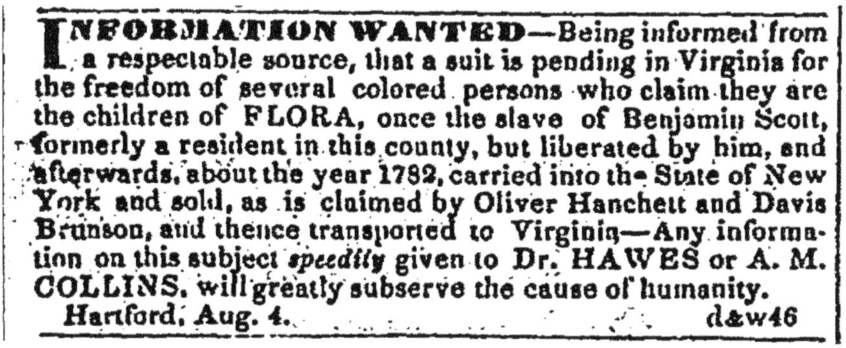

> **INFORMATION WANTED**—Being informed from a respectable source, that a suit is pending in Virginia for the freedom of several colored persons who claim they are the children of FLORA, once the slave of Benjamin Scott, formerly a resident in this county, but liberated by him, and afterwards, about the year 1782, carried into the State of New York and sold, as is claimed by Oliver Hanchett and Davis Brunson, and thence transported to Virginia—Any information on this subject *speedily* given to Dr. HAWES or A. M. COLLINS, will greatly subserve the cause of humanity.
> Hartford, Aug. 4.   d&w46

FIGURE 6. Joel Hawes placed this advertisement in the *Hartford Courant* in an effort to locate witnesses who could testify to Flora's status before she was taken from Connecticut and, ultimately, to Virginia. (*Hartford Courant*, August 5, 1842, Newspapers.com)

send you this line, that should, the information which we expect to obtain not reach you in season, you may get the case postponed to another ~~next~~ session of your court."[10]

Hawes's response reached Anderson just two weeks before Unis was due back in court for the trial that had been postponed in March. When the court convened, on August 27, both Anderson and Daniel Hoge filed affidavits requesting a further delay of the trial. Hoge concentrated on the challenges currently facing Unis and her attorneys in light of the fact that so many of their potential witnesses had failed to appear at the court's last session and that the change in their attorneys rendered their absence very damaging to the plaintiffs' case. "In his opinion," Hoge maintained, "the plaintiffs cannot safely go into trial, on account of the absence of material testimony. None of the original counsel of the plaintiffs—now engaged in the cause, are in attendance; and it is not in the power of this affiant to speak, from his own personal knowledge, as to the materiality of the testimony of any of the absent witnesses except Mrs. Richardson, with whome, at the last term of this court, this affiant had some conversation on the subject of her testimony & which he then regarded as very material." Anderson, for his part, emphasized the significance of the testimony he expected to secure from Connecticut in the near future concerning "Flora's emancipation in Hartford and subsequent fraudulent removal to the state of New York" and the problem created by changes in the plaintiffs' legal representation: "The present counsel for the plaintiffs not having the aid of the counsel originally engaged in these causes but having to rely upon the illiterate paupers." As a result, Anderson concluded, "this affiant is seriously apprehensive that if the plaintiffs should be forced into the trial of these causes in their present state of preparation & in the absence of all the original counsel who are familiar with the proceedings heretofore had, that a great injustice may be done."[11]

Their arguments failed to persuade the judge, perhaps because the court had arranged a substitute to replace the recused Edward Johnston and wanted to keep that arrangement as brief as possible. Despite her lawyer's unfamiliarity with the case and despite the promise of important evidence that was not yet available, Unis's trial began on August 27, 1842. Not surprisingly, Francis Anderson (and perhaps Daniel Hoge) seems to have relied on the same evidence Unis's earlier attorneys had assembled and based his argument on the same point of law: that Flora, Cena, Unis should have been freed when they were brought into Virginia illegally. None of the surviving depositions taken after the last trial in Smyth County introduced any evidence pointing to a different strategy. The depositions that Andrew had secured from Henry Carty and Francis Charlton in 1840 simply supported earlier testimony that it was James Simpkins who brought Flora and her daughters to Virginia. Three additional witnesses were deposed in March or early August 1842, after Hoge and/or Anderson had begun working with the plaintiffs, but their testimony focused on whether or not the earlier witnesses James Simpkins, John Lawrence, and Thomas Lawrence could be trusted. Presented with essentially the same evidence that prior juries had seen, the Roanoke County jury reached the same conclusion. After three and a half days of testimony and arguments, the jurors retired to consider the evidence. "After some time [they] returned into court and declared that they could not agree in verdict."[12]

After this fifth inconclusive trial, the cases of Flora's descendants were continued yet again, and when the court next convened, in March 1843, Edward Johnston was back on the bench. This time he effected a permanent solution to his conflict of interest. Circuit superior courts of law and equity—the type of court in which these cases were then being heard—were presided over by judges from Virginia's General Court. Each judge was assigned to a circuit in one of the state's judicial districts and moved from county to county within that circuit, holding court twice each year in each county. When the court reconvened in Salem, Judge Johnston declared,

"[T]he judge of the Court being so situated as to render it improper in his judgement for him to preside at the trial of these four causes . . . , it is ordered that they be removed to the Circuit Superior Court for the County of Rockbridge, that being one of the counties within an adjoining Circuit, to be there tried and determined." So, in March 1843, the cases of Flora's descendants moved again.[13]

Moving the cases to Rockbridge County meant more travel for many of those involved in them. Lexington, the seat of Rockbridge County, lay some seventy-five miles northeast of Christiansburg, so witnesses faced much longer journeys to appear in court than they had when traveling to the Roanoke County courthouse, in Salem. It also kept the cases in a jurisdiction where slavery was more common than it was in Montgomery County. Rockbridge County farmers grew much less tobacco than those in Roanoke County did. Rockbridge lay in the Shenandoah valley, which was the breadbasket of antebellum Virginia. Farmers there concentrated on grain production, especially wheat. That required less labor than tobacco, but large-scale, commercial production of wheat and flour still earned enough to make slavery worthwhile, and enslaved workers made up a quarter of the county's population during the 1840s.[14]

The move to Rockbridge County and the change in lawyers representing the plaintiffs also led to yet more delays in hearing the cases. First, two of the files were lost temporarily. Those of Unis and Phillis against James Charlton's administrator were transferred in April, and their cases were placed on the docket of the Rockbridge court when it met in September. The files of Rhoda Ann and Randall, however, could not be found. Frederick Johnston, clerk of the court in Roanoke County, explained to his Rockbridge counterpart that the four files had moved together as the cases made their way through "various counties in Southwestern Virginia," and that all four had been in his office that winter. By April, however, those of *Rhoda Ann v. Currin's Admin.* and *Randall v. Swope* had "disappeared." Johnston declared that he had made a "diligent search" of his own office and, finding no sign of the files, was convinced that "some one of the many counsel (eight in number) has unintentionally mislaid them." He promised to make every effort to find the files and forward them to Rockbridge, but he also tried to minimize the impact of their loss: "It will make, perhaps, no real difference to the parties, as the two cases now sent you embrace every interest in contest." Johnston's effort to minimize the loss was never put to a legal test, though, because eight months later the missing files finally turned up. They had been, Johnston explained, "mis-placed by one of the counsel, and were found among his papers a few days ago." They made their belated way to Rockbridge in January 1844 and were docketed when the court there next met, in April 1845.[15]

Even with their records fully available in Rockbridge County, the cases of Flora's descendants were continued from term to term for another two years. These continuances were ordered for "reasons appearing to the court," and the court never explained what those reasons were, but they may have been connected to Francis Anderson's new strategy of basing the plaintiffs' claim of freedom more on their descent from a free woman than on their illegal importation into Virginia. By August 1842, shortly after he began working with Flora's descendants and while their cases were still before the court in Roanoke County, Anderson had learned from correspondents in Connecticut that witnesses there might be able to confirm that Flora had been freed before she was taken to New York and sold. At that time, he did not know who those witnesses might be, but he was confident they existed and had argued unsuccessfully that his clients should not be "forced into trial without proper evidence in hand." No doubt he made a similar argument before the judge in Rockbridge when the cases were docketed there, and this may have been the reason they were continued.[16]

Obtaining the evidence he sought in a form the court would accept took time. As described earlier, in the summer of 1842 Francis Anderson had written to several "gentlemen" in Hartford seeking their help obtaining information about Flora's time in Connecticut. His letter to Joel Hawes had prompted the latter to place announcements in Connecticut newspapers soliciting information about Flora's history. One of those responding to Hawes's request was the Rev. Daniel Hemenway, a Congregational minister and teacher who had just opened a new school in Suffield, where Flora had once lived. A week after the publication of Hawes's request for information about Flora, Hemenway organized the taking of affidavits from three Suffield residents—Gustavus Austin, Hannah King, and Susan Sheldon. Each of the three had known Flora when she lived with Benjamin Scott, and each testified that she had lived with Scott's family. Neither Austin nor Sheldon said explicitly that Flora had been free, though Austin did say that people had considered Flora's seizure and sale to be "unlawful." Hannah King, however, stated categorically that Flora had been "a free woman and not a slave" and that she and her children "were carried away and held as slaves." The three affidavits were recorded on August 13, 1842, and promptly dispatched by a local justice of the peace to Francis Anderson in Virginia. These were, no doubt, the affidavits that Joel Hawes promised Anderson would provide "facts very materially affecting the case committed to your advocacy." Unfortunately, no record has survived showing when, or even if, Anderson actually received the affidavits, but if he did, they never made it into the surviving legal record. This is probably because they had been taken without a commission from the court hearing the case and without any advance notification to the defendants of the time and place at which the affidavits would be taken. As a result, they would have been inadmissible as evidence in a Virginia court.[17]

The Suffield affidavits probably arrived in Virginia just as Unis's case came to trial in Roanoke County and while Francis Anderson was still familiarizing himself with his clients and their cases. Then, six months later, the trials were transferred to Rockbridge County. It is hardly surprising that it took time for Anderson to write Hawes and Hemenway and explain the need to follow proper legal procedures. When he did so remains unknown, but in early 1845 Daniel Hemenway wrote to a young lawyer in Farmington, Connecticut, asking him to come to Suffield and "help him look up some evidence in an important slave case in Virginia." The lawyer Hemenway approached was John Hooker. A descendant of Thomas Hooker, the "Father of Connecticut," John had attended Yale for two years before ill-health forced him to abandon his studies without graduating. He then spent two years at sea before returning to Connecticut, where he began to study law and married the youngest daughter of Lyman Beecher, one of the nation's most celebrated ministers and long a supporter of the American Colonization Society and its effort to resettle emancipated African Americans in Liberia. It was at this point in his life that Hooker became an active abolitionist, perhaps as a result of influence exerted by his wife or father-in-law. Growing up in Farmington, Hooker had been aware of slavery and of "the universal disregard of the rights of colored people" but had thought little about the matter until the early 1840s. "Before that time I had not taken much interest in the anti-slavery movement," Hooker later wrote, "though I had attended a few public meetings of the abolitionists, but now I looked thoroughly into the question and became convinced they were right and that it was my plain duty to join them." Newly

converted to abolitionism, Hooker responded at once when Reverend Hemenway sought his help.[18]

Together, Hooker and Hemenway began searching for residents of Suffield or Southwick who remembered Flora and could confirm that she had
been freed before she was taken to New York and sold. "Very few people of
the time survived," Hooker recalled, but he and Hemenway ultimately found
at least twenty men or women who claimed to have known Flora personally
or to have known about her when she lived in New England. Hooker then
went before a local justice "as agent of the Pffs. [plaintiffs]" and provided a
sworn affidavit that the individuals he named were "material and important
for the Pffs." He probably did this twice, once each for two different groups
of witnesses, though only the second affidavit has survived. These affidavits
were then sent to Francis Anderson, who used them to secure commissions
from the Rockbridge County Court to examine the witnesses, take depositions from them, and have those depositions read in court as evidence in
all four of the cases brought by Flora's descendants. The first commission,
awarded in April 1845, was for Susan Sheldon, Hannah King, and Gustavus
Austin—the three witnesses who had provided affidavits in 1842; a second
commission naming seventeen more witnesses was granted in September.
Once the commissions were issued, the Rockbridge County clerk sent letters addressed to "any two judges or justices of the peace" in the appropriate
Connecticut and Massachusetts jurisdictions, commanding them to "dili-
gently examine" the named individuals under oath and send him certified
copies of their depositions.[19]

It is unclear from the surviving evidence how many of the twenty witnesses named in the two commissions actually provided depositions. James
Paxton, another Virginia lawyer working with Francis Anderson, informed
Anderson that "the depositions of all the persons were not taken" but offered no details. The chancery file containing most of the surviving evidence
from the cases includes six depositions taken in 1845, though endorsements
on letters sent in connection with the first commission indicate that three
other depositions were received that do not appear in the file. That would
still bring the total to just nine. Others may have been lost between Connecticut and Virginia. A letter written by John Hooker in September 1849
and an affidavit submitted that same month by John McCandless Taylor,
the administrator of James Charlton's estate and a defendant in two of the
four suits brought by Flora's descendants, indicate that both men believed

some number of depositions taken in 1845 may have been sent from Connecticut to Rockbridge County but never reached their destination.[20]

Whatever the actual number, Hooker wrote later, "the difficulties attending the taking of the evidence can hardly be exaggerated." Simply coordinating the schedules of twenty witnesses, two magistrates, and four lawyers spread across three states would have been challenging in the best of circumstances. In this case, however, matters were further complicated by the ages of the witnesses, most of whom were in their seventies, and their physical condition. "The deponents were," explained John Hooker, "very old, several bed-ridden, many quite deaf, and some with failing memories, and all in a condition to be embarrassed by cross-examination." Challenges notwithstanding, in June 1845 the taking of depositions began.[21]

Hooker claimed later that he served as "counsel" for the plaintiffs with the help of Daniel Hemenway. None of the surviving depositions, however, support that claim, and most identify Samuel S. Cowles as the individual asking questions "in behalf of the Plffs." Cowles was even more deeply involved in Connecticut's antislavery movement than Hooker was. Unlike Hooker, Cowles had been steeped in abolitionism since birth. His parents, Horace and Mary Ann Cowles, were stationmasters on the Underground Railroad in Farmington, Connecticut, until their deaths in 1841 and 1837, respectively, and men and women escaping slavery regularly passed through the couple's home while Samuel was growing up. Samuel continued that work after his parents died and also served as editor of the *Charter Oak*, a weekly newspaper published by the Connecticut Anti-Slavery Society. When the Rockbridge court requested depositions from witnesses in Connecticut and Massachusetts, Cowles was a justice of the peace in Hartford County and one of two magistrates before whom the first witness took the necessary oath and testified. As the process then moved to witnesses living in Massachusetts, however, Cowles seems to have changed roles, and most of the depositions taken in 1845 identify Cowles as the attorney asking questions on behalf of the plaintiffs.[22]

The identity of the defendants' representative in the taking of depositions is equally muddled. The only individual identified by name as an attorney for the defendants was Samuel E. Hartwell, a Connecticut lawyer living in Suffield, but John Hooker's memoir and a letter he wrote to Francis Anderson in 1849 suggest that Benjamin F. Wysor also represented the defendants. Wysor, a prominent attorney from Pulaski County (which had been the western half of Montgomery County until 1839), was related to the Charlton family through his mother, Cynthia Charlton Wysor. He was certainly part of the defendants' legal team in 1849 and may have participated in the taking of depositions in 1845 as well, but he was not identified as one of the defendants' lawyers in any of the documents produced at that time.[23]

Many of the questions that Samuel Cowles, the plaintiffs' representative, directed at witnesses focused on the history and legal status of Flora and her husband, Ex. On behalf of the plaintiffs, Cowles and a "Mr. Washburn," who represented the plaintiffs at the first deposition, sought to show that Flora had been married to Ex, that she had been taken from Massachusetts against her will, and that she had been a free woman at the time Hanchett seized her. This, of course, was precisely the sort of information that Francis Anderson needed to argue that the plaintiffs deserved their freedom as the descendants of a free woman. The deposition of Sally Coit, for example, bears an annotation—perhaps by Cowles or Anderson—summarizing its importance to the plaintiffs' case: "Proves marriage of Flora to Ex in 1781 & residence for 10 months in Southwick in Mass with Ex & disappearance in 1782."[24]

For their part, counsel for defense sought to provide grounds for challenging both the veracity and the admissibility of any evidence these new witnesses might provide. Hartwell asked several witnesses about the physical appearance of the Flora they had known—her color, her size—in an apparent effort to suggest she was not the Flora other witnesses had met in Virginia. He also attempted to question witnesses' impartiality. He asked several by whom and for what reason they had been asked to testify, and with Shubael Stiles he got right to the point: "Are you an abolitionist?" Virginia law barred members of "any society instituted for the purpose of emancipating negroes" from service on the jury hearing a freedom suit, and Hartwell clearly hoped to label Stiles and the other witnesses with the nefarious identity of abolitionist. Hartwell also asked questions intended to exclude completely many witnesses' testimony. He repeatedly asked witnesses what they knew of Flora through "your own knowledge" as opposed to information that had been "common report" in the neighborhood when Flora lived there. This was clearly in order to challenge the evidence as hearsay and have it excluded it from trial.[25]

Before 1813 many states, including Virginia, had recognized an exception to the rules of evidence barring hearsay and had permitted such evidence in order to establish an individual's genealogy in freedom suits. Hearsay evidence was often critical in freedom suits, especially those based on descent from a free woman. Plaintiffs in such cases frequently based their claims on the status of mothers or grandmothers who had died or been sold away years, even decades, before their suits were launched. In many instances, stories passed from one generation to another among White owners or neighbors—often the only ones permitted to offer evidence in southern courts—were the only way in which to establish the status of an individual from whom an enslaved man or woman claimed descent. By the late eighteenth century, however, growing concern about the threat that freedom suits allegedly posed to public safety and to the property rights of slave owners had led some jurists to question the acceptance of hearsay evidence. Maryland's attorney general, for example, decried the success of several enslaved families who had employed hearsay evidence to win their cases. "In all these," he declared, "and in many other similar cases, hundreds of negroes have been let loose upon [the] community by the hearsay evidence of an obscure illiterate individual." As a result, some judges had begun to deny the admissibility of hearsay evidence in freedom suits, and in 1813 the issue came before the United States Supreme Court.[26]

Three years earlier, in 1810, an enslaved woman named Mina Queen had brought a freedom suit in Washington, DC, on the basis of her descent from Mary Queen, a free woman brought to Maryland as an indentured servant in 1715 and illegally held as slave when her term of service ended. Mary Queen had died in 1759, but before her death she had related her story to a young White man named Fredus Ryland. Ryland, in turn, recounted what Queen had told him in a deposition taken in 1796 and read as evidence in several successful freedom suits brought by descendants of Mary Queen who were enslaved in Maryland. But when Mina Queen brought suit in Washington, DC's District Court, that court excluded Ryland's testimony because it was hearsay and because Mary Queen had been enslaved at the time she provided it. Without Ryland's testimony, Mina Queen lost her case, but her attorney appealed the lower court's decision to the United States Supreme Court. There Queen lost again. Writing for the court, John Marshall emphatically ruled that hearsay evidence was inadmissible in freedom suits:

> However the feelings of the individual may be interested on the part of a person claiming freedom, the Court cannot perceive any legal

distinction between the assertion of this and of any other right which will justify the application of a rule of evidence to cases of this description which would be inapplicable to general cases in which a right to property may be asserted. . . . Its intrinsic weakness, its incompetency to satisfy the mind of the existence of the fact, and the frauds which might be practiced under its cover combine to support the rule that hearsay evidence is totally inadmissible.

Samuel Hartwell, it seems, was well aware of the *Queen* decision and with his careful distinction between personal knowledge and common report was laying the groundwork for efforts by the defense to bar much of the evidence collected by the plaintiffs' New England allies from ever being heard in court.[27]

Taking the depositions was finished by early November 1845, and they were sent under seal to the clerk in Rockbridge County. They did not arrive in time, however, for the court's November term, and the cases of Flora's descendants were again continued "for reasons appearing to the court." When the depositions finally did arrive, Francis Anderson believed they "greatly strengthened the cause," but he also seems to have worried that many of the witnesses from whom he had sought testimony had not been deposed. His own letter asking about the missing depositions has not survived, but the response of James Paxton, a colleague in Lexington, has. Paxton confirmed that "the depositions of all the persons were not taken" but could not say why. He speculated that Hooker thought it "unnecessary" to take more because, as Paxton wrote, "Mr. Hooker thinks that they will be sufficient to establish the facts which were intended to be proved by them." At any rate, he continued, it was too late to secure additional depositions.[28]

According to Wendell Phillips, Anderson also tried to secure evidence from the State of Massachusetts to support the claim that Flora had been free when Oliver Hanchett sold her in New York. By the 1840s, Phillips was one of the leading figures in the American abolitionist movement and one of its most celebrated orators. Late in 1845 he spoke at Boston's Faneuil Hall to a mass meeting called to oppose the admission of Texas to the United States as a slave state. In the course of his speech, Phillips also referred to the case of Flora's descendants and described a letter sent to Massachusetts's secretary of the commonwealth. He did not name the letter's author, but it must have been Francis Anderson:

It comes from the attorney of slaves in Virginia, fifty in number, the descendants of a woman of color, who two years after the adoption of our Bill of Rights, was stolen from the town of Southwick, in Massachusetts; and now, after the lapse of two generations, each handing down the memory that their mother was free, these, her posterity, ask a certificate of the State of Massachusetts, that the Constitution of 1780 was broad enough to cover the rights of the long forgotten slave of 1782.

Phillips then lauded the authors of the Massachusetts constitution and declared, "The Constitution they framed in 1780 for the Bay State, in 1845 sweeps fifty human beings from the grasp of the Old Dominion, and places them beneath the broad shield of its own State Freedom."[29]

It is impossible to say whether or not Anderson ever received any statement from Massachusetts. No reply has survived in his correspondence, no letter from Anderson has been found in the records of the secretary of the commonwealth, and surviving court records in Virginia include no reference to a "certificate" or any other official statement concerning Flora's status under Massachusetts law. It does seem unlikely, however, that Massachusetts could have produced the sort of "shield" that Wendell Phillips invoked. As noted in chapter 1, it seems that the Massachusetts Supreme Judicial Court had ruled in *Exeter v. Hanchett* that Flora had been legally enslaved under Connecticut law and that Oliver Hanchett had been within his rights when he reclaimed his property by dragging Flora from her bed and hauling her away.[30]

Wendell Phillips's speech at Faneuil Hall also points to the changing political context surrounding the freedom suits of Flora's descendants. Arguments over the expansion of slavery in American territory had eased somewhat with adoption of the Missouri Compromises in 1820–21, but when Texas gained its independence from Mexico, in 1836, and began seeking annexation by the United States, supporters and opponents of slavery found new grounds on which to resume their battle. The fight grew increasingly bitter when President John Tyler announced his intention to see Texas admitted to the union. Between 1843 and 1845, Americans argued vociferously over the issue in the halls of Congress, in the press, and in meetings such as that Wendell Phillips addressed in Boston. Supporters of slavery claimed that the admission of Texas would benefit the nation and also knew that it would provide additional votes in Congress to help defend slavery in the future. Opponents feared that Texas would enhance the "slave power" they believed was corrupting American life. Ultimately, advocates of annexation failed to secure the two-thirds vote needed to ratify a treaty in the Senate, but a joint resolution of Congress, which required only a simple majority, squeaked through in 1845. Texas joined the union, but the debate over slavery had been reinvigorated and would continue to rage with increasing fury.[31]

With or without a certificate from Massachusetts, when the Rockbridge court next convened, in April 1846, Anderson was ready. The trial began on April 15 and lasted four days, and though they appear in the court's order book as four separate proceedings, the cases were heard together in a single trial before a single jury. Francis Anderson seems to have been the lead attorney for the plaintiffs, though he was joined in the courtroom by his brother, John T. Anderson, and two other lawyers from the region surrounding Lexington: James L. Woodville, who lived in Botetourt County, and James Garland, of Campbell County. Nothing suggests that any of the three lawyers who joined Francis Anderson in court for the trial had any significant involvement in the case prior to their appearance in court. Garland certainly did not; he had been asked to participate less than a month before the trial began. Both Woodville and Garland, however, were prominent men from distinguished families, and their presence added further gravitas to the plaintiffs' legal team. All four of the attorneys were also slave owners, as were at least nine of the twelve jurors who heard the case.[32]

More evidence has survived from this trial than from any other involving Flora's descendants. In addition to the depositions and the objections made to them, a letter from Francis Anderson to John Hooker describing the trial has survived, as have newspaper accounts, and the case file from Virginia's supreme court of appeals, to which the verdict in the case was subsequently appealed. Francis Anderson clearly did not abandon the argument that his clients were entitled to their freedom because of violations of the 1778 nonimportation act. Both a widely circulated newspaper account and the records of the supreme court of appeals indicate that who brought Flora and her children to Virginia and whether or not that person did so legally remained a part of the plaintiffs' case. But Anderson seems to have placed much greater emphasis on the claim that Flora had been a free woman who was kidnapped and sold into bondage illegally and that her descendants, therefore, were entitled to freedom through their descent from a free woman. To do so he relied heavily on the depositions gathered by John Hooker and Samuel Cowles. "The evidence taken through your agency in Massachusetts greatly strengthened the cause," he wrote Hooker, "and I doubt not had great weight with the jury."[33]

But getting that evidence before the jury was no easy matter. Lawyers for the defendants objected to the depositions taken in Massachusetts and Connecticut on multiple grounds. The deposition of Sarah Nelson bears an endorsement stating: "Defdts except to this depos 1st because it has no relation to the issue there is nothing in the cause to identify the Flora spoken of here with the Flora the ancestor of the plfffs. 2nd so far as witness gives hearsay in evidence & for want of notice to defts." The defense objected to each of the other depositions "for the same reasons Sarah Nelson's excepted to" and in the case of Shubael Stiles and Thomas Noble raised an additional objection "because witness gives in evidence the hearsay of a negro."[34]

Initially, the most significant of these objections proved to be "insufficiency of notice." The defendants did not claim they had not been notified of the time and place at which the depositions would be taken, and the case file includes the notice sent to them shortly after the commission to take the depositions had been granted. Rather, according to Francis Anderson, they objected to the lawyer who had questioned the witnesses in their name. No evidence has survived showing who asked Samuel Hartwell to question the witnesses on the defendants' behalf or what direction he may have received from them, but according to Anderson, once the trial began this became a major issue. In a letter to John Hooker, Anderson described "the defendants disclaiming the authority of the gentleman who cross-examined the witnesses on their behalf, to act for them" and indicated this was the grounds for their objection. The judge sustained this objection, and it seemed that he might exclude entirely the evidence that Hooker and Cowles had helped to gather. Anderson's case, however, depended on that evidence, and he was determined to take whatever measures were available to ensure the jury heard it. "Regarding this testimony as very important," he wrote, "and being unwilling to risk the cause if it were excluded, I moved the court for permission to withdraw a juror, unless the defendants waved [sic] their objection." Withdrawing a juror was a tactic by which a lawyer could seek to effect a mistrial when "unexpected contingencies arise." If Anderson's request were granted, he would have to arrange a new round of depositions in order to avoid similar objections in the future, but he was willing to gamble that the defendants were unwilling to end the trial and see the case continued. When the judge indicated that he was inclined to grant Anderson's request to withdraw a juror, the gamble paid off. According to Anderson, "after consultation the defendants agreed to withdraw their exceptions, rather than submit to the continuance."[35]

That still left the matters of hearsay evidence and hearsay from a Black source. Black evidence, of any sort, was barred by state law, and Marshall's decision in the *Queen* case had made hearsay evidence inadmissible in freedom suits. When the defense objected to the admission of "so much of these depositions as was hearsay," the judge tried to respect the *Queen* decision without excluding the depositions entirely. He could do so, he thought, because of the reason for which the plaintiffs had introduced the evidence. As part of the plaintiffs' case, Anderson had introduced depositions from John Lawrence and Elijah Meacham—witnesses who claimed that Flora had been free before being kidnapped, taken to New York, and sold by Oliver Hanchett. In response, lawyers for the defense sought to challenge the credibility of Lawrence and Meacham. They first introduced an earlier deposition that Meacham had provided before the one introduced by the plaintiffs. This earlier deposition had been taken in 1826, when Flora first sought permission to bring a freedom suit, and in it, Meacham had stated that Flora had been freed when the Connecticut legislature "passed a law giving freedom to all the slaves of the said State." The defense then introduced evidence that Connecticut had passed no such law; it had passed a gradual emancipation act providing that Black and mulatto children born in the state after March 1, 1784, would become free at age twenty-five, but it did not emancipate any individuals who were already enslaved on that date—as Flora had been. In addition, the defense called other witnesses who provided oral testimony "tending to impeach the character [of Lawrence and Meacham]."[36]

It was at this point that Anderson introduced depositions taken in Connecticut and Massachusetts that included the common reports of Flora's freedom. He did so, he maintained, "for the purpose of sustaining and corroborating the testimony of the witnesses Lawrence and Meacham" and not to prove that Flora had been free before being taken to Virginia. The defense immediately objected to the depositions because of the hearsay evidence they included. The judge overruled the objection, however, and permitted the depositions to be read, but in doing so he instructed the jurors to consider the hearsay evidence only "in connection with oral testimony as to the general character of Lawrence and Meacham, for the purpose alone of corroborating their testimony." Jurors were directed not to consider the hearsay evidence for any other purpose: "so much thereof as was hearsay, related to the common report that Flora had been considered a free woman in Massachusetts, and had been abducted and carried off by Hanchett or Bronson & Hanchett, must not be taken as primary evidence thereof, proving or tending to prove that Flora was actually free." With that restriction, the depositions were read to the jury.[37]

It is impossible to say whether or not the jurors followed the judge's directive, but Francis Anderson believed the evidence contained in the depositions "had a great weight with the jury," and the outcome of the trial supports that conclusion. After five hung juries, this one reached a verdict in just thirty minutes. "The plaintiffs are free persons and not slaves," the jurors announced. Then, having found for the plaintiffs, they further declared the defendants guilty of assault, battery, and false imprisonment and ordered them to pay damages. The plaintiffs had sought damages of ten thousand dollars when they filed their suits, but Virginia juries were reluctant to award the plaintiffs in freedom suits much beyond their freedom. As was customary, this jury awarded the plaintiffs damages of one cent plus the costs incurred in prosecuting their suits. The judge accepted this verdict and ordered that the plaintiffs receive their freedom, damages, and costs.[38]

Twenty years after Unis first entered a courtroom, she, her sisters, their children, and their grandchildren were free. One can only imagine how the enslaved plaintiffs felt when they heard the verdict. None of Flora's descendants left any account that has survived of their feelings in court that day, but Lucy Delaney, who won a freedom suit in 1844, described her experience in a memoir published many years later. Flora's descendants may have reacted in much the same way:

> I had taken my seat in such a condition of helpless terror that I could not tell one person from another. Friends and foes were as one, and vainly did I try to distinguish them. My long confinement, burdened with harrowing anxiety, the sleepless night I had just spent, the unaccountable absence of my mother, had brought me to an indescribable condition. I felt dazed, as if I were no longer myself. I seemed to be another person—an on looker—and in my heart dwelt a pity for the

poor, lonely girl, with down-cast face, sitting on the bench apart from anyone else in that noisy room. . . . Then the verdict was called for and rendered. . . . Oh! the overflowing thankfulness of my grateful heart at that moment, who could picture it? None but the good God above us! I could have kissed the feet of my deliverers, but I was too full to express my thanks, but with a voice trembling with tears I tried to thank Judge Bates [her lawyer, Edward Bates] for all his kindness.[39]

Newspaper accounts said the number freed was "about 45," and papers from Boston to New Orleans reported their story. The most complete account appeared in the *Charter Oak,* which was edited by Samuel Cowles, one of the lawyers who had helped the plaintiffs gather evidence of Flora's claim to freedom. It printed a letter from John Hooker recounting the case's long history and included a letter that Francis Anderson sent Hooker describing the most recent trial and its outcome. Other papers simply reprinted all or parts of an article that first appeared in the *Lexington Gazette,* published in the seat of Rockbridge County on April 30. Northern papers, however, omitted the *Gazette*'s concluding statement that the case "recommends the fact to the canting fanatics of the north, who aver with such brazen impudence and effrontery, that the negro has no chance of law or justice in a Southern clime."[40]

Like so much else about these cases, what happened next remains a mystery. Francis Anderson wrote John Hooker that, "by the verdict of the Jury and the judgement of the Court, the negroes are entitled to their freedom at once," and according to Anderson, the formerly enslaved descendants of Flora immediately began planning their new lives. Just ten days after the jury announced its verdict, Anderson told Hooker, "they have agreed that one of their counsel shall hire them out until their attorneys are compensated" and asked Hooker how much they owed him. The defendants, however, immediately tendered a bill of exception and, Anderson noted, "may make an effort to get an appeal to the Supreme Court of Appeals." The defendants did make such an appeal and also asked the supreme court to issue a writ of *supersedeas* staying any enforcement of the lower court's verdict or judgment, though the writ was not actually issued until November 11, 1846. Moreover, its execution was contingent on the defendants posting a bond to pay the trial court's judgement if the verdict was affirmed, and that bond was not posted until March 22, 1847—eleven months after a jury declared the plaintiffs free. It is impossible to say what the plaintiffs' status was during those eleven months, but it seems highly unlikely they were actually free. The defendants' intention to appeal meant that the case was not yet resolved, and if the plaintiffs had been freed there would have been no way the court could guarantee their return to slavery if the jury's verdict was eventually overturned. Anderson's comment notwithstanding, it seems far more likely that Unis and the others remained in bondage pending the outcome of the defendants' appeal.[41]

While they waited, Unis and her fellow plaintiffs may have seen what seemed to be another sign that they might actually be freed; in May 1846 a court in Montgomery County ruled in a separate but related case that Flora's descendants could not be sold. The death of James Charlton had made each of his heirs the lawful owner of a share of his estate, and even though the suits brought by Unis and the others made it impossible to effect a final division of the estate, an "undivided equal ninth part of the estate of the said James Charlton dec^d." represented a tangible financial asset. Because a married woman in Virginia was legally subsumed into her husband's identity, the share due Charlton's daughter, Matilda, fell under the control of her husband, Joseph Miller, and before his own death, in 1842, Miller alienated his wife's share twice. In 1831 he executed a deed of trust with Hugh Mc-Gavock Kent by which he transferred the undivided equal ninth part of the estate to Kent in return for Kent's guarantee to hold the property, use it to provide support and maintenance for Matilda and the couple's children during Matilda's lifetime, and to divide the property fairly among the children following Matilda's death. Then, in 1841, Joseph Miller executed a second deed of trust to Eli Pfleger by which he used Matilda's still undivided share of her father's estate to secure a bond Miller had signed to cover a debt he owed Robert Gardner.

Ten months later, Joseph Miller died, and in accordance with terms of the second deed of trust, Eli Pfleger, the trustee, announced his intention to sell at auction Matilda Miller's undivided share of her father's estate in order to settle the debt due Robert Gardner. Matilda then obtained a temporary injunction to prevent the sale, while Gardner brought suit to collect what was due him through Matilda's share of the profits earned hiring out the slaves of James Charlton. After several years of legal preliminaries, the Montgomery County case was finally resolved in May 1846, just a month after the jury in Rockbridge County declared that Flora's descendants were free. The court in Christiansburg ruled that the earlier deed of trust between Joseph Miller and Hugh McGavock Kent took precedence, and the judge "perpetuated" the injunction barring the sale of James Charlton's enslaved property. It also dismissed Gardner's suit. The rulings had no effect on the actual status of Flora's descendants, but they may well have taken the court's order that they not be sold as another sign of their impending freedom.[42]

That freedom, however, remained in limbo for more than a year awaiting a decision by Virginia's supreme court of appeals. Flora's descendants might have waited much longer had their case been heard in Richmond, where the volume of cases pending before the court had created a massive backlog. A decade earlier, however, the growth of population and business in western Virginia had led the General Assembly to require the supreme court of appeals to meet in Lewisburg each July, and there, it seems, things moved much more quickly. The court heard the case in July 1847, just fifteen months after the jury in Lexington had rendered its verdict.[43]

Ultimately, the appeals court considered a number of issues arising from the defense's effort to impeach the credibility of John Lawrence and Elijah Meacham. It first declared that it had been appropriate to introduce Meacham's earlier deposition in order to impeach the accuracy of his later testimony. It had not been proper, however, for the defense to introduce additional evidence, such as the Connecticut legislation, and such additional evidence should have been excluded had the plaintiffs objected. Having allowed the "improper" evidence to go to the jury without objection, though, the plaintiffs should not have been allowed to counter it with their own "illegal and improper" evidence in the form of hearsay evidence in the depositions from Connecticut and Massachusetts. It was not enough, the court ruled, that the trial judge had instructed jurors to consider the hearsay evidence only as it related to the credibility of Lawrence and Meacham. "Such illegal testimony may make an improper impression upon the minds of the jury, notwithstanding any instruction of the court," ruled the supreme court; so it should never have been heard at all. Thus, the supreme court concluded that the trial judge had erred in admitting the depositions "for the purpose of corroborating the testimony of said John Lawrence and Elijah Meacham . . . or for any other purpose," and it set aside the verdicts. All four cases were sent back to be tried again, and this time, the court directed, "so much of the said depositions as was excepted to . . . are to be specifically designated by the court and excluded from the jury if again objected to."[44]

The news must have been heartbreaking for the plaintiffs. For fifteen months, Flora's descendants had dared to hope they were free. They would, they believed, soon gain control of their lives, and they had already begun planning what they might do once they obtained their long-delayed freedom. It is unlikely they had enjoyed any actual change in their daily lives during the months waiting for their appeal to be heard; they almost certainly remained in bondage, hired out to White people and, perhaps, separated from their spouses, parents, or children. But they must have taken comfort in the fact that, unlike the bondage of their enslaved peers, the end of their captivity was in sight. Once the jury's verdict was upheld, the freedom they had won in principle would become real. That, of course, did not happen. The supreme court of appeals crushed their hopes—overturning the verdict and plunging them back into slavery. They refused to surrender, though, and returned to court almost immediately, determined to win the freedom they had been denied.

❖ 6 ❖

Back to Christiansburg

The decision of Virginia's supreme court of appeals to overturn the jury's verdict declaring Flora's descendants to be free people was a bitter blow to the plaintiffs and their lawyers, but they refused to give up. Decisions setting aside the jury's verdicts—one for each of the four cases—were officially entered in the Rockbridge County Court in September 1847, and each of the cases was returned to the court's docket for trial. Within a month, counsel for the plaintiffs was back in court to resume the process of building their case. Francis Anderson was still involved in the case, and it was still his strategy informing the plaintiffs' approach, but it was James G. Paxton who appeared in court this time. Paxton came from a prominent, slave-owning family in Rockbridge County, though he himself seems to have owned relatively few slaves. He was still in his mid-twenties and had just begun his legal career, but his name carried weight in the county, and he soon went on to serve a decade in the House of Delegates and briefly in the state senate.[1] In October 1847, Paxton provided the court a sworn affidavit identifying nine men and women living in Connecticut and Massachusetts as "material witnesses for the plaintiffs," and six months later, in April 1848, the court awarded the plaintiffs a commission to take depositions from a total of seventeen witnesses in Connecticut and Massachusetts, including seven of the nine identified in Paxton's affidavit. All seventeen of those named in the commission had been among the witnesses from whom Francis Anderson sought depositions in 1845, though only five had actually been deposed that year. Clearly, the plaintiffs' lawyers, at least, still believed that basing their clients' claims to freedom on

Flora's having been free before she was abducted offered a viable route to victory.[2]

As they had before, lawyers for the plaintiffs relied on John Hooker to coordinate their efforts in New England. Francis Anderson wrote to Hooker soon after the court granted the plaintiffs a commission to take depositions in Massachusetts and Connecticut. Hooker then set out to determine which of the individuals named in the commission were still alive and to arrange dates and venues for deposing them. In January 1849 he sent Anderson a proposed schedule for taking twelve depositions beginning as soon as proper notice could be served to the defendants. The plaintiffs immediately requested and obtained summons to depose the witnesses identified by Hooker, plus several others whose testimony had been sought but not taken in 1845. In spite of Hooker's urging Anderson to move as quickly as possible, none of the new depositions were taken before August 1849. Meanwhile, the defendants had also located a witness in Connecticut. On August 3, 1849, John McCandless Taylor appeared before Robert Gardner, a justice of the peace in Montgomery County, and swore that William Hartwell "will be an important witness" in the case and requested a commission to take his deposition. Unfortunately, no deposition from Hartwell has survived, and it is impossible to say how Taylor learned of him or what he expected to gain from his testimony.[3]

With the preliminaries completed, a second round of depositions were taken in Connecticut and Massachusetts during August and September 1849. Samuel Cowles continued his role as the plaintiffs' representative, and this time Benjamin Wysor definitely represented the defendants. Together, Cowles and Wysor reinterviewed two of the witnesses questioned in 1845 and questioned at least seven others who had been identified in 1845 but had not, apparently, been deposed at that time. All but one of those deposed in 1849 were elderly men or women who had lived in Suffield or Southwick when Flora and Ex had, and most had known either Flora or Ex personally. As he had before, Cowles focused on establishing that Flora and Ex had been married, that they had been free, and that Oliver Hanchett had seized Flora and Cena against their will, taken them to New York, and sold them. For his part, Wysor again sought detailed descriptions of Flora's physical appearance in an effort to demonstrate that she had not been the woman who had lived in Montgomery County, and in order to flag hearsay evidence he repeatedly asked witnesses how much of what they reported was a result of their own personal knowledge and how much was based on "common talk."[4]

Meanwhile, in Virginia, the defense introduced two new motions on September 13, 1849. First, it sought a change of venue in order to move the cases back to Montgomery County. The defendants' counsel submitted a sworn affidavit from John McCandless Taylor, administrator of the Charlton estate, asserting that conditions in Montgomery County had changed significantly since 1829, when the suits had been transferred from Montgomery to Giles County. At that time the defense had asked for a change of venue "in consequence of the excitement of public feeling in the said county in favor of the claim of the slaves to freedom." Since then, however, Taylor claimed that "a new generation has sprung in that county wholly unacquainted with the cause & unprejudiced on either side." In addition, Taylor maintained that a potential conflict involving the judge responsible for the judicial circuit that included Montgomery County was no longer an issue. In 1832, the superior court judge hearing the cases in Giles County, James E. Brown, had ordered the suits moved to Smyth County, in a different circuit, because he felt "a delicasy" in presiding over the cases "in consequence of the connection existing between his family and that of William B. Charlton one of the distributees of James Charlton Dec[d]." In 1849, Taylor told the court in Rockbridge County that "the impediment in the way of Judge Brown's sitting in the causes he now understands is removed & that judge no longer has any objection to try the causes." Taylor failed to explain how the impediment had been removed, but he assured the court that "the Hon. Judge Brown has stated to him recently that he had no objection now to presiding over the trials of the causes." Finally, Taylor pointed out that most of the parties in the suits and most of the witnesses lived in either Montgomery or Pulaski County and had to travel repeatedly to Lexington, "making the costs of the trials very heavy." The judge was not convinced, though, and the request was denied.[5]

The defendants had slightly better luck with their second motion that day. Counsel for the defense presented another sworn affidavit from John McCandless Taylor, this one asserting that evidence detrimental to the plaintiffs' case may have been suppressed. According to Taylor, he had been informed by the defendants' agent present during the first round of depositions taken in Connecticut, in 1845, that one of the witnesses had provided "a very erroneous description of Flora their common ancestor."

The defendants' agent had assumed this deposition was then sent to Rock-bridge County along with the others taken at that time. but Taylor had reason to believe that "sd depositions never were sent on or filed . . . but that others, as he believes of the same witnesses, were taken after his agents return home & are now filed in the cause." To support this claim, Taylor asserted that while his agent had been engaged taking the current round of depositions, he had been informed by one of the magistrates who had taken the first round, in 1845, that "those depositions are still in sd magistrates possession." Taylor believed that the evidence in these "suppressed" depositions would be "most material to the defense of sd suits if his information concerning them is correct," and his attorney asked the court to order the plaintiffs to produce them. This motion the presiding judge believed had merit, and he ordered the plaintiffs to "cause said depositions to be filed or show cause to the contrary on the first day of the next term." When that next term began, however, the plaintiffs' counsel denied any possession of or knowledge of the allegedly suppressed depositions, and Taylor's charge was quickly dismissed.[6]

The court's September 1849 term also saw another documented instance of participation in the official legal proceedings by one of the enslaved plaintiffs. On September 14, Andrew Lewis, a son of Unis and grandson of Flora and still legally enslaved, came before Robert White, a Rockbridge County justice of the peace, and made a sworn affidavit that he believed Henry Wysor could testify to the fact that "some years before" Flora's descendants had initiated their freedom suits, Flora herself had gone to a local justice in order to open such a suit herself. According to Lewis, Wysor would testify that Flora had gone to the home of Ezekiel Howard but that James Charlton had followed her and brought her back before she could accomplish her goal. He then "abused her and threatened to whip her if she ever went to Howard's again." If presented in court, Wysor's testimony might enable the plaintiffs to gain their freedom by overcoming the presumption that, if Flora and her daughters had been brought into Virginia legally, their owner had taken the oath required under the state's nonimportation law. But Henry Wysor lived in Pulaski County, more than one hundred miles from Lexington, and Lewis asked that he be allowed to provide a deposition rather than travel to Rockbridge County to testify in person. The court order book contains no reference to the matter, but it seems the request was granted because the affidavit is endorsed: "Send Comm. with a copy this aft to Staples & Preston attos." This endorsement suggests that the court did issue a commission to take the deposition and sent it along with a copy of Andrew Lewis's affidavit to Waller Staples and William Ballard Preston, attorneys in Christiansburg, in order to provide the defense proper notification of when and where Henry Wysor would be deposed. It also suggests that William Ballard Preston, who had originally been one of the plaintiffs' attorneys, may now have been working for the defense in some capacity, though no other evidence has survived to indicate how.[7]

No deposition by Henry Wysor has yet been found, but the fact that Andrew Lewis went into court himself seeking a commission to depose Wysor is extraordinarily revealing. Clearly, Flora's descendants had an impressive understanding of legal procedures. They understood that in order for Wysor's testimony to be admissible, they first had to secure a commission to depose him and had to notify the defendants of their intention to do so, and Lewis did so in a way that satisfied the court. Equally surprising are the simple fact of Lewis appearing in court that day and the court's response to his appearance. At the time, Andrew Lewis was enslaved in Montgomery County, but he traveled seventy-five miles to Lexington in order to appear in court. Was he permitted to travel alone? Was he escorted by a sheriff or another White custodian? The record, unfortunately, is silent about the circumstances of his trip. Then, as an enslaved Black man, Lewis "made oath" that he was speaking the truth, and the court seems to have accepted that oath and the truth of his statement. The court did manage, however, to demonstrate that Andrew Lewis was still something less than fully equal. Whoever wrote out the affidavit initially wrote that "Andrew Lewis, one of the Plaintiffs" appeared before Justice White. The surname Lewis was then stricken from the document—one of three "corrections" made in a different hand, and Andrew Lewis became simply Andrew. Enslaved Virginians often had surnames, but those who enslaved them generally chose to ignore these signs of their status as human beings.[8]

Henry Wysor was not the only witness living far from Lexington, and ensuring that their witnesses appeared in court remained a challenge to all the parties as they prepared to retry the four cases. Depositions from the witnesses living in Massachusetts and Connecticut arrived in September 1849, but the cases were continued pending resolution of the possible suppression of earlier depositions described above. That matter was resolved when the court next met, in April 1850, but thirty-three witnesses summoned to testify in person, twenty-six for the plaintiffs and seven for the defense, failed to appear, and the cases were continued until September. When the court convened in September, at least five witnesses had submitted affidavits or doctor's certification that they were too ill or too old to travel safely to Lexington, but enough others were present to allow the proceedings to continue, and yet another trial opened on September 16, 1850.[9]

This trial ran for six days, but little else about it is known for sure because it generated no known bills of exception. Presumably, both plaintiffs and defense employed many of the same tactics and introduced much of the same evidence they had before. The plaintiffs still seem to have pursued two lines of argument in making their case: that Flora had been a free woman and that once enslaved she had been brought to Virginia in violation of the 1778 nonimportation law. In arguing that Flora had been a free woman, they no doubt sought to introduce the most recent depositions from witnesses in Connecticut and Massachusetts. Most of these witnesses had lived in Suffield or Southwick when Flora and Ex had. Some had known Ex or Flora personally, while others had heard their story from other residents, and in response to questions posed by the plaintiffs' representative they had testified that Flora and Ex had been legally married, had lived in Massachusetts, and had been freed before Flora was kidnapped by Oliver Hanchett and sold as a slave. It is impossible to say, however, whether or not the jury actually heard any of that testimony read in court.[10]

Absent any other evidence from the trial, we have only the depositions themselves, each of which bears an endorsement detailing objections from attorneys for the defendants. In most cases, the defense challenged the evidence as hearsay and, thus, inadmissible. The presiding judge in the case, Lucas P. Thompson, was the same judge whose earlier decision to admit hearsay evidence under restrictions on its use by the jury had been overruled by the supreme court of appeals. The supreme court found that Judge Thompson had erred in allowing any use of hearsay evidence, and it seems unlikely he would have been willing to make the same mistake again. Many of the depositions, therefore, may have been barred at trial. Indeed, it seems that counsel for the plaintiffs themselves may have decided not even to try entering some of their evidence. Depositions by Mary Warner, Horace Noble, and Abraham Rising all bear endorsements from the defense objecting to them as hearsay and notes in a different hand reading "not to be offered" or "do not off." The only new deposition that was not described as hearsay was that of Sylvester Graham, the celebrated advocate of dietary reform who urged Americans to avoid meat, dairy, and alcohol in favor of products—including Graham Crackers—made from coarse, whole-wheat flour. In this instance, Graham's significance lay in the fact that it was his father who presided at the wedding of Flora and Ex. In his deposition, Graham read from the contemporaneous written record that his father had made of the marriage. This the defense objected to on the grounds that the record itself was not produced in court.[11]

For their part, the plaintiffs objected to at least one defense witness. Three days before the trial began, Topal O. Watkins sat for a deposition to be offered in evidence on behalf of the defendants. Watkins declared that he would not believe anything said under oath by either John or Thomas Lawrence, who had testified in earlier depositions that Flora, Unis, and Cena had been purchased and brought to Virginia by James Simpkins, who had no right to do so under the state's nonimportation law. Under cross-examination by the plaintiffs' lawyer, Watkins explained that his brother had married a daughter of James Simpkins and through her had inherited part of Simpkins's estate but had to post "a refunding bond" in case Flora's descendants won their suit and the estate was obliged to repay the money James Charlton had paid for Flora, Cena, and Unis. Watkins himself stood as security on his brother's bond, and counsel for the plaintiffs objected to his offering evidence because he had a vested interest in the outcome of the trial. "If the Pllfs. are successful," their lawyer argued, "Simpkins' estate is responsible to Charlton for the value of the Pllfs. who were sold by Simpkins to Charlton."[12]

It is impossible to say if the objections from either side prevailed because whatever evidence was ultimately heard in the courtroom was insufficient to generate a verdict that could be appealed. After hearing five days of evidence and arguments by counsel, the jury retired to deliberate and "after some time" returned "not being able to agree in a verdict." The jurors were then dismissed, and the suits continued to the next term.[13]

When the court reconvened, in April 1851, the cases were continued again "for reasons appearing to the court." It remains unclear what those reasons were, but the continuation may have come at the request of the plaintiffs, who were still seeking additional evidence to strengthen their case. At least ten individuals the plaintiffs considered "material witnesses" to their case had failed to appear when the suits had last come to trial, and the plaintiffs now sought to take depositions from at least five of them who lived in Montgomery or Pulaski County. No court record has survived of a commission to depose the five, but one does seem to have been issued, because in May 1851 William Barnitz Jr., a lawyer in Christiansburg, wrote Francis Anderson to say that he had received "some papers relating to the taking of depositions." Barnitz informed Anderson that notice had been served to the defendants' lawyer but that he was confused as to who would be representing the plaintiffs. Because Anderson had set the date for taking the depositions, Barnitz thought that Anderson planned to attend, but James Paxton, an attorney working with Anderson, had said nothing about that in the letter that accompanied the papers. This left Barnitz confused, and he asked Anderson "to write me whether you wish me to attend."[14]

It is impossible to be certain, but it seems that by this point Francis Anderson had withdrawn from the case. Court records rarely mention lawyers by name, so the absence in those records of any reference to Anderson is not surprising. Anderson's own papers, however, include no sign of his active participation in the cases of Flora's descendants after the summer of 1849. Anderson replied almost immediately to William Barnitz's 1851 letter asking if Anderson planned to attend the taking of the depositions in Christiansburg, but what he wrote remains unknown, and ultimately neither Anderson nor Paxton nor Barnitz attended. Apparently, the plaintiffs themselves took the depositions.[15]

This may be the most striking example of just how involved Flora's descendants were in prosecuting their suits, but it also suggests the limits of their ability to do so. As described above, the plaintiffs planned to depose a number of witnesses living in Montgomery or adjacent Pulaski County, but their attorneys were apparently unable or unwilling to make the trip down from Rockbridge County. Undeterred, Flora's descendants took the depositions themselves. Unfortunately, it is impossible to say who participated, how they conducted themselves, or what they asked because the depositions were never entered into the record. It seems that while Flora's descendants understood the procedure for seeking a deposition, they did not understand exactly how to take one that would stand up in court. In September 1851, when the Rockbridge court reconvened, Andrew Lewis traveled again to Lexington, "made oath" before the court, and explained what had happened. The plaintiffs had intended to depose five witnesses they believed could prove "very important facts" on their behalf. Unfortunately,

Lewis explained, "they were unable to procure the services of an attorney to attend to taking the said depositions and they were consequently so defectively taken that they are [now] informed by their counsel that they are not fit to be used on the trial." Moreover, Lewis told the court, an additional witness had recently been identified in Indiana who could also provide "very important facts" in the case. It was clear, he concluded, "the plaintiffs cannot go safely to trial without the aforementioned witnesses or their depositions," and he requested that the cases be continued.[16]

The judge agreed: "On the motion of the plaintiffs and for reasons appearing to the court, it is ordered that these causes be continued." And he went further. No evidence has been found that Andrew Lewis requested a change of venue, but the judge declared, "[F]or good cause shown to the court, it is ordered that this cause be removed from this court to the circuit court for the County of Montgomery." He then entered an identical order for each of the three other cases. Two years earlier the defense had unsuccessfully asked for just such a change in an effort to reduce the "cost & trouble" associated with holding a trial so far from the homes of the interested parties and their witnesses. Now, at the plaintiffs' request perhaps, the judge seems to have decided that it was inefficient and inconvenient to hear the cases in Lexington and ordered them transferred back to Montgomery County.[17]

This latest change of venue certainly made it easier for the plaintiffs, the defendants, and the witnesses to attend, but it also seems to have cost the plaintiffs their most effective advocate. Francis Anderson had worked more aggressively than any of the plaintiffs' earlier lawyers. The possibility that Flora had been a free woman when Oliver Hanchett took her to New York had first been raised in an 1826 deposition of Elijah Meacham that was introduced in the hearing by which Unis first gained permission to sue *in forma pauperis*. But for almost twenty years lawyers for the plaintiffs made no serious effort to develop that argument on their clients' behalf. Only Francis Anderson took action to locate witnesses in Connecticut or Massachusetts who might be able to offer convincing evidence that Flora had been free before she was brought to Virginia. Much of the evidence he found, of course, was eventually ruled inadmissible by the supreme court of appeals, but that does not diminish the effort that Anderson put into advancing his clients' cause. He was the most ardent advocate that Flora's descendants had ever had and the only one who had yet convinced a jury they should be free. By the time their cases moved back to Montgomery County, though, he seems to have left their legal team.

Anderson's successor was probably Daniel H. Hoge, a planter-lawyer from Montgomery County who had briefly assisted the plaintiffs in 1842, when they found themselves without counsel before the court in Roanoke County. The only evidence suggesting this is the fact that when the case eventually rose from Montgomery County to the supreme court of appeals, in 1855, the attorney representing Flora's descendants before the appellate court was identified as "Hoge." This could have been another Hoge; Daniel's brother James was also a lawyer in the county. Given Daniel Hoge's earlier connection to the plaintiffs, though, he seems the more likely candidate.

The change of venue also brought the cases back into an environment that had changed significantly since they left. In some ways, Montgomery County had changed relatively little between 1825 and 1851. It had been and remained a region with many smaller farms and a handful of larger plantations, most of them producing a variety of agricultural products. Much of what they produced was still consumed locally or sold to travelers passing through the county because while the number and quality of turnpikes in southwest Virginia had increased recently, transportation in and out of the region was still limited to roads and turnpikes. Neither canals nor railroads had reached Montgomery County by 1851. Physically, the county was actually smaller than it had been in 1830 due to the fact that several new counties had been formed from Montgomery during the 1830s, and a portion of eastern Montgomery County had been transferred to Roanoke County in the 1840s. These changes also reduced the county's population; both its White population and its enslaved population were smaller in 1850 than they had been in 1830. As a share of the total population, though, slavery had grown in the county since 1830. When Unis and her family initiated their suits, enslaved workers had represented just over 16 percent of the county's population; by 1850 that figure had risen to 20 percent, and the pace of change was beginning to accelerate dramatically.[18]

Driving that change was the coming of the railroad. Advocates of internal improvement had tried for years to establish a railway through southwest Virginia, but their efforts had repeatedly foundered on political or economic obstacles. Hopes rose, however, in 1849, when the General Assembly granted a charter to the Virginia and Tennessee Railroad, and this time those hopes were finally realized. Between 1850 and 1856, crews worked from east and west to construct a two-hundred-mile-long link between Lynchburg, Virginia, and Bristol, Tennessee. Its completion, in conjunction with the simultaneous completion of the Southside Railroad between Lynchburg and Petersburg, filled a gap between rail lines in eastern Virginia, which connected to those of the Atlantic seaboard, and those in Tennessee that connected to the Ohio and Mississippi valleys. Montgomery County residents did not have to wait for the line's completion to see changes in their community. Trains reached eastern Montgomery in the fall of 1853 and Christiansburg the following April. Almost immediately, the Virginia and Tennessee began providing daily service between Christiansburg and Lynchburg, and from there passengers and freight moved on to Petersburg, Baltimore, and beyond.[19]

Opening Montgomery County to rail traffic would lead to rapid and dramatic changes in the local economy. Reducing transportation costs would open new markets for county products and widen existing ones. Quarrying increased as cheaper transportation made it profitable to ship millstones and building material from the county, and commercial coal mining began, though on very small scale. The most striking changes, though, came in agriculture and especially in tobacco production. Improved acreage in the county rose 23 percent between 1850 and 1860, adding more than thirteen thousand acres in ten years. Some of this went into pasture, contributing to a 44 percent increase in the value of livestock in the county, and some of it was devoted to wheat, the production of which tripled during the decade, but much of this new land supported vastly expanded tobacco production. Between 1850 and 1860, Montgomery County's annual tobacco harvest increased fifteenfold. In 1850, just 24 of the 561 farmers identified on its agricultural schedule (4.3 percent) had reported raising any tobacco at all, and the largest producer in the county that year, Jubal Early, had grown just four thousand pounds. Ten years later, nearly half the farmers in Montgomery County included tobacco among their farm products, and seven of them raised more than ten thousand pounds each. And as it did elsewhere in Virginia, tobacco production in Montgomery County often relied on enslaved labor.[20]

Between 1850 and 1860, the number of enslaved workers in the county rose by 51 percent, far exceeding anything that might be regarded as natural growth. Montgomery County's White population also grew during the 1850s, but its rate of growth—just over 20 percent for the decade—was less than half that seen in the county's enslaved population. Certainly, part of the growth among the enslaved was natural, and part, no doubt, was a result of existing residents buying more workers. A significant part, however, seems to have been the result of farmers farther east moving west with their enslaved workers. In many parts of eastern Virginia, farming had become more difficult as years of tobacco cultivation reduced the soil's fertility and as population growth made it ever more difficult for new generations to establish themselves. More efficient transportation promised to make tobacco cultivation practical in southwest Virginia, and as railroads advanced farther west, so did migrants from Tidewater and Southside Virginia. Thomas Henry Fowlkes, for example, had farmed in Lunenburg County for two decades before deciding, in 1848, to shift part of his operations to Montgomery County. When he and his sons moved to the county, they brought with them several enslaved families and quickly put them to work raising tobacco in the county's Childress Store neighborhood.[21]

Data collected by the Freedmen's Bureau shortly after slavery was abolished in Montgomery County clearly demonstrates a pattern of forced migration into the county. In the summer of 1866, bureau officials recorded the places of birth of 431 adult men and women who had been enslaved in the county when the Civil War ended. Just under half had been born in Montgomery County and 60 percent in Montgomery and the immediately adjacent counties. More than a third, though, had been born elsewhere, and the overwhelming majority of these coerced immigrants had come from counties farther east in Virginia. Southside, in particular, was home to a great number of men and women later enslaved in Montgomery County. In all, 19 percent of the formerly enslaved who reported a place of birth in 1866 had been born in Southside, with the largest numbers coming from Bedford, Lunenburg, and Campbell Counties.[22]

These technological, economic, and demographic changes in Montgomery County may also have been accompanied by intellectual and political change. Throughout the South, the late 1840s and early 1850s saw growing anxiety about the security of slavery and that of the White society it supported. The depth of this anxiety in any particular region of the South often seems to have been proportional to the importance of slavery there. Thus, as slavery expanded in Montgomery County, and as economic, cultural, and personal connections multiplied between southwest Virginia and eastern regions of the state in which slavery was even more established and considered even more essential to the happiness and prosperity of White residents, concerns about the institution maintaining the existing racial hierarchy may have become more pronounced in Montgomery County as well. Such concerns may also explain why the cases moved so quickly toward a final resolution following their return to Montgomery County.[23]

All four were placed on the circuit court's docket in May 1852 and immediately continued until the next term. With the cases being heard in Christiansburg, it was much easier for most witnesses to attend, and in the cases of those living elsewhere, both parties had been taking depositions for more than twenty years. Apparently, by now neither side had reason to delay, so when the court next convened, in September, all four cases came to trial together. Once again, it is impossible to say anything definite about either the strategy or the evidence employed because the trial generated no bills of exception that have survived and there was no verdict to appeal. The trial lasted three days and ended with another hung jury.[24]

It does seem likely, though, that in this latest trial the focus of attention may have shifted back to the question of whether or not Flora, Cena, and Unis had been brought to Virginia in violation of the 1778 nonimportation statute and away from the issue of Flora's legal status before her importation. Evidence submitted by the defendants during the 1846 trial in which Flora's descendants had won their freedom and then explicitly referenced by the supreme court of appeals when it overturned that verdict had clearly established that Connecticut had not taken action to emancipate any slaves while Flora was living in the state. This would have weakened significantly any effort to argue that she had been a free woman when Oliver Hanchett, a Connecticut resident, dragged her out of bed, took her to New York, and sold her to Jacob Lawrence. Moreover, the supreme court of appeals had also ruled decisively that hearsay evidence was entirely inadmissible, which excluded much—if not all—of the evidence included in the depositions gathered on the plaintiffs' behalf in Connecticut and Massachusetts and further weakened any effort to show that Flora had been a free woman sold illegally into slavery.[25]

Additional evidence of this shift in focus came as the parties prepared for yet another trial. When jurors failed to reach a verdict in September 1852, the suits were continued to the next term, which opened the following April. They were then continued again and scheduled for trial during a special term of the circuit court to be held in June 1853. Shortly before that trial began, lawyers for the defendants took three more depositions from residents of Montgomery County who had known Flora personally. Together the three were clearly intended to strengthen the defendants' claim that it was James Stephens who purchased Flora, Cena, and Unis and brought them to Virginia, which as a new migrant to the commonwealth he was permitted to do under the 1778 law, and that the defendants should enjoy the presumption that Stephens had taken the requisite oath that he had not brought the enslaved into Virginia with the intent to sell them.

None of the new witnesses had been present when Flora and her daughters were sold, but two of them, Samuel Pearce and John Gardner, had known James Simpkins and declared him to be a man who could be trusted to speak the truth. Simpkins had explained in an 1833 deposition that while he did act as a surrogate for James Stephens when selling the latter's deerskins in New York, he had not done so when Stephens bought Flora, Cena, and Unis. "Stephens made the bargain himself," Simpkins had testified. He further stated that while he had lent Stephens part of the money paid for the enslaved trio, he had been repaid in full and had "no interest either direct or indirect in the said slaves." He had then repeated this point under cross-examination. When asked by the plaintiffs' lawyer, William Ballard Preston, "Did you ever own either Flora, Caena or Unis," Simpkins declared simply, "No, I never did." Now, both Pearce and Gardner testified that Simpkins was an honest man, and the defense apparently hoped this would buttress its claim that it was Stephens who brought Flora and her daughters into Virginia.[26]

As for his then taking the required oath, the defendants seem to have hoped these new witnesses would help to buttress the presumption that he had. In 1818, Virginia's supreme court of appeals had ruled that in freedom suits involving an allegation that the defendant had failed to take the oath required under the 1778 nonimportation act, "the fact of the master's having taken the oath . . . should be presumed from twenty years possession of them as slaves without their claiming their freedom." Flora had been enslaved by James Charlton for at least twenty-nine years after being brought to Virginia, and each of these new witnesses declared emphatically that, as far they knew, Flora had made no claim to freedom during that time. Moreover, they called into question the source of claims that she had. Samuel Pearce explained that he "never heard of such a thing until Elijah Meacham stated it," while the others, Jane Burke and John Gardner, both declared that Meacham's character was suspect and that they would not believe him under oath.[27]

The plaintiffs also took action during the spring of 1853 that suggests the focus of the case had returned to the 1778 nonimportation act and the legality of the importation of Flora and her daughters. As the trial opened, on June 21, 1853, the attorney for Unis et al. and Phillis et al., plaintiffs suing the estate of James Charlton, filed an interrogatory seeking information from John McCandless Taylor, the estate's administrator. The plaintiffs asked that Taylor be required to answer under oath whether or not he had a bill of sale from James Simpkins or Samuel Langhorn to James Charlton for the sale of Flora, Cena, or Unis; whether or not he had ever seen such a bill of sale among Charlton's papers or anywhere else; and whether or not he had ever heard from any of Charlton's heirs that such a document existed. This information had no bearing on whether or not Flora had been free when Oliver Hanchett took her to New York, but it could shed light on whether or not she had been brought into Virginia illegally by James Simpkins rather than legally by James Stephens. Taylor denied all knowledge of such a paper, and the trial began.[28]

The trial lasted four days, and the only evidence of what happened during that time is the appellate decision published in 1855.[29] That decision indicates that the plaintiffs did raise the issue of Flora's status before she was taken to New York and did introduce some of the evidence collected in Connecticut. Shubael Stiles had declared in an 1845 deposition that Flora "was free according to our laws" when she married Ex. Counsel for the plaintiffs must have felt safe introducing Stiles's testimony because the relevant portion of his deposition seemed to rest on his own personal knowledge rather than on "common report" in the neighborhood. The question of Flora's status before she was brought to Virginia, however, seems to have been much less prominent in the 1853 trial than it had been in 1846, no doubt because so much of the evidence concerning her life in Connecticut and Massachusetts was hearsay that would certainly be ruled inadmissible. Beyond Stiles's deposition, all of the evidence discussed in the appellate decision relates to the 1778 nonimportation act. Thus, it seems likely that the central question of the 1853 trial was whether or not Flora's descendants were entitled to their freedom because her importation had violated the nonimportation act.

In arguing that the plaintiffs were entitled to their freedom because of Flora's illegal importation, Hoge employed two strategies. First, he maintained that if, as the defendants claimed, it was James Stephens who brought

Flora, Cena, and Unis to Virginia, he should within ten days have taken the necessary oath that he did not import them "with an intent of selling them." Absent conclusive proof that Stephens had taken the oath, the defense could only benefit from the presumption that he had if Flora had made no claim to freedom during the twenty years immediately after her importation. To negate that presumption, the plaintiffs introduced a deposition provided by Henry Carty in 1832 in which Carty declared that "she [Flora] told me at different times that if she had her just rights she would be a free woman." Carty had also testified that Ezekiel Howard, a county magistrate who died in 1824, had once told him that Flora had applied to him for her freedom.

Simultaneously, Hoge employed a second approach that might also prove the plaintiffs were entitled to their freedom on the grounds of illegal importation. In 1778 the law had permitted new settlers, such as James Stephens, to bring their enslaved workers with them to Virginia as long as they took the oath mentioned above within ten days. This did not, however, apply to men such as James Simpkins, who already lived in Virginia. Whether they took the oath or not, residents of Virginia were only permitted to bring into the commonwealth slaves that they already owned or had received through marriage or inheritance, and the law required that any they did acquire through purchase and import into Virginia "shall, upon such importation become free." At least five witnesses declared in their depositions that James Simpkins, then a resident of Virginia, had purchased Flora and her daughters in New York and brought them with him back to the commonwealth. In his own deposition, however, Simpkins had denied ever owning them, so the plaintiffs' lawyer sought to undermine the jurors' confidence in Simpkins's credibility by introducing "evidence to prove that he had made statements inconsistent with his deposition."

The defense successfully countered each of these with objections to the admission of the plaintiffs' evidence. Counsel for the defense objected to the introduction of Shubael Stiles's deposition claiming that Flora had been free when she was kidnapped and sold in New York on the grounds that no notice had been given of the time and place for the taking of the deposition and that no commission had been awarded to authorize the taking of his testimony. The judge sustained the objection and excluded Stiles's deposition. The defense also objected to the admission of Henry Carty's testimony that Flora had asserted her status as a free woman and had gone before Ezekiel Howard to challenge her enslavement, testimony that threatened to undermine the presumption that James Stephens had taken the oath required to make Flora's importation legal. The judge also sustained this objection. It was, he ruled, impossible to say in what year Flora made her claim of freedom, and it seemed that Howard's report of Flora approaching him for legal redress was made more than twenty years after her importation and, thus, too late to negate the presumption of compliance with the law. Finally, the defense objected to the plaintiffs' introduction of evidence that James Simpkins had made statements inconsistent with the deposition in which he denied that he had ever owned Flora or her daughters. The allegedly inconsistent statements, argued the defense, had not been taken under oath, and no foundation had been laid for their introduction into evidence. The judge agreed, sustained the objection, and excluded the evidence of Simpkins's alleged inconsistencies.

Counsel for the defense also blocked the plaintiffs' use of a deposition provided by Robert Gardner while the cases had been before the court in Rockbridge County. Gardner's deposition is not among the surviving records of the case; thus, it is impossible to say what Gardner claimed or how his testimony might have factored in the plaintiffs' case, but it clearly included something the defense wished to exclude from the jury's consideration. What is known is that Gardner had been deposed in Christiansburg on April 11, 1850, the day before the circuit court was scheduled to open in Lexington, ninety miles away. The defense objected to the introduction of Gardner's testimony on the grounds that the defendants had only been notified on April 8, 9, and 10 that Gardner was to be deposed and could not be in Christiansburg on April 11 and in Lexington the next day. The judge agreed and excluded Gardner's deposition.

The defense did more than simply object to the admission of evidence offered by the plaintiffs. It also offered evidence of its own to rebut the plaintiffs' case. Unfortunately, only one element of that evidence appears in the appellate record. After the plaintiffs had introduced depositions from several witnesses stating that it was James Simpkins who purchased and imported Flora, Cena, and Unis and sold them to James Charlton "with a general warranty of title," the defense not only challenged those depositions, as described above, but also sought to introduce a deposition from Simpkins himself denying that he had ever owned or sold any of the three enslaved individuals.

This time it was the plaintiffs' turn to object. Their counsel immediately sought to block the admission of Simpkins's deposition on the grounds that the witness had a personal interest in the outcome of the case. If Simpkins had owned Flora and her daughters when they were brought into Virginia, the 1778 statute declared that they should have been freed immediately, and Simpkins would have had no legal title to them when he sold them to James Charlton. Thus, if the plaintiffs won, Simpkins would be liable for damages suffered by the defendants as a result of his selling them property to which he had no legal title. The defense countered the objection with a release from James McCandless Taylor, executor of Charlton's estate, waiving all right of recovery from Simpkins and, as a result, eliminating any personal interest Simpkins had in the outcome of the case. Counsel for the plaintiffs then argued that Charlton's estate was the defendant in just two of the four cases before the court and that Simpkins remained vulnerable to suits by John Swope and the estate of William Currin if the plaintiffs gained their freedom. The judge, however, overruled the plaintiffs' objection because all of the parties in all four cases had agreed that "evidence taken in one case should be read in all." Simpkins's deposition was allowed.

Beyond testimony mentioned in the appeal, it is impossible to say precisely what evidence the jury heard. Significantly, though, the decision rendered in that appeal reveals that "all the testimony offered on the trial of these causes was in the form of depositions." This means that almost all of the evidence introduced in 1853 had already been heard by earlier juries. This probably included little of the evidence collected in Massachusetts and Connecticut because so much of it had been declared inadmissible hearsay. This was evidence that Francis Anderson believed "had a great weight with the jury" during the 1846 trial in which Flora's descendants won their freedom, but even without it the plaintiffs had secured hung juries in 1850 and 1852. The only new evidence known to have been gathered after 1852 were the three depositions described above that the defense took in May 1853 in an effort to strengthen its claim that it was James Stephens, not James Simpkins, who purchased Flora, Cena, and Unis and brought them to Virginia and to undermine the credibility of witnesses claiming that Flora had challenged her enslavement within twenty years of her importation to Virginia. Perhaps this was enough to sway undecided jurors. Perhaps the rising tension between supporters of slavery and those seeking to contain or abolish it had made Virginians less willing to take any action that might suggest slavery was in any way improper. Or perhaps this particular group of men simply reacted differently to the evidence than earlier juries had. Whatever the reason, when they completed their deliberations, these men had reached a different conclusion: "We the jury find the defts. not guilty & that the plaintiffs are slaves."[30]

Again, one can only imagine the response of Flora's descendants to the jury's verdict. Their suits had now been in progress for almost thirty years. Some of the plaintiffs had not even been born when their cases began. They had grown up hearing that their grandmother or great-grandmother had been free until she was kidnapped and sold into slavery and that, finally, it was time to right that wrong. Through the many years and the many trials, the plaintiffs had kept alive the dream of their eventual freedom. They had even heard one jury agree that they were free, only to see that verdict overturned on what must have seemed to them a mere technicality totally unrelated to genuine justice. But as disheartening as this new verdict must have been, Flora's descendants were not beaten. Through their counsel they immediately filed bills of exception, initiating an appeal to the supreme court of appeals, and sought writs to suspend the lower court's judgment pending the outcome of that appeal. A suspension would not overturn the jury's decision. It would, however, bar the defendants—John Swope and administrators of the estates of James Charlton and William Currin—from exercising their ownership rights over the property in question before the appeal was heard. Swope would be forbidden to sell Rhoda, or any children she might have had, and the estates' administrators would be blocked from distributing among the heirs of Charlton or Currin any of Flora's descendants held by those estates. The supreme court of appeals granted this request, and for the second time in eight years, plaintiffs and defendants awaited their turn before Virginia's highest court.[31]

The Court Speaks

When Unis first set off for the courthouse, in September 1825, she had reason to hope that she would prevail in the freedom suit she planned to launch. Previous freedom suits in Montgomery County had often succeeded, and Unis had every reason to believe that hers might too. Slavery was still widespread in Virginia, but at least some White Virginians were willing to consider its eventual abolition. As time passed, though, the obstacles confronting Flora's descendants had grown. As described in previous chapters, the chances of winning their freedom through the courts had certainly been hurt when judges refused to admit depositions from witnesses in Connecticut and Massachusetts who testified that Flora had previously been free. Equally damaging may have been the changes that occurred in Montgomery County as plans to connect southwest Virginia to a growing network of railroads began transforming the county's economy and demography. Those were not the only changes underway, though. Nationally, the environment in which the cases were heard changed significantly between the 1820s and the 1850s, and these changes probably lengthened the odds that Flora's descendants faced as they awaited a decision from the supreme court of appeals.

Tension over the expansion of slavery had been rising steadily since the United States declared war against Mexico in 1846. Opponents of the war immediately denounced it as act of naked aggression waged on behalf of evil slaveholders anxious to acquire more territory in which to establish their immoral system of coerced labor. In an effort to stop them, Pennsylvania congressman David Wilmot introduced a resolution in the House of

Representatives to ban slavery in any territory the United States might acquire through its war with Mexico. Congress ultimately rejected the Wilmot Proviso, but the issue arose again almost immediately as Congress moved to organize land acquired through the war into American territories. These discussions were further complicated by disputes concerning two other issues related to slavery: northern objections to the existence of slavery in Washington, DC, and southern anger at northerners' refusal to enforce the Fugitive Slave Act of 1793. The result was months of bitter debates in Congress as Henry Clay tried unsuccessfully to settle all of these issues through a single great compromise (his "Omnibus Bill"), and Stephen Douglas coordinated efforts to accomplish each of the different elements of Clay's proposal though individual pieces of legislation. These passed thanks to a shifting array of majorities and were known collectively as the Compromise of 1850.

In the course of the debates surrounding the compromise, White southerners saw any effort to prevent the expansion of slavery into new territory or to question its morality as an insult to their honor, a threat to their economy, and a danger to the racial supremacy on which their society was built. In Congress they spoke eloquently and fought doggedly to protect their interests, and when they feared their efforts might fail, they considered alternative measures. In the summer of 1850, while Congress prepared to vote on Clay's Omnibus Bill, delegates from nine southern states, including Virginia, met in Nashville for a convention called to consider a southern response to what they saw as northern attacks on their way of life. Radical members of the convention called for secession as the only means to guarantee the preservation of slavery and the southern culture it made possible. Moderates ultimately prevailed in the convention, and its final resolutions avoided any call for secession. But the debates in Nashville provided a platform for slavery's strongest advocates to voice their concerns about its future and to fuel southern anxiety about northern opposition to the institution.

Southern anxiety was not reduced when Congress finally cobbled together the Compromise of 1850. Supporters of slavery had wanted an explicit provision allowing its expansion into at least some of the territory acquired from Mexico. They did not get such a guarantee. Instead, California had been admitted to the Union as a free state, while the rest had become Utah Territory and New Mexico Territory with no provision for the future of slavery in either. Under the doctrine known as popular sovereignty, settlers in those territories would, at some point in the future, decide themselves whether or not to permit slavery. Southerners did get a stronger fugitive slave act through the Compromise of 1850, but the new law was met immediately with strong opposition throughout the North, where private citizens as well as state and local officials took steps to render the law almost unenforceable.

Sectional animosity and southern anxiety were further inflamed in the years that followed. The publication of Uncle Tom's Cabin, in 1852, and its runaway success with the northern public intensified criticism of slavery and of slaveholders on moral grounds. That, in turn, made southerners even more determined to defend themselves and their institutions, and in June 1853 that determination may have played a role in the jurors' decision that Flora's descendants were not entitled to their freedom. Then, while the jury's verdict awaited review by the Virginia supreme court of appeals, tensions rose even more when Congress passed the Kansas-Nebraska Act. In order to open a northern route across the Great Plains for a proposed transcontinental railroad, Stephen Douglas envisioned organizing a new territory in the region. Southerners refused to support such a plan, though, because the new territory would lie north of the Missouri Compromise line and, as a result, would be closed to slavery. In an effort to secure southern votes for his plan, Douglas agreed to include in it a repeal of the Missouri Compromise. When the bill finally passed, in May 1854, it established two territories, Kansas and Nebraska, and opened them to the possible introduction of slavery through the same doctrine of popular sovereignty employed in the Utah and New Mexico territories. This was immensely popular in the South. The Kansas-Nebraska Act infuriated northerners, though, and that anger quickly led to the formation of the Republican Party, which pledged to stop the expansion of slavery into any United States territory. The act also prompted both pro- and antislavery groups to call on their supporters to head for Kansas in order to control the local government taking shape there.[1]

It was in this fevered environment, that Virginia's supreme court of appeals heard Unis & als. v. Charlton's Adm'r & als. The four cases brought by Flora's descendants were combined into a single case that the court of appeals heard in Lewisburg during its July term, 1855. Counsel for the plaintiffs, probably Daniel H. Hoge, based the appeal on the five points described in chapter 6. Writing for the court, Judge William Daniel quickly dismissed four of the five. Concerning the admissibility of Shubael Stiles's deposition, Hoge argued that the presence of counsel for the defense when the deposition was taken and the ability of the defense to cross-examine the witness "dispensed with the necessity of producing the commission." Judge Daniel bluntly disagreed. He declared that the plaintiffs had to show either that they had met the statutory requirements for an admissible deposition or that the defendants had explicitly waived those requirements. Noting "an absence of all proof to show that the plaintiffs had complied with the conditions on the performance of which their right to read the deposition depended," he upheld the exclusion of Stiles's testimony.

Hoge had no more success with his second exception. Henry Carty had maintained that Flora challenged her enslavement within twenty years of her importation, which would negate the presumption that James Stephens had taken the oath required under the 1778 nonimportation act. The relevant portion of Carty's deposition had been had excluded, however, because the trial judge ruled that it was impossible to say when Flora had declared that "if she had her just rights she would be a free woman" and that "her application to the justice Howard [to initiate a freedom suit] was not made within twenty years." Hoge argued before the supreme court that it was up to the jury, not the judge, to decide whether or not Flora's actions had come within the magic twenty years. Judge Daniel dismissed this objection as quickly as he had Hoge's first. The presumption of compliance after twenty years was settled law established by "repeated adjudications of this court." As for who should decide when Flora's statements and actions had taken place, Daniel admitted that "how such a claim should be asserted in order to have the effect of repelling this presumption has never been decided by this court." It did not need to be decided in this case, though, because "it is obvious . . . that no matter what may be the essentials of such a claim, or how it must be asserted, it can be of no avail unless made within the twenty years before presumption." Carty's deposition was taken more than forty-five years after Flora's importation, and "these declarations, from aught that appears to the contrary, may have been made long after the presumption had attached; and were therefore plainly inadmissible as testimony for any purpose."

Judge Daniel was no more willing to entertain the plaintiffs' claim that James Simpkins should be barred from giving evidence because if the plaintiffs won their case, he might be liable for damages for selling Flora, Cena, and Unis to James Charlton when he had no legal title to them. Simpkins had obtained a release from John McCandless Taylor, Charlton's administrator, but not from any of the other defendants. Daniel quickly dismissed this matter. As "Charlton's representative," only Taylor had any grounds for a suit against Simpkins, "and no good reason is suggested why such a release should be made by anyone but Taylor." Moreover, Daniel added, because the parties had agreed that evidence taken in one case could be read in all, "I see no reason why the agreement should not be allowed to cure the omission in the releases."

Judge Daniel was equally dismissive of Hoge's argument that the trial judge had improperly excluded the deposition of John Gardner. Gardner had been deposed in Christiansburg the day before the Rockbridge County Superior Court opened, and Judge Daniel pointed out that the defendants "could not have attended the taking of the depositions and then have reached the court by the commencement of its session." They had a right to attend both, and their objection to the admission of Gardner's deposition was, Daniel declared, properly sustained.

Only one of the plaintiffs' exceptions merited extended consideration by the supreme court of appeals. During the trial, counsel for the defense had introduced a deposition from James Simpkins in which Simpkins categorically denied purchasing Flora and her daughters in New York or owning them when they were imported to Virginia. This was an effort to counter the plaintiffs' claim that they were entitled to their freedom because Flora, Cena, and Unis had been brought into Virginia by a resident of Virginia, Simpkins, in violation of the state's 1778 nonimportation act. In response the plaintiffs sought to introduce evidence that Simpkins had made statements elsewhere that were inconsistent with the testimony offered in his deposition. The trial judge had excluded the plaintiffs' evidence, however, on the grounds that it had not been made under oath and the defense had had no opportunity to question Simpkins about the allegedly inconsistent statements and whether or not he actually made them. Counsel for the plaintiffs had unsuccessfully objected to the trial judge's ruling and now argued before the supreme court of appeals that the state's highest court, itself, had previously ruled on the matter in a way that supported the plaintiffs' objection. Eight years earlier, when the cases of Flora's descendants first came before Virginia's supreme court, it had ruled that "previous statements of a witness, whether oral or written, may be introduced in evidence to impeach his credibility." Citing this precedent, Daniel Hoge argued that the evidence of Simpkins's inconsistent statements should have been admitted.

In Judge Daniel's view, however, the question before the court this time was not whether or not such evidence could be introduced; that, he agreed, had been established in the earlier appeal. Rather, the issue before the court this time involved the way in which that evidence had been obtained: "whether a witness who has testified in a cause may be impeached by the proof of contradictory or inconsistent statements, alleged to have been made by him on other occasions, before the foundation for such impeaching testimony is first laid, by an examination of the witness touching the fact of his having made such statements." In other words, could Simpkins's earlier, contradictory statements be admitted as evidence if Simpkins had not been directly questioned about them when he was deposed and provided the opportunity to deny that he had made them or to reconcile them with his later testimony. This question, Judge Daniel noted, had never come before the Virginia court, but an examination of English and American precedents provided a rule that seemed "safe, just, and convenient" to the matter at hand.

The guiding principle, Judge Daniel believed, must be to maintain "a sense of justice to the witness"—in this case to James Simpkins. "As the direct tendency of the [plaintiffs'] evidence is to impeach his veracity," Daniel wrote, "common justice requires that by first calling his attention to the subject, he should have an opportunity to recollect the facts, and if necessary to correct the statement already given, as well as by a re-examination to explain the nature, circumstances, meaning, and design of what he is proved elsewhere to have said." Courts in England and in "a large majority" of the American states had previously reached this conclusion, and just eighteen months earlier, in *Conrad v. Griffey*, the Supreme Court of the United States had ruled, "[A] witness cannot be impeached by showing that he had made contradictory statements from those sworn to, unless on his examination he was asked whether he had not made such statements to the individuals by whom the proof was expected to be given."

James Simpkins's deposition made clear that he had never been afforded such an opportunity. The plaintiffs' lawyer had been present when Simpkins was deposed and had cross-examined him at the time. He had not, however, asked any questions about Simpkins's earlier statements. Thus,

Judge Daniel concluded, the trial judge had been correct in refusing to admit any subsequent challenge to Simpkins's earlier, allegedly inconsistent, statements unless the plaintiffs secured a new commission for a second deposition in which Simpkins was asked directly about those statements and provided an opportunity to explain them. "As it does not appear that any predicate was laid in the course of the examination, for the introduction of proof of the inconsistent declarations offered on the trial to impeach the witness," Daniel concluded, "the court did right, I think, in refusing to allow such proof to go to the jury."[2]

After considering each of the plaintiffs' five grounds for appeal, Judge Daniel could find no error in the proceedings of the circuit court. With the other judges concurring in his opinion, he affirmed the judgment of the lower court, and the jury's verdict remained the final word: "the plaintiffs are slaves." After thirty years, nine trials, and two hearings before the supreme court of appeals, the effort that Unis Lewis had begun to secure the freedom of herself and her extended family was over. The supreme court of appeals rendered its opinion during its August 1855 term and issued separate orders regarding each of the four cases between August 20 and August 24 of that year. These orders were not officially entered into the record at the Montgomery County Superior Court until the following March, but by then the distribution of James Charlton's enslaved property had already begun.[3]

Unfortunately, reconstructing that distribution and measuring the full extent of its impact on Flora's descendants is complicated by a variety of factors. First, the number of plaintiffs in the cases had increased over time, though their exact number and identities became less clear (fig. 7). Flora's youngest daughter, Phillis, had at least five more children while her suit was before the courts. And Phillis's older children had children of their own. Her daughter Mary had three between 1826 and 1844, though neither the names of the children nor those of their father or fathers were recorded. Mary then entered a relationship with Thomas Brown in 1853 that they later registered as a legal marriage, and their first child, Eunice, was born about 1854. Three of Phillis's other daughters also had children while the suits were pending. By 1844, Matilda and Helen each had two children, though their names and ages remain unknown, as do the identities of their fathers, and Flora had at least two children, Mary Susan and Robert, whose fathers' names are also unknown. In all, the number of plaintiffs tripled before their suits were finally resolved. When they were first allowed to proceed, in

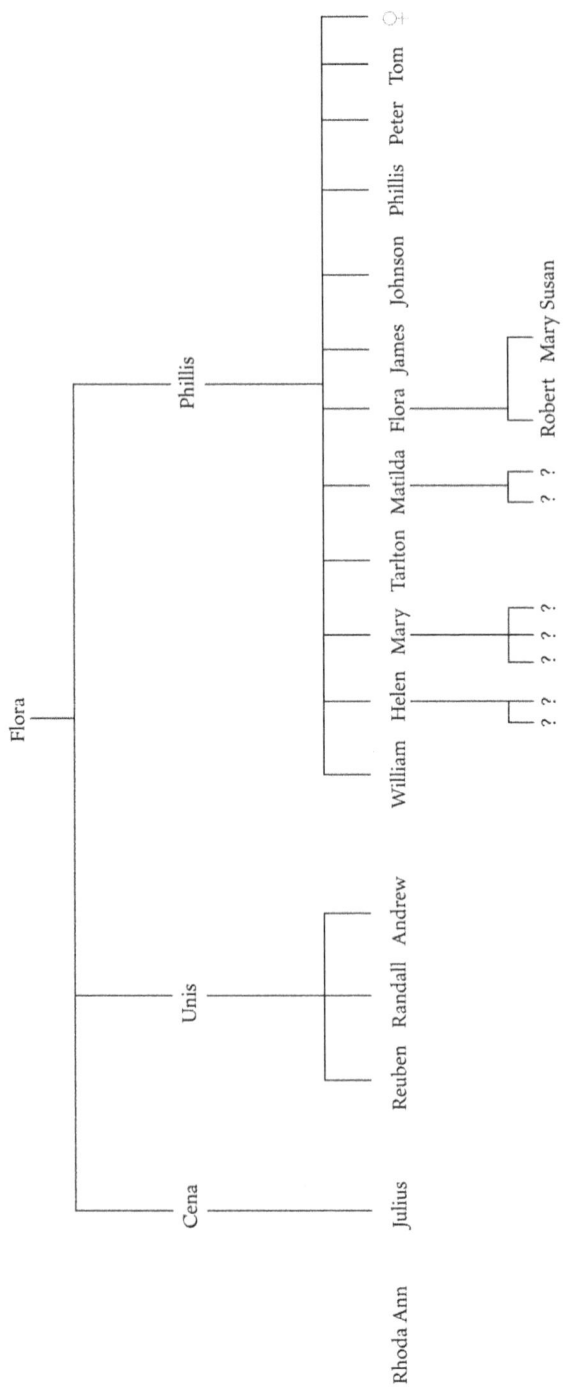

FIGURE 7. Descendants of Flora in 1844

1826, the four suits involved a total of fifteen plaintiffs—all of them children or grandchildren of Flora and each of them identified by name in court papers. By 1844, the number had grown to at least twenty-nine and probably more; a deponent identifying Flora's descendants still held by the estate of James Charlton in that year admitted, "there may be some young children whom I do not know." Two years later, in 1846, newspaper reports put the number at forty to forty-five, and by 1855 it was probably even larger. The number of these plaintiffs known by name, however, barely changed over the suits' thirty-year history. In all, just twenty-two of the forty-five or more plaintiffs in the suits can be identified by name.

In addition, the number of individuals who were not plaintiffs in the suits but were affected by their outcome also grew. Phillis's son William married an enslaved woman named Mary Johnson in 1847, and the couple had at least one child, a daughter Sarah, while waiting to learn the outcome of William's freedom suit. Unis's son Reuben may also have married while his case was pending. He seems to have had at least one child, a son named Peter, by 1855, though nothing is known of the boy's mother. Neither Sarah nor Peter ever became plaintiffs in their fathers' freedom suits, however, because freedom in Virginia descended through the mother's line. They would certainly be affected by the suits' outcome, though; if their fathers remained enslaved, they might be sold away when James Charlton's estate was finally distributed among his heirs and creditors. Similarly, the children of William's brother Tarlton never became plaintiffs because he married a free woman of color. Sometime around 1845, Tarlton married Jane Campbell. Members of her family had been living as free people in Montgomery County since the 1790s, at least, and by the 1840s were the largest free Black family in the county. Between 1845 and 1855 Tarlton and Jane had at least five children—Mary Elizabeth, Ann Eliza, James, David Wade, and William. Because their mother was already free, the couple's children were free regardless of the outcome of Tarlton's freedom suit, but they might lose their father and Jane her husband if he remained enslaved.[4]

When the suits were finally resolved and James Charlton's enslaved property was actually distributed, the individuals least affected by the outcome were probably Unis's son Randall Lewis and any wife or children he may have had. Certainly, the supreme court's decision dealt a crushing blow to any dreams of freedom Randall had nourished, but it probably had relatively little impact on his immediate situation. From the beginning of his legal odyssey, Randall had been the putative property of John Swope, and no evidence has yet been found to suggest that Swope ever transferred his interest in Randall to anyone else. Thus, the supreme court's order simply provided official confirmation that the Commonwealth of Virginia considered Randall the property of John Swope. And because Randall was a male, the outcome of his suit was never going to change the legal status of any children he may have had. If Randall had any children, their condition would follow that of their mother, and her status was never an issue in the suit against John Swope.

What actually happened to Randall once his freedom suit failed, though, remains a mystery. Census records from 1820 through 1850 identify John Swope as the owner of a single adult, male slave. This enslaved man was reported to be between the ages of twenty-six and forty-five in 1820, between twenty-four and thirty-five in 1840, and forty years old in 1850—an obvious inconsistency, but not unprecedented in census records of the enslaved. Swope died in 1856, the year after Randall's freedom suit was decided, and according to the inventory of his estate his property included "One Negro Man George." It is possible that Randall and George were the same individual known by two names, but this seems unlikely. References to enslaved individuals and to free people of color in antebellum Virginia did sometimes indicate that those individuals might be known by different names; court papers concerning Flora's descendants, for example, mention that Unis had originally been known as Rose. Nowhere in the dozens of documents generated by the case of *Randall v. Swope*, however, is there any indication that Randall had ever been known by another name. Nor is it possible to follow George in any later records because the final accounting of the sale of Swope's property, dated April 10, 1857, reported that George died "immediately after sale."[5]

It is possible that Swope sold Randall after the supreme court reached a final decision in the case and bought George. It is also possible that between 1825 and 1855 he sold his claim to Randall pending the suit's outcome and purchased George. As detailed below, several of James Charlton's heirs did sell their shares in their father's estate while the suits against it were still unresolved. When Randall initiated his suit, Swope had been ordered to post a bond of six hundred dollars to ensure he would "have the said Randall forthcoming to answer the judgement of the court," but that would not preclude his selling his claim to Randall as long he was confident the purchaser would allow Randall to conduct his business before the court. Neither possibility can be confirmed, though. Outside of estate sales, few sales of enslaved individuals seem to have been recorded in Virginia courthouses, and if Swope did sell Randall, it is impossible to say to whom he was sold or what happened to him after 1855.[6]

The fate of Rhoda Ann remains equally obscure. She was a granddaughter of Flora, though it has proven impossible to determine who her mother was or when she was born. Rhoda Ann had probably been given by James Charlton to his daughter, also named Rhoda, perhaps when she married William Currin, in 1804, and had ultimately become the property of William Currin. She was included in the inventory of Currin's estate following his death, in 1828, and the administrator of that estate remained the named defendant in her freedom suit through its final resolution. By then, Rhoda Currin had also died, but she and William had at least four surviving children and several grandchildren by a son who had died young. Rhoda Ann might have passed to one of those heirs or might have been sold so the money could be more easily divided among multiple heirs, and it has proven impossible to determine her fate. Nor is it possible to say if she had children of her own. They would also have been plaintiffs in her freedom suit, but the fact that no other plaintiffs were named in her suit does not mean that none existed. Court records make it clear that several named plaintiffs had children who were also recognized as plaintiffs but were never identified by name in material generated by their freedom suits.[7]

Only in the case of individuals belonging to the estate of James Charlton is it possible to say with any certainty what happened to Flora's descendants when their freedom suits failed, but here too the picture is muddled and incomplete. That portion of James Charlton's estate that consisted of enslaved workers remained undivided until 1855. The widow's dower had been assigned within months of Charlton's death, but when Hannah Charlton died, in 1827, her dower reverted to the estate.[8] No other division of Charlton's estate took place until 1834, when William B. Charlton, one of James's sons, petitioned the court to order a division of his father's real and personal property. Other heirs consented to this request, and the court appointed four commissioners to effect the partition. They divided Charlton's land successfully, but the personal property—his enslaved workers—proved more difficult because so many of those workers were suing for their freedom. The commissioners finally reported: "after several days trying to make division it was agreed by the representatives of said Charlton that it was not expedient to make division of the personal estate until the decision of the said suit." William B. Charlton petitioned the county court a second time, in 1836, and once again the court appointed commissioners "for the purpose of dividing equally amongst the legal heirs of James Charlton deceased, all the slaves belonging to said estate." No report from these commissioners has survived, however, making it impossible to say whether or not they managed to accomplish their task this time. Even if they did, though, the court's order also stipulated that "the said slaves after being divided are to remain in the hands of the administrator [of Charlton's estate]," and John McCandless Taylor, the estate's administrator, stated in 1844: "they are all in my possession (as administrator) at this time." That 1844 statement is the last-known evidence concerning the status of Charlton's enslaved property until its division in November 1855, three months after the supreme court of appeals affirmed the verdict denying the plaintiffs their freedom, and until that time it seems that none of the individuals enslaved by James Charlton were actually transferred to any of the estate's beneficiaries.[9]

By the time that division did finally begin, in the fall of 1855, the beneficiaries of the estate had changed almost as much as the number of enslaved individuals belonging to it had. William B. Charlton bought the share of his sister Juliet Charlton Saunders in 1830 and two years later bought the share of his sister Nancy Charlton Thompson, who had died in 1826. This may explain why William was so anxious to have the county court order the division of his father's estate. By the time he made his requests he was entitled to a third of the estate and may have wanted to secure his property as quickly as possible. Three other shares changed hands as a result of their owners' deaths. Rhoda Carlton Currin, Matilda Charlton Miller, and Lucinda Charlton Robinson all died between 1841 and 1855, and each was predeceased by her husband. Their shares of their father's estate passed to their children and grandchildren. And one of the original shares passed out of the family entirely. Between March 1830 and December 1831, James Charlton's son, John Lynch Charlton, executed three deeds of trust by which he used his share of his father's undivided estate to secure debts he had incurred. When he was unable to repay one of those debts, in 1837, the trustee did so by selling at public auction Charlton's share of his father's personal estate, including his share of the enslaved suing for their freedom.

The buyers were two local men, Thomas Bowyer and Creed Taylor. Bowyer then died by 1840, and his enslaved property seems to have passed to his children collectively.[10]

These many changes make it impossible to determine what happened to most of the individuals held by James Charlton's estate following the conclusion of their freedom suits. Some of the enslaved may have passed directly to an individual with a claim to part of Charlton's estate, but given the number of claimants and the range of appraised values that must have existed among the dozens of enslaved men, women, and children belonging to the estate by 1855, it would have been much easier for the administrator to sell some or all of the enslaved and divide the proceeds among those entitled to a share. Administrators and executors of estates often employed this strategy when an estate was too small to divide into viable portions or too complicated to divide equally among the heirs. They might arrange private transactions through which the heirs compensated one another in order equalize their shares, or they might organize a public sale and distribute the proceeds among the heirs. Unfortunately, very few records have been found indicating how Charlton's personal property was finally divided, and the ones that have been found provide little clarity about what happened.

The only share of James Charlton's personal property for which the disposition can be documented is that belonging to his daughter Matilda. Matilda L. Charlton had married Dr. Joseph Miller in 1812, and the couple had four surviving children when Joseph died, in 1842. Matilda herself died in 1854, and while her estate was being settled her father's personal property was finally divided following the resolution of the freedom suits brought by Flora's descendants. The report of Matilda's estate administrator states that on November 8, 1855, the administrator received on behalf of Matilda's estate a portion of her father's personal property, but the wording of the report is confusing: "said Admr. received negro woman (Flora) her two children (Mary Susan & Robert) and negro boy (Jack) of the slaves belonging to the estate of James Charlton dec.[d] suing for their freedom in which slaves M. L. Miller's interest was $1946.76 of the proceeds of which negroes distribution has been made among those entitled, by the administrator." The naming of Flora (a daughter of Phillis and granddaughter of the original Flora), Mary Susan, Robert, and Jack suggests that those four individuals passed in person to the estate of Matilda Miller, but the penny-perfect accounting that "M. L. Miller's interest was $1946.76," and the reference to its coming from "the proceeds of which negroes distribution" seem to indicate that Matilda's estate received a share of the money realized from a sale rather than actual individuals.[11]

Further complicating the picture is the fact that two days later Matilda's son, Charles A. Miller, used part of his share of his mother's estate to settle a debt he owed to Joseph S. Edie. Edie was Miller's brother-in-law, and as the husband of Matilda Miller's daughter Amanda was also a beneficiary of Matilda's estate. Charles Miller had purchased a house and lot from Edie in 1854 and signed a promissory note for $166.67 to cover part of the cost (see fig. 8). That note was later endorsed: "This was paid with its int up to Nov. 10th 1855 by transfer of my Int in slaves of my mother's estate." The debt was considerably less than Charles's "Int in slaves in my mother's estate" should have been (that is, one-quarter of $1,946.76). He might have paid the debt with part of the money received through his mother's estate if his grandfather's enslaved personal property had been sold and the proceeds divided among the heirs; or he and Matilda's other heirs could have arranged a very quick public sale of Flora, Mary Susan, Robert, and Jack, though it seems very unlikely they would have held such a sale with so little time to advertise it; or the heirs could have negotiated how to divide Matilda's share of her father's estate among themselves and Charles could have credited Edie $166.67 from his share. It is simply not possible to say how Matilda Miller's share of her father's property was actually divided or what happened to Flora, Mary Susan, Robert, and Jack.[12]

One point that is clear is that some of Flora's descendants were sold following their distribution among those holding shares of James Charlton's estate. As noted above, Mary Johnson Brown, a daughter of Flora's daughter Phillis, had at least four children by the time her freedom suit came to an end. Mary's fate in the immediate division of James Charlton's estate is unclear, but she eventually passed somehow to Floyd Smith, a tanner, farmer, and deputy sheriff living outside Christiansburg, and several of her children were sold to interstate traders and taken out of Virginia forever. Two of Mary's daughters, Eunice Brown and Ellen Brown Lynch, described childhood memories of auctions, "n——r traders," and the sale of family members. In an undated interview conducted by the Depression-era Works Progress Administration, Eunice simply described the auction block in Christiansburg and sales in general. Her sister's memories, however, were more complete and more personal. Ellen's granddaughter, Janie Gayles Milton, told an

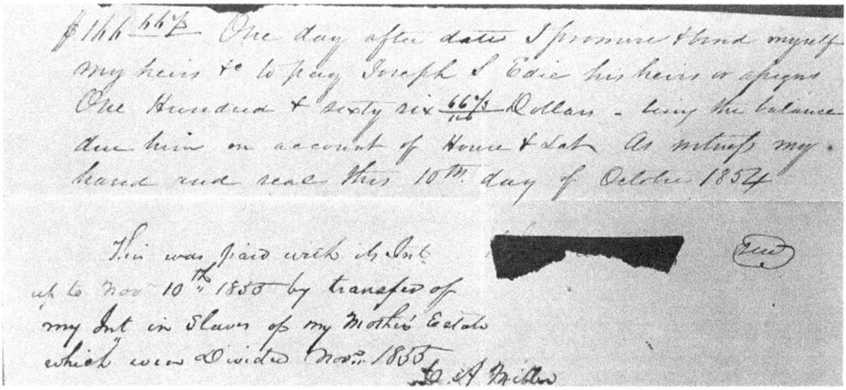

FIGURE 8. In November 1855, Charles Miller noted that he had used a portion of his share of Flora's descendants to settle this promissory note. (Rev. Charles Alexander Miller Family Papers, Special Collections and University Archives, Virginia Tech)

interviewer in 1982 that she had heard her grandmother describe the sale of her siblings "[like] cattle and sheep." "They didn't sell the girls," Milton explained, but "her brothers were sold away from her and they never did see them again. . . . They sold the boys to what's called n——r traders and they took em off down south. And they never seen em anymore."[13]

The sale of another of Flora's descendants may even be the subject of a well-known image by Lewis Miller. Miller was a Pennsylvania-born carpenter and a prolific folk artist. During his lifetime, he executed hundreds of ink and watercolor sketches depicting scenes of daily life around him. Most of these works were done in and around York, Pennsylvania, where Miller was born in 1796 and where he spent much of his life. He also sketched during his travels, though, including his frequent visits to Virginia. Miller's brother Joseph had settled in Christiansburg, where he married James Charlton's daughter, Matilda, and Lewis began visiting the couple no later than 1831. Over the years, he grew very close to his nephew, Joseph's son Charles A. Miller, and continued visiting him after Joseph and Matilda died. The Civil War interrupted the visits, but shortly after the war ended Miller moved south for good and settled in Christiansburg, where he remained until his death in 1882.[14]

Among the sketches Miller made in Christiansburg is one entitled *Miss Fillis and child, and Bill, Sold at publick Sale* (see fig. 9). It depicts an auctioneer soliciting bids from a trio of potential buyers of a Black man and a Black

FIGURE 9. This painting by Lewis Miller may depict the sale of Flora's granddaughter Phillis Johnson and other members of her family following the conclusion of their freedom suits. (The Colonial Williamsburg Foundation; gift of Dr. and Mrs. Richard M. Kain in memory of George Hay Kain)

woman nursing an infant. Miller did not identify the individuals being sold beyond the names Miss Fillis and Bill, and the only date on the work is May 12, but circumstantial evidence suggests that the individuals being sold may have been among the descendants of Flora who had sued for their freedom and lost.

Several factors suggest that the woman in the painting could be Phillis Johnson, the daughter of Phillis and Jack Johnson and a granddaughter of Flora, the ancestor of all the plaintiffs in these cases. An 1844 deposition included "young Phillis" among those enslaved by James Charlton and suing for their freedom and identifies her as the daughter of Flora's daughter Phillis. Postemancipation records in Montgomery County include the marriage license of a woman named Phillis Johnson, who identified her parents as Phillis and Jack Johnson and the year of her birth as 1837. She would have been "young" in 1844 and by 1855 old enough to be the woman Lewis Miller painted. The man could be her older brother William, who would have been in his early forties when the suits ended, or one of her cousins (four older sisters of "young Phillis" had children who were never identified by name in court records), or another William who may or may not have been married to Phillis at the time of their sale. Other, dated, works show that Lewis Miller was in Christiansburg in May 1856, nine months after the supreme court of appeals rendered its decision in the suits and two months after those decisions were officially entered in the Christiansburg circuit court. And at the time he was almost certainly staying with his nephew, Rev. Charles A. Miller, who through his mother had recently inherited part of James Charlton's personal property and who knew all of the others who had inherited shares of Charlton's property. Though it cannot be proven conclusively, it is quite possible that the Phillis depicted in Lewis Miller's sketch (and perhaps Bill as well) was a grandchild of Flora and was among the unsuccessful plaintiffs in the cases known as *Unis v. Charlton*.[15]

Whether by sale, direct transfer, or some other means, "the slaves belonging to the estate of James Charlton dec^d suing for their freedom" were finally distributed among their new owners. Phillis Johnson, youngest daughter of the original Flora, seems to have passed to William B. Charlton. Phillis's son William apparently became the property of Charles Gardner, who was married to a granddaughter of James Charlton, and worked as a farmhand for the Gardners until slavery was abolished. Another son, Tarlton, seems to have been acquired by Rice D. Montague, a prominent businessman in Christiansburg and clerk of the county court. Tarlton, however, died in 1860, leaving a widow and six children. Yet another son, James, came to belong to Charles Bowyer, whose father had purchased a share of the Charlton estate when John Lynch Charlton failed to pay his debts. James also worked as a farmhand. Phillis's daughter Mary Johnson Brown may have passed initially to Dr. Joseph Spears Edie, the husband of Matilda Charlton Miller's daughter Amanda. As described above, though, Mary and her daughters soon passed to Floyd Smith, while her sons were sold to interstate slave traders and taken south. Mary cooked for the Smiths, while her daughter Eunice served the family as a "house girl."[16]

Slavery in Montgomery County lasted another decade after the suits brought by Flora's descendants came to an end, but in the spring of 1865 the surviving plaintiffs finally gained the freedom that Virginia courts had denied them. Unfortunately, not all were there to enjoy it. No record has yet been found of Unis, Andrew, or Randall Lewis after 1855, nor has any evidence emerged that Cena, Flora's eldest daughter, or Cena's son, Julius, or Rhoda Ann were still alive after 1855. Unis and Cena would have been in their seventies by then, and it would hardly be surprising if they died before 1865. Andrew, Randall, Julius, and Rhoda Ann were younger, but were all adults as their suits made their way through Virginia's legal system. Like Tarlton Johnson, they may have died by 1865; the registry of deaths in Montgomery County is very incomplete, especially for enslaved individuals. Or, like Mary Brown's sons, they may have been sold to interstate traders and sent south. Or they may have freed themselves and fled the region. Absent any evidence, none of these options can be proven or disproven. Andrew Lewis and Randall Lewis are relatively common names. The 1870 federal census includes several Black men with those names and of approximately the right age living in other counties or states, but it is impossible to say if any of them were Unis's sons. As for Julius and Rhoda Ann, the absence of surnames makes their fates even more difficult to determine.

For those who did live until 1865, freedom finally came that April. Word quickly spread through southwest Virginia that the Confederate government had collapsed and that Robert E. Lee had surrendered his army at Appomattox. Almost immediately, it seems, slave owners in Montgomery County recognized that slavery was dead. The little evidence that has survived of this process suggests that slave owners in the county were remarkably matter-of-fact about it. Mary Johnson Brown's owner, for example, simply declared, "Well, Mary you alls set free today." To the formerly enslaved workers, on the other hand, it must have been an occasion of extraordinary joy, excitement, and fear. Flora's descendants had struggled for thirty years to win their freedom through the courts. Those efforts had failed, but failure had not dampened their thirst for freedom. They must have rejoiced that their long-awaited liberation had finally come to pass. But they must also have recognized the challenges they faced. They owned nothing, enjoyed few rights under existing Virginia law, and could hardly expect their former enslavers to welcome their freedom or to offer them much help establishing their new lives. Mary Brown's response to the announcement that she was free was to ask, "Well Master, what am I gonna do?"[17]

What she and her family did was begin to build lives of their own, and with the end of slavery it is possible to identify a number of Flora's descendants and glimpse the new lives they built for themselves. The end of slavery meant that African Americans began to appear by name much more frequently in state and federal records. In March 1865, Congress established the Bureau of Refugees, Freedmen, and Abandoned Lands (more commonly known as the Freedmen's Bureau) to provide emergency assistance to newly freed African Americans, and by July the Bureau had established a presence in Christiansburg. That summer, and again in 1867, staff at the Freedmen's Bureau attempted to take censuses of freedpeople in the county, and in 1866 they enrolled formerly enslaved couples on a cohabitation register to legalize their marriages and the births of their children under legislation passed by Virginia's General Assembly.[18]

These records do make it easier to document the lives of African Americans in Montgomery County, but none of the records are complete, and mysteries abound in the stories of Flora's descendants. Even with these new records, only one branch of Flora's family tree can be followed for very long. As noted above, no trace has survived of Flora's daughter Cena or her family after the close of their freedom suit; nor is there any mention of Flora's daughter Unis or of Unis's sons Randall and Andrew Lewis after 1855. Unis's third son, Reuben Lewis, does seem to appear on the 1870 census as a farmworker living in Pulaski County, and marriage records from that county suggest that his son Peter married there in 1868 and his daughter Laura in 1874. But after that, all three vanish from the historical record. Only in the case of Unis's youngest daughter, Phillis, and her descendants is it possible to reconstruct the postemancipation lives of this story's protagonists to any significant degree, and even then the stories that emerge often contain gaps or contradictory information.[19]

Phillis herself seems to have enjoyed only a few years of freedom before her death. She was already in her early seventies by the time slavery ended, and a census of freedpeople in Montgomery County taken during the summer of 1865 included her among those identified as "infirm" and "unable to support themselves." At the time, Phillis was married, for at least the second time, but was not living with her husband, a sixty-six-year-old barber named Spencer Haden. This was not unusual in 1865. After emancipation it often took time for couples who had been held by different owners to establish homes together, and according to the 1865 census many of the formerly enslaved couples in the county were still living apart that summer. Spencer Haden does not appear on the 1865 census, but Phillis and her daughter Flora were living in the household of Charles Gardner, whose wife was a granddaughter of James Charlton and had inherited part of her mother's share of Charlton's enslaved workers. By 1867, Phillis and Spencer Haden were living together in their own household, along with Spencer's son, Samuel, and his family, and by the standards of the day the family was doing very well. The census taker estimated that their property was worth five hundred dollars, which was a very large estate for a Black family in Montgomery County at that time. That is the last known record of Phillis Johnson Haden, who seems to have died sometime between 1867 and 1870.[20]

At least seven of Phillis's children also lived in Montgomery County after gaining their freedom, and their histories reflect two elements already noted in their mother's. First, just as Flora may have cared for Phillis immediately after their emancipation, the siblings sometimes lived together and helped one another make the transition to lives as free men and women. Second, initially at least, the lives of Phillis's children often intersected with those of members of the Gardner family. The Gardners were a prominent family in Christiansburg with links to the Miller and Charlton families. Members of the Gardner family seem to have inherited or acquired a number of Flora's descendants following the distribution of James Charlton's estate, and several of those descendants worked in Gardner households following their emancipation.

Phillis's daughter Flora, for example, may have remained with the Gardners until her death. When her freedom suit failed and James Charlton's enslaved workers were distributed among his heirs, in 1855, Flora had passed to the estate of Matilda Charlton Miller along with "her two children (Mary Susan and Robert)." The three may then have passed to the Gardners. Charles B. Gardner was married to one of Matilda Miller's daughters, Mary, and in 1852 had been named guardian of the children of another, Emeline Miller Craig. The 1865 census showed Flora working for Elizabeth Gardner, Charles's mother, and with her were three children—Mary Jane, Robert, and Rebecca. They were not identified on the census as Flora's children, but Mary Jane and Robert may well be the Mary Susan and Robert named in 1855, and later census records suggest that Rebecca was also Flora's daughter. Two years later, the 1867 census of freedpeople identified Flora as a servant working for Charles Gardner. Robert and Rebecca were listed with her, but neither a Mary Susan nor a Mary Jane appeared on that census. In 1870, Flora married Philip Carder/Carter, another Gardner servant, and that year's federal census included the couple in the household of

Charles Gardner. Philip was working as a farm laborer and Flora as a cook, and listed immediately after Flora on the census schedule was ten-year-old Rebecca Calloway. A decade later, the 1880 federal census identified Philip and Flora Carter as a waggoner and a cook, with Rebecca Johnson, age twenty-one, listed as Philip's "stepdaughter." Together, these records suggest that Rebecca was Flora's daughter by a man named Calloway with whom Flora had a relationship while she had been enslaved. While the family was no longer living with the Gardners in 1880, they may have continued working for them because when Philip died, sometime after 1900, a newspaper article describing his passing declared that "up to the time of his death [he] had been the 'right hand man' of the members of the Gardner family and connections" and identified Flora as "another ex-slave of the family, who preceded him to the grave many years ago." What happened to Rebecca Calloway/Johnson remains a mystery.[21]

William Johnson, Phillis's eldest son, also had a connection to the Gardners. According to Montgomery County's cohabitation register, Charles Gardner was William's last owner, though he did not remain with Gardner for long after gaining his freedom. William did not appear on the 1865 census, but by 1867 he was working as a farm laborer for a man named Thomas Wilson. Living with him were his wife, Mary, and their four children and perhaps his sister Matilda, who, as described more fully below, was cooking for Wilson, and Matilda's daughter Helen. William, Mary, and their children (including their daughter Sarah, who in 1871 married Thomas Burks) all appeared on the federal censuses of 1870 and 1880, but no later evidence of them has been found.[22]

The record of Phillis's daughter Matilda is equally abbreviated. As noted above, Matilda appears on the 1867 census as a cook working for Thomas Wilson, who also employed her brother William. She may actually have been living with William because her own marriage had apparently ended recently. The Freedmen's Bureau agent who compiled the 1867 census of freedpeople in Montgomery County used a system of dots to identify women who had previously had partners but by 1867 had lost them through sale, death, or the decision not to legalize their relationship by entering it on the cohabitation register. Matilda appears on the census as such a woman with a one-year-old daughter named Helen. On a subsequent census Helen was identified as Helen Beverly, and when she married, in 1887, she named her mother as Matilda Beverly. This suggests that Matilda Johnson had been in a previous relationship with a man named Beverly but that by 1867 he had died or been sold away or the couple had chosen not to convert their "cohabitation" into a legally recognized marriage. Neither Matilda nor Helen appeared on the 1870 census, but by 1880 both were working in the household of Fleming Gardner, a brother of Charles B. Gardner. Matilda was cooking for the family, while Helen worked as a servant. That is the last-known record concerning Matilda, and Helen disappeared following her marriage to Charles Hunter in 1887. An 1844 deposition identifying descendants of the original Flora belonging to the estate of James Charlton indicated that Matilda had two children at that time, but neither was named, and discovering anything else about them has proven impossible.[23]

Nor is much known about Phillis's daughter Helen or her children. The same 1844 deposition that included Matilda Johnson and her children also identified Helen as a daughter of Phillis and indicated that she had two children of her own. Helen did not appear on the county's cohabitation register or on either the 1865 or 1867 censuses of freedpeople. She did appear on the 1870 federal census with another woman, Phillis Johnson, who at age twenty-nine was old enough to have been one of the children referred to in 1844 or to have been Helen's sister—the "little Phillis" whose sale may have been sketched by Lewis Miller. The women were living on their own in Christiansburg, where Helen was "keeping house" while Phillis worked as a washerwoman. That is the last-known reference to Helen, while Phillis—her sister or daughter, married Jonathan Bramblett in 1872 and promptly vanished from the historical record.[24]

Unlike the lives of most of her siblings, that of Mary Johnson is known in more detail, and her descendants can be followed to the present. At the time her freedom suit was finally rejected, Mary was in her late thirties and had recently married a man named Tom Brown. Mary had borne at least three children before her marriage to Tom Brown, but, as described above, they had been sold to interstate slave traders when the estate of James Charlton was divided among his heirs. Between 1853 and 1865, Mary and Tom had three daughters of their own—Eunice, Ellen, and Celia. Tom lived elsewhere, while the girls lived with their mother on the farm of Floyd Smith, where Mary worked as a cook and Eunice as a "house girl." When freedom came, Mary and her daughters remained with the Smiths at least through the summer of 1865, but by 1867 the family had moved on. According to the census of freedpeople taken that summer, the Browns were working for David Wade—Tom as a farm laborer and Mary as a laundress. The Browns never acquired land of their own, and Tom continued working as a laborer for other men, but by 1870 Mary had stopped working for other people and was "keeping house" for her own family. Mary Brown died early in 1895.[25]

Tom and Mary Brown's daughter Celia apparently died between 1865 and 1867, but her sisters, Eunice and Ellen, lived well into the twentieth century. Eunice had begun performing domestic work as an enslaved child and continued working as a cook or laundress after gaining her freedom. She never married but seems to have had six children of her own. Three of the six left few records that have survived, but the other three—Nannie, Mary, and Jennie—all became domestic workers in Christiansburg, lived near one another and their mother for decades, and produced children of their own, and descendants who remain in Christiansburg to this day. Eunice died in 1946. Her sister Ellen married John Wyatt Lynch, a railroad worker originally from Campbell County, Virginia, in 1878. The couple remained together until Lynch died, in 1932; Ellen followed a decade later. They had at least five children between 1882 and 1892, all of whom married, and through them came grandchildren, great-grandchildren, great-great-grandchildren, and great-great-great grandchildren of Ellen Brown Lynch. Through the generations, many of Ellen's descendants remained in southwest Virginia or in adjacent counties of West Virginia (see fig. 10). Others, however, moved on to Indiana, Texas, and North Carolina. And while some continued to work as domestics, others became railroad workers, municipal workers, soldiers, nurses, and, more recently, professional athletes, doctors, and financial planners.[26]

Phillis Johnson's son James also left a more visible trail in the historical record and descendants who can be identified today. Through the division of James Charlton's estate, James came to be the property of four children of the late Thomas Bowyer. The elder Bowyer, who died in 1840, had acquired a share of the estate when that belonging to John Lynch Charlton had been sold to cover a debt in 1837. The Bowyers lived on Meadow Creek, not far from Seven Mile Farm, so James may have been able to keep in touch with family after they were separated. In 1856, shortly after passing to the

FIGURE 10. Descendants of Flora at a family reunion in 2023. (Photograph by the author)

Bowyers, James married Dicie Sephas, who was also enslaved by the Bowyers, and the couple began raising a family. By 1865, they had four children—including daughters named Phillis and Flora, after James's mother and grandmother, and over the next thirteen years they had at least seven more. As a free man, James worked as a farm laborer until his death, sometime around 1900. Dicie was a laundress in 1867, but after that she left the paid workforce until James died, when she began supporting herself as a dress-maker. And the couple stayed in touch with James's family; in 1880 James and Dicie were living next door to Tom and Mary Brown, James's sister and brother-in-law. The children of James and Dicie tended to remain in southwest Virginia or southern West Virginia, though their son Joseph had moved his family to Philadelphia by 1900, and most worked as domestics, hotel porters, or laborers. Subsequent generations, however, moved to Ohio, Michigan, and New York and established themselves in a variety of blue-collar occupations as well as the ministry, dentistry, teaching, and law.[27]

Forty years after Unis Lewis first entered a Virginia courtroom and initiated her family's legal battle against their enslavement, Flora's descendants finally gained the freedom they had been seeking for so long. And like millions of other formerly enslaved African Americans, they suddenly found themselves in a new world in which they had to make lives for themselves with few resources and with little support beyond that of family and friends. In the century and a half that followed, they struggled to make the most of the freedom their ancestors dreamt of and fought for. Some succeeded more than others, but all enjoyed a degree of independence that Flora never had.

Afterword

As the years passed, Flora's descendants forgot or never learned the story of their ancestors' long struggle for freedom. None of the living descendants who have been identified thus far had any prior knowledge of their family's freedom suits. Even Janie Milton, who heard stories of slavery from a grandmother who had been born to one of the plaintiffs just five years after her freedom suit failed, recalled nothing of her family's legal challenge to their bondage in an extensive interview she recorded in 1982. This historical amnesia was not just a tragedy for the families; it was part of a broader tragedy affecting the wider population. Many Americans today have only a generic understanding of "the American slave" and know little of the individual men, women, and children held in slavery. Thus, they know few of the personal stories of the enslaved, their individual triumphs and tragedies, including their use of freedom suits to escape slavery.

Close examination of cases the cases making up *Unis v. Charlton* offers a rare window into these personal stories, but it also provides important evidence of a broader truth concerning the enslaved population in antebellum America. Enslaved men and women clearly understood significant parts of the legal system and, when they could, actively employed that system in an effort to better their lives. Unis Lewis and her fellow plaintiffs initiated their suits without the assistance of any White allies; on their own, they learned about the promise of freedom suits and the steps necessary to begin one. Then, as the legal process unfolded, they actively assisted their court-appointed attorneys in building the strongest case they could—identifying witnesses and suggesting ways to employ their testimony. And when those attorneys failed to act, the enslaved plaintiffs acted for themselves—questioning witnesses, appearing in court, and doing as much to advance their cause as the racially biased legal system of antebellum Virginia would permit. These were not ignorant, impotent creatures passively waiting for others to determine their fate. They clearly understood the parameters of the world in which they lived, and, within the restrictions imposed on them by the institution of slavery and the laws governing it, they took the initiative in every way they could in an effort to secure their freedom.

Flora's descendants recognized that rebellion against an armed, White population with no reservations about using those arms would be suicidal. Running away en masse was equally impractical, given the wide range in the age and stamina of the descendants, but if the prime-age adults ran away by themselves, they would be leaving behind, probably forever, the friends and family they loved. Facing this bleak reality, though, they did not simply accept their fate and resign themselves to perpetual bondage. They saw in freedom suits the possibility of escaping slavery without risking their lives and with a realistic chance of taking along at least some members of their families, and they acted on that possibility as forcefully as they could. The suits brought by Flora's descendants demonstrate both the unquenchable desire of enslaved individuals to gain their freedom and the determination and ingenuity with which they sought to do so.

In the end, of course, Unis and her fellow plaintiffs failed to win the freedom for which they fought so hard. Barriers built into the legal system and embedded in the culture that produced it proved insurmountable, and the plaintiffs remained enslaved until the maelstrom of war finally destroyed slavery in Virginia. Their failure to win in the courts, however, cannot diminish the significance of the effort they made. It provides a remarkable testimonial to the ingenuity and resilience with which enslaved African Americans resisted the dehumanizing institution in which they found themselves and to the energy with which they built new lives for themselves and their families once that institution finally collapsed.

❖ NOTES ❖

1865 Census	"Census Return of the Colored Population of Montgomery Co., State of Va. August 1865." Reel 198. Records of the Field Offices for the State of Virginia, Bureau of Refugees, Freedmen, and Abandoned Lands, 1865–1872. Microfilm Publication 1913, Record Group 105, National Archives, Washington, DC.
1867 Census	"Census Returns of Colored Population of Montgomery County, State of Virginia" [1867]. Reel 68. Records of the Field Offices for the State of Virginia, Bureau of Refugees, Freedmen, and Abandoned Lands, 1865–1872. Microfilm Publication 1913, Record Group 105, National Archives, Washington, DC.
Anderson Papers	Anderson Papers, MSS 38–96. Albert and Shirley Small Special Collections Library, University of Virginia, Charlottesville.
Giles	Giles County Courthouse, Pearisburg, Virginia.
Kent	Kent Memorial Library, Suffield, Connecticut.
MC Cohabitation	"Register of Colored Persons of Montgomery County, State of Virginia, Cohabiting Together as Husband and Wife on 27th February, 1866." Montgomery County Clerk of the Circuit Court's Office, Christiansburg, Virginia.

MCCH	Montgomery County Clerk of the Circuit Court's Office, Christiansburg, Virginia.
Pulaski	Pulaski County Courthouse, Pulaski, Virginia.
RCCH	Roanoke County Courthouse, Salem, Virginia.
Rockbridge	Rockbridge County Clerk of the Circuit Court's Office, Lexington, Virginia.
Smyth	Smyth County Courthouse, Marion, Virginia.
Unis v. Charlton	*Unis v. Charlton*, Montgomery County Chancery 1853-011. Montgomery County Clerk of the Circuit Court's Office, Christiansburg, Virginia. A copy of this file is also available through the "Chancery Records Index" on the Virginia Memory website.
Virginia Tech	Special Collections and University Archives, Newman Library, Virginia Tech, Blacksburg.

INTRODUCTION

1. *Unis v. Charlton*, Montgomery County Chancery 1853-011, MCCH (hereafter *Unis v. Charlton*), 132 and 416–17; Rockbridge County Law Order Book, 1846-52:428, Rockbridge.
2. Jordan, *White Over Black*; Morgan, *American Slavery, American Freedom*; Higginbotham, *In the Matter of Color*; Berlin, *Many Thousands Gone*; Parent, *Foul Means*.
3. Russell, *The Free Negro in Virginia, 1619–1865*; Breen and Innes, *"Myne Owne Grounde"*; Berlin, *Many Thousands Gone*.
4. Gross, *Double Character*, 3–4; Kennington, *In the Shadow of Dred Scott*, 117–18.
5. Higginbotham and Kopytoff, "Property First, Humanity Second," 511–40. Jacob I. Corré also discussed the legal paradox of "thinking property" in "Thinking Property at Memphis," 437–51.
6. Jordan, *White Over Black*; Wiethoff, *A Peculiar Humanism*.
7. Higginbotham and Kopytoff, "Property First, Humanity Second," 533; Higginbotham and Higginbotham, "Yearning to Breathe Free"; Schafer, *Becoming Free, Remaining Free*, 1–33; Wong, *Neither Fugitive nor Free*; Fede, *Roadblocks to Freedom*; VanderVelde, *Redemption Songs*; Twitty, *Before Dred Scott*; Kennington, *In the Shadow of Dred Scott*; Schweninger, *Appealing for Liberty*.

8. Fede, *Roadblocks to Freedom;* Schweninger, *Appealing for Liberty;* Welch, *Black Litigants in the Antebellum South,* 165–67.
9. According to the Citing Slavery Project (https://www.citingslavery.org /court_cases/20893), it was cited in fourteen decisions between 1863 and 2001; for an example of its use in discussions of evidentiary rules, see the report of the 2017 Boyd-Graves Conference at https://cdn.ymaws.com/www .vba.org/resource/resmgr/boyd-graves/2017_booklet/2017_BG_Booklet _-_Part_1.pdf.
10. *Unis v. Charlton.* Although the record today is filed among chancery cases, the charges in each case were trespass, assault and battery, and false imprisonment, and the trials were all conducted in courts of law. The file is also available through Virginia Memory at https://www.virginiamemory .com/collections/chancery/.
11. *Unis v. Charlton;* "Chap. 111—An act reducing into one, the several acts concerning Slaves, Free Negroes and Mulattoes," Leigh, *The Revised Code of the Laws of Virginia,* 1:421–44.
12. Adams and Pleck, *Love of Freedom,* 116–17; Blanck, "Seventeen Eighty-Three"; Sword, *Wives Not Slaves,* 234–41; Shelton, "Flora's Plight" and "The Long Wait for Freedom"; Harwood, "A Twisted Road to Freedom."
13. Gross, *Double Character;* Twitty, *Before Dred Scott;* Kennington, *In the Shadow of Dred Scott;* Welch, *Black Litigants in the Antebellum South;* Penningroth, *Before the Movement.*
14. Twitty, *Before Dred Scott.*
15. Thomas, *A Question of Freedom.*

1. NEW ENGLAND BEGINNINGS

1. [Montgomery County Superior Court Order Book, 1822–1830], 153, MCCH; National Register of Historic Places Registration Form, James Charlton Farm, accessed at https://www.dhr.virginia.gov/historic-registers /060-0137/; 1820 and 1830 federal censuses; "Map of Christiansburg," 1826, Montgomery Museum of Art and History, Christiansburg, VA; Kanode, *Christiansburg,* 182; Paige and Wyatt, "'The Nigh and Best Way.'" No surviving record identifies Unis as Unis Lewis, but her sons Andrew and Randall each signed a letter using that name (Andy Lewis to Francis Anderson, July 23, 1849, box 3, Anderson Papers; Randall Lewis to John Swope, n.d., *Unis v. Charlton,* 274).
2. [Depositions of Jane Burke and John Gardner], *Unis v. Charlton,* 420–24; Kanode, *Christiansburg,* 4.

3. [Montgomery County Superior Court Order Book, 1822–1830], 153, MCCH; [deposition of Fleming Gardner], *Amiss v. Robinson*, Montgomery County Chancery 1857-022, 24–25, MCCH; "James Charlton's appraisement," Montgomery County Will Book 5:41, MCCH; National Register of Historic Places Registration Form, James Charlton Farm, accessed at https://www.dhr.virginia.gov/historic-registers/060-0137/; Leigh, *The Revised Code of the Laws of Virginia*, chaps. 96 and 104.

4. Higginbotham and Higginbotham, "Yearning to Breathe Free"; Nicholls, "'The Squint of Freedom'"; Gillmer, "Suing for Freedom"; Wong, *Neither Fugitive nor Free*; Fede, *Roadblocks to Freedom*; Kennington, "Law, Geography, and Mobility"; VanderVelde, *Redemption Songs*; Whittico, "The Rule of Law and the Genesis of Freedom"; Schweninger, *Appealing for Liberty*; Thomas, *A Question of Freedom*, 1–12.

5. The original law governing freedom suits in Virginia, passed in 1795, was "Chap. 11—An ACT to amend an act, intituled 'An act to reduce into one the several acts concerning slaves, free negroes and mulattoes, and for other purposes,'" in Shepherd, *The Statutes at Large of Virginia*, 1:363–65. At the time Flora's descendants initiated their suits, the governing statute was "Chapter 124—An act reducing into one all acts and parts of acts, providing a method to help and speed poor persons in their suits," in Leigh, *The Revised Code of the Laws of Virginia*, 1:481–82.

6. Fede, *Roadblocks to Freedom*, 2–5; Wong, *Neither Fugitive nor Free*, 149–57 (quotations on 153–54); VanderVelde, *Redemption Songs*, 1–22 (quotation on 19); Higginbotham and Kopytoff, "Property First, Humanity Second," esp. 533–34.

7. Warren M. Billings, "The Law of Servants and Slaves in Seventeenth-Century Virginia"; Banks, "Dangerous Woman"; Tarter, "Elizabeth Key (fl. 1655–1660)."

8. Taylor, *The Internal Enemy*, 35–42; Higginbotham and Higginbotham, "Yearning to Breathe Free"; Nicholls, "'The Squint of Freedom'"; Whittico, "The Rule of Law and the Genesis of Freedom"; Kennington, *In the Shadow of Dred Scott*, 26; Schweninger, *Appealing for Liberty*, 291–92; "An ACT to amend an act, intituled, 'An act to reduce into one the several acts concerning slaves, free negroes and mulattoes, and for other purposes,'" in Shepherd, *The Statutes at Large of Virginia*, 1:363–65.

9. Russell, *The Free Negro in Virginia, 1619–1865*; Heinegg, *Free African Americans of North Carolina, Virginia, and South Carolina*; Higginbotham and Higginbotham, "Yearning to Breathe Free," 1242–47.

10. Steiner, *History of Slavery in Connecticut*; Greene, *The Negro in Colonial New England*, 15–49; Romer, *Slavery in the Connecticut Valley of Massachusetts*,

8–29; Carvalho, *Black Families in Hampden County, Massachusetts;* di Bonaventura, *For Adam's Sake,* 15–22; Hardesty, *Unfreedom,* 16–22.

11. Steiner, *History of Slavery in Connecticut;* Greene, *The Negro in Colonial New England,* 72–123; Melish, *Disowning Slavery,* 11–49; Miller, "The Narragansett Planters"; Adams and Pleck, *Love of Freedom,* 29–50; Carvalho, *Black Families in Hampden County, Massachusetts,* 1–11; Romer, *Slavery in the Connecticut Valley of Massachusetts;* di Bonaventura, *For Adam's Sake,* 15–22, 102, and 266–306; Forbes, "Grating the Nutmeg"; "Suffield History."

12. Greene, *The Negro in Colonial New England,* 172–90; Zilversmit, *The First Emancipation,* 7–24; Piersen, *Black Yankees,* 25–36, 145–46; Sweet, *Bodies Politic,* 60–63, 92–95, and 156–57; Romer, *Slavery in the Connecticut Valley of Massachusetts,* 31–44; di Bonaventura, *For Adam's Sake,* 16–22, 123–32, and 285–306; Adams and Pleck, *Love of Freedom,* 11–17, 29–50; Blanck, *Tyrannicide,* 24–26; Hardesty, *Unfreedom,* 16–22; Clark, "'Their Negro Nanny Was with Child by a White Man.'"

13. Sheldon, *Documentary History of Suffield,* 5–29; McDonald and Tercentenary Commission of the State of Connecticut, Committee on Historical Publications, *The History of Tobacco Production in Connecticut,* 1–6; Northeastern Friends of the Pleistocene, *A Drainage History for Glacial Lake Hitchcock;* Karmazinas, *Historic and Architectural Resources Inventory for the Town of Suffield, Connecticut,* 10–19; "Suffield History"; "Slavery in Suffield," [file] 12, IX Slaves, Kent. Details of Flora's life can only be reconstructed from depositions filed in multiple lawsuits over seventy years. Not surprisingly, witnesses disagreed on a number of points, and it is impossible to say definitively who was right. The account presented here is based on depositions filed in *Unis v. Charlton;* IX Slaves, Kent; and *Exeter v. Hanchett,* case no. 158594, Suffolk Court Files Collection, Massachusetts State Archives, accessed at https://www.sec.state.ma.us/arc/arcdigitalrecords/digitalrecordsidx.htm.

14. "Slavery in Suffield," [file] 12 and "Depositions taken in 1842 of Gustavus Austin, Hannah King, and Susan Sheldon," [file] 19, IX Slaves, Kent; [bill of sale], May 14, 1781, in *Exeter v. Hanchett,* Case no. 158594, p. 113, Suffolk Court Files Collection, Massachusetts State Archives, accessed at https://www.sec.state.ma.us/arc/arcdigitalrecords/digitalrecordsidx.htm.

15. "Slavery in Suffield," [file] 12, IX Slaves, Kent; [depositions of Abraham Rising, Sarah Nelson, Bela Spencer, and Silence Remington], *Unis v. Charlton,* 355–57, 361–62, 338–48, and 321–28; [depositions of Eliakim Pomeoy and Ebenezer Wyman], *Exeter v. Hanchett,* Case no. 158594, Suffolk Court Files Collection, Massachusetts State Archives, accessed at

https://www.sec.state.ma.us/arc/arcdigitalrecords/digitalrecordsidx.htm; Carvalho, *Black Families in Hampden County, Massachusetts,* 277. See also Blanck, "Seventeen Eighty-Three"; Adams and Pleck, *Love of Freedom,* 116–17; Hanchett, *In Defense of Captain Oliver Hanchett,* 52–59; and Sword, *Wives Not Slaves,* 234–41.

16. Sword, *Wives Not Slaves,* 234–35; Romer, *Slavery in the Connecticut Valley of Massachusetts,* 25–26; Carvalho, *Black Families in Hampden County,* 3–6.

17. [Depositions of Sally Coit, Shubael Stiles, and Abraham Rising (quoted)], *Unis v. Charlton,* 308–13, 276–81, and 355–57.

18. [Bill of sale], May 14, 1781 in *Exeter v. Hanchett,* Case no. 158594, Suffolk Court Files Collection, Massachusetts State Archives, p. 113, accessed at https://www.sec.state.ma.us/arc/arcdigitalrecords/digitalrecordsidx.htm; "Flora—Copy of judmt assigning her in service to Oliver Hanchett Oct. 29, 1781," box 14, Anderson Papers; Carvalho, *Black Families in Hampden County, Massachusetts,* 3–4.

19. Greene, *The Negro in Colonial New England,* 183–84; Zilversmit, *The First Emancipation,* 107–38; Melish, *Disowning Slavery,* 50–83; Sweet, *Bodies Politic,* 248–49; Dodge, "The Southwick Jog."

20. "Flora—Copy of judmt assigning her in service to Oliver Hanchett Oct. 29, 1781," box 14, Anderson Papers; Sword, *Wives Not Slaves,* 236–38; Blanck, "Seventeen Eighty-Three," 38–42; Hanchett, *In Defense of Captain Oliver Hanchett,* 52–59; Harper, "Slavery in Connecticut."

21. [Depositions of Mary Warner and Submit King], *Unis v. Charlton,* 329–38.

22. Zilversmit, *The First Emancipation,* 112–15; Sword, *Wives Not Slaves,* 236–41; Blanck, "Seventeen Eighty-Three," 25–29; Blanck, *Tyrannicide,* 97–104; Melish, *Disowning Slavery,* 64–65 and 95–96; Romer, *Slavery in the Connecticut Valley of Massachusetts,* 206–8; Hardesty, *Unfreedom,* 174–76; "Legal Notes by William Cushing about the Quock Walker case [1783]," Massachusetts Historical Society, MHS Collections Online, accessed at https://www.masshist.org/database/viewer.php?item_id=630&mode=dual&img_step=11#page11.

23. Zilversmit, *The First Emancipation,* 112–15; Blanck, "Seventeen Eighty-Three," 29–31; Romer, *Slavery in the Connecticut Valley of Massachusetts,* 206–22; [depositions of Shubael Stiles, Susanna Clark, Sally Coit, Sarah Nelson, Jeremiah Nelson, and Bela Spencer (quotation)], *Unis v. Charlton,* 276–81, 378–82, 308–13, 294–96, 298–301, and 338–48.

24. Adams and Pleck, *Love of Freedom,* 116–17; Sword, *Wives Not Slaves,* 236–41; Blanck, "Seventeen Eighty-Three," 38–42; Van Cleve, *A Slaveholder's Union,* 56; Blanck, *Tyrannicide,* 104–11.

25. Blanck, "Seventeen Eighty-Three," 32–38.
26. Melish, *Disowning Slavery,* 101–7; Van Cleve, *A Slaveholders' Union,* 88–89; Hardesty, *Unfreedom,* 174–76; [depositions of Shubael Stiles, John Lawrence, and Thomas Lawrence], *Unis v. Charlton,* 276–81, 213–19; Dutchess County Historical Society, *The Year Book of the Dutchess County Historical Society: 1926;* Carvalho, *Black Families in Hampden County, Massachusetts,* 277; Hooker, *Some Reminiscences of a Long Life,* 32.
27. McColman, *Descendants of Elder John Lawrence,* 1; Groth, *Slavery and Freedom in the Mid-Hudson Valley,* 1–5; Kim, *Landlord and Tenant in Colonial New York,* 3–43; federal census of 1790.
28. Groth, *Slavery and Freedom in the Mid-Hudson Valley,* 1–9; Gellman, *Emancipating New York,* 18–21; federal census of 1790.
29. Groth, *Slavery and Freedom in the Mid-Hudson Valley,* 9–19 and 44; Zilversmit, *The First Emancipation,* 118–24; Gellman, *Emancipating New York,* 15–25 and 45–55.
30. Federal census of 1790; [depositions of Massa Simpkins and John Lawrence], *Unis v. Charlton,* 177–78 and 213–16.
31. [Depositions of Thomas Stevens, William Stevens, John Lawrence, Thomas Lawrence, Massa Simpkins, and James Simpkins], *Unis v. Charlton,* 184–85, 192–94, 213–16, 216–19, 177–78, and 246–49; McColman, *Descendants of Elder John Lawrence,* 1.
32. [Depositions of William Stevens, Thomas Stevens, John Lawrence, Thomas Lawrence, and James Simpkins], *Unis v. Charlton,* 182–85, 192–97, 213–19, and 246–49.

2. BOUND FOR VIRGINIA

1. Fischer and Kelly, *Bound Away,* 74–134.
2. Newberry Library's *Atlas of Historical County Boundaries;* Kanode, *Christiansburg,* 1–2.
3. It is impossible to provide precise population data for Montgomery County before 1790, when the first federal census reported a White population of 12,394 in the county. The 1782 tax list found 1,339 White tithables in the county, but the abrupt end of this document suggests that it may be incomplete (Montgomery County Land Book and Personal Property, 1782, Personal Property Tax Lists, Department of Taxation, Library of Virginia). An online transcription of the tax list, which does not indicate its source, includes an additional 101 taxpayers, suggesting that the Library of Virginia's copy may be missing a page (https://www.newrivernotes.com

/montgomery-county-personal-property-tax-list-1782/). Wyatt, "'There Are Few More Favored Sections.'"

4. The final page of the tax list in the Library of Virginia ("Montgomery County Land Book and Personal Property, 1782," Personal Property Tax Lists, Department of Taxation, Library of Virginia), which may be incomplete, shows there were 565 slaves in the county, while the transcription on New River Notes (https://www.newrivernotes.com/montgomery -county-personal-property-tax-list-1782/) shows a total of 556. Piersen, *Black Yankees*, 146.

5. "Montgomery County Land Book and Personal Property, 1782," Personal Property Tax Lists, Department of Taxation, Library of Virginia; Fischer and Kelly, *Bound Away*, 202–7; Troutman, "Slave Trade and Sentiment in Antebellum Virginia," 419–20; federal censuses of 1790, 1800, 1810, 1820, and 1830.

6. "Montgomery County Land Book and Personal Property, 1782," Personal Property Tax Lists, Department of Taxation, Library of Virginia; Billings, "The Law of Servants and Slaves in Seventeenth-Century Virginia"; McColley, *Slavery and Jeffersonian Virginia*, 57–76; Schwarz, *Twice Condemned*, 6–34.

7. [Depositions of William Stevens, Thomas Stevens, Francis Charlton, and Henry Carty], *Unis v. Charlton*, 192–94, 195–97, 208–9, and 201–2.

8. Kanode, *Christiansburg*, 122; [undated Charlton family history], box 1, folder 8, Charlton Family Papers, Ms 1980-001, Virginia Tech; Montgomery County Court Order Books 1:260, 6:169, 18:118, 20:272, 22:372, MCCH; Ferguson, "County Court in Virginia, 1700–1830."

9. [Deposition of Jane Burke], *Unis v. Charlton*, 420–24; Allen, *James Charlton, Sr. Home*; National Register of Historic Places, Registration Form for James Charlton Farm, accessed at https://www.dhr.virginia.gov/historic -registers/060-0137/; "James Charlton's appraisement," Montgomery County Will Book 5:41, MCCH.

10. [Depositions of Jane Burke, and John Gardner], *Unis v. Charlton*, 420–24; [deposition of Fleming Gardner], *Amis v. Robinson*, MC-Chancery, 1857-022, 24–25, MCCH; [deposition of Elijah Meacham], in *Charlton v. Unis*, Virginia Court of Appeals, Ms 79–83, West Virginia State Archives, 07-010, Charleston; "James Charlton's appraisement," Montgomery County Will Book 5:41, MCCH.

11. [Depositions of Jane Burke, John Gardner, Henry Carty, and Elijah Meacham], *Unis v. Charlton*, 420–24, 201–2, and 219–20; [deposition of Elijah Meacham], Virginia Court of Appeals, Ms 79–83, West Virginia State Archives, 07-010, Charleston.

12. "Mrs. H. Charlton dower," Montgomery County Will Book 4:143, MCCH; National Register of Historic Places Registration Form, James Charlton Farm, accessed at https://www.dhr.virginia.gov/historic-registers/060 -0137/; "James Charlton's appraisement," Montgomery County Will Book 5:41, MCCH; "Jas. Charlton Sale Bill," Montgomery County Will Book 5:43, MCCH.

13. Loveland, *Southern Evangelicals and the Social Order, 1800–1860,* 219–56; Touchstone, "Planters and Slave Religion in the Deep South"; Richey, Rowe, and Schmidt, *The Methodist Experience in America,* 1:158–60; Whitt, "'Free Indeed!'"

14. "List of Official Members and Records of Quarterly Meetings, June 2, 1827 to Dec. 23, 1854" and "Register of Christiansburg Station, Roanoke District, Baltimore Conf., M.E. Church, South," [1861–85], St. Paul Methodist Church, Christiansburg, VA; "Record of Baptisms, 1859–1878" [in the Blacksburg Station], box 3, folder 1, Whisner Memorial Methodist Church Records, Ms 64-003, Virginia Tech; "Records of the Church Session, 1827," Christiansburg Presbyterian Church, Christiansburg, VA; "Records of the Session of the Blacksburg Church," Blacksburg Presbyterian Church, Blacksburg, VA; "Inventory of Membership by Race of Baptist Churches in Virginia in 1860 by County and City," in Whitt, "'Free Indeed!'" 2928–37.

15. "John Charlton Sr., Home," *Historical Inventory of Montgomery County,* [1937], Virginia Tech (this is a copy made from WPA microfilm series 509 housed in the Virginia State Library); Leitch, *Baptized into One Body,* 25–45; "Records of the Church Session, 1827," Christiansburg Presbyterian Church, Christiansburg, VA.

16. Gutman, *The Black Family in Slavery and Freedom,* 230–44; Genovese, *Roll, Jordan, Roll,* 443–50; Taylor, *The Internal Enemy,* 256–58; "List of Official Members and Records of Quarterly Meetings, June 2, 1827 to Dec. 23, 1854" and "Register of Christiansburg Station, Roanoke District, Baltimore Conf., M.E. Church, South," [1861–85], St. Paul Methodist Church, Christiansburg, VA.

17. [Deposition of Samuel Pearce], *Unis v. Charlton,* 418–20.

18. [Depositions of Henry Carty], *Unis v. Charlton,* 201–2 and 224.

19. Twitty, *Before Dred Scott,* 81–83.

20. [Depositions of Jane Burke, John Gardner, Henry Carty, and Elijah Meacham and petition of Andrew], *Unis v. Charlton,* 420–24, 201–2, 224, 219–20, and 366.

21. According to Jane Burke's deposition in *Unis v. Charlton* (420–24), when James Charlton moved to Seven Mile Farm, Flora remained at the

Meadow Creek house "until Lynch Charlton was married and who upon his marriage moved into the house and then Flora went to the Seven Mile Tree Place." John Lynch Charlton married Christiana Currin in February 1813.

22. "James Charlton's appraisement," Montgomery County Will Book 5:41, MCCH; [deposition of Fleming Gardner] in *Amiss v. Robinson,* MC Chancery 1857-022, 24–25; Andrew Lewis to Francis Anderson, July 23, 1849, box 3, Anderson Papers; Randall Lewis to John Swope, April 22, 1845, *Unis v. Charlton,* 274–75; MC Cohabitation; [list of members], Records of the Church Session [1827–1869], Christiansburg Presbyterian Church, Christiansburg, VA; [marriage license of Flora Jackson], Montgomery County Marriage Licenses, 1870:35, MCCH.

23. Troutman, "Slave Trade and Sentiment in Antebellum Virginia," 18–116; Deyle, *Carry Me Back,* 35–38; Troutman, "A 'Sorrowful Cavalcade'"; Featherstonaugh, *Excursion through the Slave States,* 36–37.

24. Wong, *Neither Fugitive nor Free,* 137–43; Delaney, *From the Darkness Cometh the Light* (quotation from 15–16).

25. [Depositions of Henry Carty and Elijah Meacham], *Unis v. Charlton,* 201–2 and 219–20; Kennington, *In the Shadow of Dred Scott,* 41–66.

3. VIRGINIA COURTS AND ENSLAVED PLAINTIFFS

1. [Montgomery County Superior Court Order Book, 1822–1830], 153, MCCH.

2. Washington, *Up from Slavery,* 8; Escott, *Slavery Remembered,* 66; Lussana, *My Brother Slaves,* 125–46; Kennington, *In the Shadow of Dred Scott,* 29–30 and 43–47.

3. Gross, *Double Character,* 42–44; Twitty, *Before Dred Scott,* 71–95; Kennington, *In the Shadow of Dred Scott,* 43–47; Milewski, *Litigating across the Color Line,* 20–24; Welch, *Black Litigants in the Antebellum South,* 27–36; Penningroth, *Before the Movement,* 3–26.

4. Montgomery County Court Order Books 17:181, 20:272, and 21:2, MCCH.

5. *Rachel Viney v. Henry Patton,* Montgomery County Chancery 1815-006, MCCH; *Rachel Viney, for her son Jupiter v. Andrew Johnston,* Montgomery County Superior Court Order Book From 1814 to No. 2:65–68, MCCH; "The Veney Family of the Northern Neck: Sarah's Story," The UnCommonwealth: Voices from the Library of Virginia, June 2, 2021, accessed at https://uncommonwealth.virginiamemory.com/blog/2021/06/02/the

-veney-family-of-the-northern-neck-sarahs-story/; "The Veney Family of the Northern Neck: Rachel's Story," The UnCommonwealth: Voices from the Library of Virginia, June 9, 2021 accessed at https://uncommon wealth.virginiamemory.com/blog/2021/06/09/the-veney-family-of -the-northern-neck-rachels-story/; Kegley, "Indian Slavery and Freedom Suits."

6. Finkelman, "The American Suppression of the American Slave Trade," esp. 436–38; Whittico, "The Rule of Law and the Genesis of Freedom," 443–45; Hening, *The Statutes at Large*, 9:471–72 and 12:182–83.

7. *Nanny Pegee v. John Hook*, Montgomery County Chancery 1807-014, MCCH; finding aid to the John Hook Papers, RL.00573, Duke University Archives & Manuscripts, accessed at https://archives.lib.duke.edu/catalog /hookjohn. Nanny Pegee's original complaint has not survived, and the jury's verdict found in Montgomery County Chancery 1807-014 mentions both the failure to take the required oath and the fact that Nanny Pegee was the daughter of a white woman.

8. *Pegee v. Hook*, Montgomery County Chancery 1807-014, MCCH; *Hook v. Nanny* (Enslaved) (alias: Nanny Pegee), Augusta County Chancery, 1809-095, accessed at virginiamemory.com; Franklin County (Va.) Judgments (Freedom Suits), 1808, local government records collection, Franklin County Court Records, Library of Virginia.

9. *Ruth v. James Sallust*, Montgomery County Chancery, 1826-005, MCCH; Montgomery County Superior Court Order Book No. 3:171, MCCH; Higginbotham and Higginbotham, "Yearning to Breathe Free," 1254–55; Sallust v. Ruth, 25 Va. 67, 4 Rand. 67 (1826).

10. Montgomery County Superior Court Order Book From 1814 to No. 2:7 and 12. Alexander Baine's will, which did emancipate Ann and Roderick, is in Montgomery County Will Book 1:299, MCCH.

11. Montgomery County "Sup Court May 1809 No. [illegible]":137, 149–50, and 164–65, MCCH. The court declared Sarah and Rhoda freed on April 4, 1806; Bob and James were bound under "An Act to amend the several laws concerning slaves" passed January 26, 1806, in Shepherd, *The Statutes at Large of Virginia*, 3:251–53. Shanklin's deed of emancipation is in Montgomery County Will Book 1:267, and his will is in Montgomery County Will Book 1:330, both in MCCH.

12. H. R. McIlwaine, *Minutes of the Council and General Court of Virginia*, 604; "An ACT to amend an act, Intituled 'An act to reduce into one the several acts concerning slaves, free negroes and mulattoes, and for other purposes,'" in Shepherd, *The Statutes at Large of Virginia*, 1:363–65; "An

act reducing into one all acts and parts of acts, providing a method to help and speed poor persons in their suits," in Leigh, *The Revised Code of the Laws of Virginia*, 1:481–82. I am grateful to one of the anonymous readers for bringing to my attention the precedent in the records of the General Court.

13. Leigh, *Revised Code of Virginia*, chap. 124; Twitty, *Before Dred Scott*, 96–125; Kennington, *In the Shadow of Dred Scott*, 67–92; Schweninger, *Appealing for Liberty*, 239–66.

14. Fede, *Roadblocks to Freedom*, 147–50; VanderVelde, *Redemption Songs*, 8–9, 17–19 (quotation on 19); Schweninger, *Appealing for Liberty*, 239–66 (quotations on 242 and 262).

15. Leigh, *Revised Code of Virginia*, chap. 124; Genovese, *Roll, Jordan, Roll*, 392 and 535–40; "List of Official Members and Records of Quarterly Meetings, June 2, 1827 to Dec. 23, 1854," Feb. 9 and May 3, 1845, and Nov. 9, 1846, St. Paul Methodist Church, Christiansburg, VA; "Negro Book," Series II: Anderson Ledgers, Anderson Papers; Montgomery County Order Book 23:167 and 243, MCCH; [order showing court costs in Smyth County], Sept. 30, 1839, *Unis v. Charlton*, 71.

16. Montgomery County Superior Court Order Book From 1814 to No. 2:69; [notice of deposition], April 15, 1828, *Unis v. Charlton*, 10–11. Economists employ a variety of methods to provide modern equivalents to historical monetary values. Based on purchasing power, Sallust's eight-dollar fine would be the equivalent of approximately three hundred dollars in 2025 (https://www.measuringworth.com/index.php).

17. *Viney v. Patton*, Montgomery County Chancery 1815-006, MCCH; Montgomery County Superior Court Order Book From 1814 to No. 2:69 and 236–37, MCCH; Montgomery County Superior Court Order Book, 1822–1830, 154–55, MCCH.

18. *Viney v. Patton*, MC Chancery 1815-006, MCCH; Montgomery County Superior Court Order Book From 1814 to No. 2:69 and 113, MCCH.

19. Three other men—John James Allen, James Francis Preston, and John B. I. Logan—may also have provided legal assistance to the enslaved plaintiffs. Allen signed an 1829 bill of exception by which the plaintiffs objected to the court's allowing James Simpkins to appear as a "competent witness" for the defense (*Unis v. Charlton*, 20–21). Preston was the recipient of an 1849 letter from the clerk of the Rockbridge County Court sent at the request of the plaintiffs' lawyer in Rockbridge County to provide Preston, who was then practicing law in Christiansburg, "the names of the defendants in certain pauper suits depending in our circuit superior court" (Samuel McDowell Reid to James F. Preston, July 6, 1849, box 3,

Anderson Papers). Logan wrote Francis Anderson about sending the daughter of Phillis—probably the plaintiff Phillis Johnson—to Rockbridge County, where Unis's case was then being heard (Logan to Anderson, June 8, 1846, box 3, Anderson Papers).

20. Root, *Sons of the Fathers,* 134–40; [sale of the estate of William Godbey], Feb. 8–9, 1833, Montgomery County Will Book 5:142, MCCH; Montgomery County Personal Property Tax Records, Library of Virginia; *Admrs. of William Ballard Preston v. William Linkous,* Montgomery County Chancery 1869-006, MCCH; federal census of 1860, slave schedule. My thanks to Talmage Stanley for alerting me to Preston's purchase of Fanny, Henry, and Tom.

21. Schweninger, *Appealing for Liberty,* 54; Leigh, *Revised Code of Virginia,* chap. 124.

22. "Andy Lewis" to Francis T. Anderson, July 23, 1849, box 3, Anderson Papers, MSS 38–96.

23. Ibid.; federal census of 1850, population and slave schedules; Montgomery County Will Book 8:515, MCCH.

24. [Depositions of John Lawrence, Henry Carty, Francis Charlton, and Henry Roope], *Unis v. Charlton,* 213–16, 224, 226, 236–37; [affidavit of Andrew Lewis], Sept. 15, 1851, *Unis v. Charlton,* 416–17. A deposition by John Draper includes the statement "question by Andrew defendant," which may be a case of the clerk mistakenly writing defendant rather than plaintiff (*Unis v. Charlton,* 234–35).

25. [Affidavit of Andrew Lewis], Sept. 14, 1849 and [affidavit of Andrew Lewis], Sept. 15, 1851, *Unis v. Charlton,* 366–67 and 416–17; Rockbridge County Law Order Book 1846–52:428, Rockbridge.

26. [Depositions of Henry Carty and Francis Charlton and affidavit of Francis T. Anderson, August 29, 1842], *Unis v. Charlton,* 224, 226, and 243–44; John B. I. Logan to Francis T. Anderson, June 8, 1846, box 3, Anderson Papers; federal census of 1850; [deposition of Fleming Gardner], *Amiss v. Robinson,* Montgomery County Chancery 1857-022, MCCH.

27. Schweninger, "The Vass Slaves"; *Viney v. Patton,* Montgomery County Chancery, 1815006, MCCH; Montgomery County Superior Court Order Book From 1814 to No. 2:133, MCCH.

4. THE TRIALS BEGIN

1. Montgomery County Superior Court Order Book, 1822–1830:131 and 153, MCCH; Montgomery County Court Order Book 23:138, 152, 167, and 243, MCCH; Kanode, *Christiansburg,* 137; *Code of Virginia* (1819), chap. 124.

2. Montgomery County Superior Court Order Book, 1822–1830:153; Leigh, *Revised Code of Virginia*, chap. 124.

3. [Complaint of Unis], *Unis v. Charlton*, 364–65; *Code of Virginia* (1819), chap. 124; "James Charlton's appraisement," Montgomery County Will Book 5:41, MCCH; Montgomery County Superior Court Order Book, 1822–1830:153–54, MCCH.

4. Montgomery County Superior Court Order Book, 1822–1830:153 and 224, MCCH; [deposition of Elijah Meacham], *Charlton v. Unis*, 26–27, Virginia Court of Appeals, Ms 79–83, West Virginia State Archives, 07-010, Charleston.

5. Montgomery County Superior Court Order Book, 1822–1830:153, 169–70, and 225, MCCH; [deposition of John McC. Taylor], *Matilda Miller etc. v. Robert Gardner etc.* and *Robert Gardner v. Matilda L. Miller etc.* Montgomery County Chancery 1846-010, 26, MCCH; *Code of Virginia* (1819), chap. 104.

6. Gillmer, "Suing for Freedom," 567–68; Schweninger, *Appealing for Liberty*, 51–69. Despite the fact that the record of these cases is now found among chancery files in the Montgomery County courthouse and in the Library of Virginia's online "Chancery Records Index," court order books make it very clear that the cases originated in Montgomery County's Superior Court of Law and were heard in law courts. Separate, and very brief, criminal files do exist for *Randall v. Swope* (series 2, No. 411, MCCH) and for *Rhoda Ann v. Wm. Currin* (series 2, No. 418, MCCH), though none have been yet found for the other two cases.

7. While there are separate files in Montgomery County for *Rhoda Ann v. William Currin* and for *Randall v. Swope* (Common Law, series 2, numbers 411 and 418), each consists of a single page: the original complaint with a few endorsements noting developments and verdicts in the case. Everything else regarding all four cases is in a single chancery file (originally 1846, no. 6; now Chancery 1853-011) that was originally, and confusingly, labeled "Andrews, Unis v. James Charlton's Adm"; (quotation from F. Johnston to Clerk of the Superior Court of Law & Chancery for the County of Rockbridge, April 15, 1843, *Unis v. Charlton*, 76–77).

8. Leigh, *Revised Code of Virginia*, chap. 124.

9. Montgomery County Superior Court Order Book 1822–1830:169–70, MCCH; Montgomery County Order Book 26:117 and 346, MCCH; "James Charlton division of lands," Montgomery County Will Book 5:262, MCCH.

10. [Account of William B. Charlton in administrator's report, Feb. 3, 1845], Montgomery County Will Book 7:230–43, MCCH. For evidence of shares

in the estate changing hands while the suits were pending, see Montgomery County Deed Book K:497 and 559 and Deed Book L:69, 237, 242, and 330, MCCH; *Amiss v. Robinson*, Montgomery County Chancery 1857-022, MCCH; and *Bowyer v. Robenson*, Montgomery County Chancery, 1858-020, MCCH. It is also possible that Andrew Lewis, a son of Unis, was hired to David Page, a carpenter living in Christiansburg. Andrew Lewis wrote a letter to Francis Anderson in 1849 (box 3, Anderson Papers) about the case and indicated that Anderson should reply to Mr. Joseph Page, Christiansburg. That seems to be William Joseph R. Page, the fifteen-year-old son of David Page (federal census of 1850; Montgomery County Will Book 8:515, MCCH). According to the 1850 census, David Page had a male slave, age forty-five, who was Andrew's approximate age. When David Page died, in 1854, neither his will nor his inventory made any mention of a slave, which could indicate that the man listed in 1850 had been hired (Montgomery County Will Book 8:515 and 539, MCCH).

11. "James Charlton settlement," Montgomery County Will Book 7:230-43 and 322-27, MCCH; "M. L. Miller settlement," Montgomery County Will Book 9:116-18, MCCH; Montgomery County Personal Property Tax Records, Library of Virginia.

12. Leigh, *Revised Code of Virginia,* chap. 124.

13. [Summons, July 6, 1826; record of petition of Randall, April 12, 1826; record of petition of Rhoda Ann, April 12, 1826], *Unis v. Charlton,* 2, 43, and 46; *Randall v. Swope*, Montgomery County Common Law, Series 2, No. 411, MCCH; *Rhoda Ann v. Currin*, Montgomery County Common Law, Series 2, No. 418, MCCH; Montgomery County Superior Court Order Book 1822-1830:231-32, 246, 263, 268, and 295-96, MCCH.

14. Montgomery County Superior Court Order Book 1822-1830: 246, MCCH; [deposition of John McC. Taylor], *Matilda Miller etc. v. Robert Gardner etc.* and *Robert Gardner v. Matilda L. Miller etc.* Montgomery County Chancery 1846-010, 26, MCCH. The Superior Court order book and the material in *Unis v. Charlton* disagree about this stage in the proceedings. The order book (Montgomery County Superior Court Order Book 1822-1830:290-91, 296, 311, and 314, MCCH) identifies the plaintiff in this new case as Unis from the fall of 1827 until mid-1829, while material preserved in the chancery file (*Unis v. Charlton,* 4-9 and 40-42) describes them as Unis, Andrew, Reuben, Cena, and Julius from the time Hannah Charlton died, in 1827. Order books were kept contemporaneously from notes taken by the clerk. Many of the documents in the chancery file, however, are copies made as the case moved from county to county. It appears that when records of the cases

were copied and sent to Smyth County, in 1832, they were edited to indicate that Andrew, Reuben, Cena, and Julius had been added to Unis's case when Hannah Charlton died, in 1827, rather than 1829, when then order book shows they were.

15. Lawyers for the plaintiffs are identified from a variety of documents and endorsements in *Unis v. Charlton*, 5, 22, 30, 40, 43, 46, 211, and 249.

16. Higginbotham and Higginbotham, "Yearning to Breathe Free," 1248–1255; Montgomery County Superior Court Order Book From 1814 to No. 2:224; Sallust v. Ruth, 25 Va. 67, 4 Rand. 67 (1826).

17. Hening, *The Statutes at Large*, 9:471–72.

18. "Forty-Five Slaves Set Free," *Liberator*, May 29, 1846; Higginbotham and Higginbotham, "Yearning to Breathe Free," 1248–55; Fede, *Roadblocks to Freedom*, 271–72; quotation from Unis & als. v. Charlton's Adm'r & als, Virginia Reports, 12 Gratt, 492 citing Abraham v. Matthews, 6 Munf. 159 [1818] and George v. Parker, 4 Rand. 659 [1826] (published in Michie, *Virginia Reports*, 17:673–77).

19. [Deposition of Elijah Meacham], in *Charlton v. Unis*, 26–27, Virginia Court of Appeals, Ms 79–83, West Virginia State Archives, 07-010, Charleston.

20. "An Act Concerning Slaves" (October 1785), Hening, *The Statutes at Large*, 12:182–83; *Unis v. Charlton*, 177–78.

21. [Record of proceedings in Montgomery County Superior Court, April 12, 1826–Sept. 19, 1829], *Unis v. Charlton*, 40–47.

22. Charlton's plea is not identified as part of any particular trial; rather it is endorsed "Wm. B. Charlton afft. April 1829 to get causes removed from Montgomery." In the text, however, he referred to "certain slaves belonging to the estate of James Charlton," which would preclude Randall and Rhoda Ann (*Unis v. Charlton*, 180–81).

23. [Affidavit of William B. Charlton], April 17, 1829, *Unis v. Charlton*, 180–81.

24. Montgomery County Superior Court Order Book 1822–1830:330 and 332–35, MCCH.

25. [Petition of Robert Craig, David McComas, Archibald Stuart, and William Ballard Preston] and [record of proceedings in Montgomery County Superior Court, April 12, 1826–Sept. 19, 1829], *Unis v. Charlton*, 30 and 40–47.

26. *Abstract of the Fifth Census of the United States*, 17–18.

27. Oates, *The Fires of Jubilee*; Freehling, *The Road to Disunion*, 178–96; Breen, *The Land Shall Be Deluged in Blood*.

28. Freehling, *Road to Disunion*, 178–96; Root, *Sons of the Fathers*.

29. [Bill of exception, Oct. 13, 1832; affidavit of Edward Hammet, May 5, 1832; and deposition of Nancy Bowyer], *Unis v. Charlton*, 38–39, 199, and 211; Giles County Chancery Order Book, 1831–1843: 21–22, and 45–49, Giles.

30. [Deposition of Henry Carty], *Unis v. Charlton*, 201–2.

31. [Notice of deposition, depositions of William and Thomas Stevens, and affidavit of John L. Charlton], *Unis v. Charlton*, 22 and 182–90.

32. [Bill of exception, Oct. 13, 1832], *Unis v. Charlton*, 38–39.

33. Giles County Chancery Order Book, 1831–1843, pp. 46–51, Giles.

34. *Compendium of the Enumeration of the Inhabitants and Statistics of the United States: As Obtained at the Department of State, from the Returns of the Sixth Census*, 36–38.

35. Smyth County Common Law Order Book No. 1 1832–1842:19, 26, 44, 57–58, 73, 99, and 104–6, Smyth; [depositions of Nancy Bowyer and James Simpkins], *Unis v. Charlton*, 211 and 249.

36. [Depositions of Henry Carty, Francis Charlton, John Lawrence, and Thomas Lawrence], *Unis v. Charlton*, 201–2, 208–9, and 213–19.

37. [Depositions of William Stevens, Thomas Stevens, and James Simpkins], *Unis v. Charlton*, 192–97 and 246–49.

38. Smyth County Common Law Order Book No. 1 1832–1842:120, 135, 155, 167 186, 199, 213, 234, 255 and 281, Smyth; [copies of court proceedings], *Unis v. Charlton*, 58–71.

39. *Compendium of the Inhabitants and Statistics of the United States: As Obtained at the Department of State from the Returns of the Sixth Census*, 38 and 168.

5. A NEW LEGAL STRATEGY

1. [Depositions of Elijah Meacham, Nancy Bowyer, and James Simpkins], *Unis v. Charlton*, 202, 211, 246–49; Smyth County Common Law Order Book, 1:281, Smyth.

2. "Andrew a pauper to John Mc. Taylor," Nov. 28, 1840, and [depositions of Henry Carty and Francis Charlton], *Unis v. Charlton*, 64, 224, 226.

3. [Affidavit of William B. Charlton], *Unis v. Charlton*, 241; Roanoke Circuit Court Common Law Orders, 1:130, RCCH.

4. [Copies of court proceedings], March 29, 1843, *Unis v. Charlton*, 72, 74–75, 78–79 (the date for *Rhoda Ann v. Currin* [p. 74] seems to have been written incorrectly as October 10, 1841); Roanoke Circuit Court Common Law Orders, 1:90, 93, 109, RCCH.

5. "D. H. Hoge's affidavit," and "Affidavit of F. T. Anderson as to reasons for not going to trial," *Unis v. Charlton*, 239–40 and 243–44 (the pages of Anderson's affidavit were digitized in reverse order).

6. Joel Hawes to Francis Anderson, Aug. 12, 1842, box 2, Anderson Papers; "Guide to the Papers of the Anderson family 1771–1952," https://ead .lib.virginia.edu/vivaxtf/view?docId=uva-sc/viu03869.xml; "Affidavit of F. T. Anderson," Aug. 27, 1842, *Unis v. Charlton*, 243–44.

7. "Affidavit of F.T. Anderson," Aug. 12, 1842, *Unis v. Charlton*, 243–44.

8. Specific details about Flora's life in Connecticut and Massachusetts were included in advertisements seeking information about her case. Neither Francis Anderson nor the author of those advertisements could have known those details on their own.

9. Joel Hawes to Francis Anderson, Aug. 12, 1842, box 2, Anderson Papers; Lawrence, *The Life of the Rev. Joel Hawes* (quotation from 343); "Frederick Douglass' First Speech in Hartford," accessed at https://www.waymarking .com/waymarks/WM153H5_Frederick_Douglass_First_Speech_in _Hartford_Hartford_CT.

10. Joel Hawes to Francis Anderson, Aug. 12, 1842, box 2, Anderson Papers; *Hartford Courant*, Aug. 5, 1842; *Connecticut Courant*, Aug. 6, 1842; "Collins, Amos M." identified in "American Abolitionists and Antislavery Activists: Conscience of the Nation," accessed at http://www.americanabolitionists .com/abolitionists-and-anti-slavery-activists.html#C.

11. "D. H. Hoge's affidavit" and "Affidavit of F.T. Anderson," both Aug. 27, 1842, *Unis v. Charlton*, 239–40 and 243–44.

12. [Depositions of Henry Carty, Francis Charlton, Anderson Howard, John Draper, and Henry Roope], *Unis v. Charlton*, 224, 226, 228–30, 234–37; Roanoke Circuit Court Common Law Orders, 1:162, 164, 165, 167, RCCH.

13. Headlee, "The Virginia State Court System 1776," 18; *The American Almanac and Repository of Useful Knowledge for the Year 1847*, 255–56; Roanoke Circuit Court Common Law Orders, 1:180, RCCH.

14. *Compendium of the Inhabitants and Statistics of the United States: As Obtained at the Department of State from the Returns of the Sixth Census*, 38 and 168; *The Seventh Census of the United States*, 257, 276, and 278.

15. Johnston to "Clerk of the Circuit Superior Court of Law & Chancery for the County of Rockbridge," April 15, 1843, and Jan. 11, 1844, *Unis v. Charlton*, 76–77 and 81–82; Rockbridge County Law Order Book, 1841–45: 245 and 316, Rockbridge.

16. Rockbridge County Law Order Book, 1841–45:304, 355, 367, and 467, Rockbridge; "Affidavit of F. T Anderson," Aug. 27, 1842, *Unis v. Charlton*, 243–44.

17. Biographical sketch of Daniel Hemenway, in "The Ledger," Litchfield Historical Society, accessed at https://ledger.litchfieldhistoricalsociety.org/ledger/students/2945; "Family School in Suffield," *Connecticut Courant*, April 16, 1842; "Depositions taken in 1842 of Gustavus Austin, Hannah King, and Susan Sheldon concerning negro woman residing in the Benjamin Scott household," Item 19, IX Slaves, Kent; Hawes to Anderson, Aug. 12, 1842, box 2, Anderson Papers.

18. Hooker, *Some Reminiscences of a Long Life*, 22, 31–33, and 338. Hooker misspelled the name and identified him as "Rev. Hemingway of Suffield," but this was clearly Reverend Hemenway (Litchfield Historical Society's biographical sketch of Daniel Hemenway, accessed at https://ledger.litchfieldhistoricalsociety.org/ledger/students/2945).

19. Hooker, *Some Reminiscences of a Long Life*, 32; "Highly Interesting Slave Case in Virginia," *Charter Oak*, June 11, 1846; [commissions to take depositions, records of court proceedings, and affidavit of John Hooker], *Unis v. Charlton*, 85–92, 95–98, 122–63, and 284; Rockbridge County Law Order Book 1841–45:406–7 and 437, Rockbridge.

20. Paxton to Anderson, March 17, 1846, and Hooker to Anderson, Sept. 4, 1849, box 3, Anderson Papers; [commission to take depositions, depositions of Shubael Stiles, Sylvester Graham, Sarah Nelson, Jeremiah Nelson, Thomas Noble, and Sally Coit, and affidavit of John Mc. Taylor], *Unis v. Charlton*, 85–92, 276–83, 290–314, and 384–85.

21. Hooker, *Some Reminiscences of a Long Life*, 32.

22. Ibid.; Snodgrass, *The Underground Railroad*, 6 and 140; [depositions of Shubael Stiles, Sylvester Graham, Sarah Nelson, Jeremiah Nelson, Thomas Noble, and Sally Coit], *Unis v. Charlton*, 276–83 and 290–314.

23. [Depositions of Sylvester Graham and Sarah Nelson and affidavit of John Mc. Taylor], *Unis v. Charlton*, 290–97, 361–62, 370–73, and 384–85; [Green], *Green's Connecticut Annual Register and United States Calendar for 1845*, 27; Hooker, *Some Reminiscences of a Long Life*, 32; Cooper, "Students of the University of Virginia, 1825–1874."

24. [Depositions of Shubael Stiles, Sylvester Graham, Sarah Nelson, Jeremiah Nelson, Thomas Noble, and Sally Coit], *Unis v. Charlton*, 276–83 and 290–314 (quotations on 315).

25. Ibid. (quotations on 279 and 295–96); [Green], *Green's Connecticut Annual Register and United States Calendar for 1845*, 27.

26. Gillmer, "Suing for Freedom," 573–78; Fede, *Roadblocks to Freedom*, 340–50; Schweninger, "Freedom Suits, African American Women, and the Genealogy of Slavery" (quotation from 60); Thomas, *A Question of Freedom*, 157–90.

27. Gillmer, "Suing for Freedom," 584–88; Fede, *Roadblocks to Freedom*, 340–50; Thomas, *A Question of Freedom*, 157–90; Queen v. Hepburn, 11 U.S. (7 Cranch) 290 (1813).

28. [Depositions of Shubael Stiles, Sylvester Graham, Sarah Nelson, Jeremiah Nelson, Thomas Noble, and Sally Coit], *Unis v. Charlton*, 276–83 and 290–314; Rockbridge County Law Order Book, 1841–45:467, Rockbridge; Paxton to Hooker, March 17, 1846, box 3, Anderson Papers.

29. "Speech of Wendell Phillips at the Anti-Texas Mass Meeting in Faneuil Hall," *Liberator*, Dec. 5, 1845. My thanks to Lee Hamberg for alerting me to this article.

30. Personal communication from Caitlin Jones, Head of Reference, Massachusetts Archives, July 24, 2023; Blanck, "Seventeen Eighty-Three," 38–42.

31. Freehling, *The Road to Disunion*, 353–452.

32. Rockbridge County Law Order Book, 1846–52:10–14, Rockbridge; "Highly Interesting Slave Case in Virginia," *Charter Oak*, June 11, 1846; federal censuses of 1840 and 1850 (1840 Population Schedule and 1850 Slave Schedule).

33. Charlton v. Unis (4 Gratt) 58–63 (published in Michie, *Virginia Reports*, 14:37–39); *Charlton v. Unis*, Virginia Court of Appeals, Ms 79–83, West Virginia State Archives 07-010, Charleston; Anderson to Hooker, April 28, 1846, printed in "Highly Interesting Slave Case in Virginia," *Charter Oak*, June 11, 1846. Another account of the case was originally published in the *Lexington (VA) Gazette*, reprinted in the *Richmond Times*, and subsequently reprinted throughout the United States. It has survived in the *Liberator* (May 29, 1846), the *Buffalo (NY) Daily National Pilot* (May 14, 1846), and the *New Orleans Daily Delta* (May 27, 1846).

34. [Marginal comments on depositions], *Unis v. Charlton*, 283, 293, 297, 303, 307, and 315.

35. [Notice of deposition], *Unis v. Charlton*, 292–93; Anderson to Hooker, April 28, 1846, printed in "Highly Interesting Slave Case in Virginia," *Charter Oak*, June 11, 1846; von Moschzisker, *Trial by Jury*, 112–17 (quotation on 114).

36. Charlton v. Unis (4 Gratt) 58–63 (published in Michie, *Virginia Reports*, 14:37–39); *Charlton v. Unis*, Virginia Court of Appeals, Ms 79–83, West Virginia State Archives 07-010, Charleston.

37. Charlton v. Unis (4 Gratt) 58–63 (published in Michie, *Virginia Reports*, 14:37–39). A slightly different version of the judge's instructions is included in the original supreme court file (*Charlton v. Unis*, Virginia Court of Appeals, Ms 79–83, West Virginia State Archives 07-010, Charleston).

38. Anderson to Hooker, April 28, 1846, printed in "Highly Interesting Slave Case in Virginia," *Charter Oak*, June 11, 1846; Rockbridge County

Law Order Book, 1846–52:13–14, Rockbridge; Higginbotham, "Yearning to Breathe Free," 1247–48; Higginbotham and Kopytoff, "Property First, Humanity Second," 530–33.

39. Delaney, *From the Darkness Cometh the Light*, 47–49.

40. *Richmond Daily Whig*, May 7, 1846; *Buffalo (NY) Daily National Pilot*, May 14, 1846; *Liberator* (Boston), May 29, 1846; *New Orleans Daily Delta*, May 27, 1846; *Charter Oak* (Hartford, CT), June 11, 1846.

41. Anderson to Hooker, April 28, 1846, printed in "Highly Interesting Slave Case in Virginia," *Charter Oak*, June 11, 1846; Rockbridge County Law Order Book, 1846–52:13–14, Rockbridge; [writ of supersedeas, Nov. 11, 1846, and bond of John Mc. Taylor, et al., March 22, 1847], *Charlton v. Unis*, Virginia Court of Appeals, Ms 79–83, West Virginia State Archives 07-010, Charleston.

42. *Matilda L. Miller v. Robert Gardner* and *Robert Gardner v. Matilda L. Miller*, Montgomery County Chancery 1846010, MCCH.

43. Sutelan and Spencer, "The Virginia Supreme Court of Appeals"; "A Short History of the Supreme Court of Virginia," accessed at https://scvahistory.org/scv/supreme-court-of-virginia/; Charlton v. Unis (4 Gratt) 58–63 (published in Michie, *Virginia Reports*, 14:37–39). My thanks to one of the press's anonymous readers for alerting me to the court's backlog.

44. Charlton v. Unis (4 Gratt) 58–63 (published in Michie, *Virginia Reports*, 14:37–39). Four copies of the appellate decision—one for each of the individual cases—are also included in *Unis v. Charlton*, 101–17.

6. BACK TO CHRISTIANSBURG

1. Federal censuses of 1830, 1850, and 1860 (according to the slave schedules, James Paxton owned one slave in 1850 and three in 1860); "Virginia Military Institute Historical Rosters Database"; "A History of the House of Delegates"; *Richmond Daily Dispatch*, Nov. 21, 1861.

2. Rockbridge County Law Order Book, 1846–52: 127–29, 131–33, 138–42, and 177, Rockbridge; [copies of court proceedings and affidavit of James G. Paxton], *Unis v. Charlton*, 128, 139–40, 149, 159, and 316.

3. Hooker to Anderson, Jan. 16, 1849, box 3, Anderson Papers; [affidavit of John Mc. Taylor and orders to take depositions], *Unis v. Charlton*, 318–19, 350, 359, and 368.

4. [Depositions of Silence Remington, Mary Warner, Submit King, Bela Spencer, Lucy Austin, Horace Noble, Abraham Rising, Sarah Nelson, and Sylvester Graham], *Unis v. Charlton*, 321–49, 353–57, 361–62, and 370–73.

5. [Affidavit of John Mc. Taylor], *Unis v. Charlton*, 389–90; Montgomery County Superior Court Order Book, 1822–1830: 336, MCCH; Giles County Chancery Order Book, 1831–1843:51, Giles; Rockbridge County Law Order Book, 1846–52: 280, Rockbridge.

6. [Affidavit of John Mc. Taylor and copy of court proceedings], *Unis v. Charlton*, 118, 129, and 384–87; Rockbridge County Law Order Book, 1846–52: 280 and 310, Rockbridge.

7. [Affidavit of Andrew Lewis], *Unis v. Charlton*, 366–67.

8. Ibid.; Gutman, *The Black Family in Slavery and Freedom*, 230–44; Genovese, *Roll, Jordan, Roll*, 443–50; Taylor, *The Internal Enemy*, 256–58.

9. John Hooker to Francis Anderson, Sept. 4, 1849, box 3, Anderson Papers; Rockbridge County Law Order Book, 1846–52:280, 310–11, and 347, Rockbridge; [affidavits of William Childress, Elijah Meacham, James Holly, and Joseph P. Edie], *Unis v. Charlton*, 392, 394, 396, 398, and 400.

10. Rockbridge County Law Order Book, 1846–52:347–58, Rockbridge; [depositions of Silence Remington, Mary Warner, Submit King, Bela Spencer, Lucy Austin, Horace Noble, Abraham Rising, Sarah Nelson, and Sylvester Graham], *Unis v. Charlton*, 321–49, 353–58, 361–63, and 370–74.

11. [Depositions of Silence Remington, Mary Warner, Submit King, Bela Spencer, Lucy Austin, Horace Noble, Abraham Rising, Sarah Nelson, and Sylvester Graham], *Unis v. Charlton*, 321–49, 353–58, 361–63, and 370–74 (quotations on 334 and 358). My thanks to Kirsten Sword for pointing out that the age and residence of Sylvester Graham, the deponent, matched exactly those of the famous reformer.

12. [Deposition of Topal O. Watkins], *Unis v. Charlton*, 402–7.

13. Rockbridge County Law Order Book, 1846–52:357, Rockbridge.

14. Ibid.: 380; Barnitz to Anderson, May 30, 1851, box 3, Anderson.

15. [Endorsement on Barnitz to Anderson, May 30, 1851], box 3, Anderson; [affidavit of Andrew Lewis], *Unis v. Charlton*, 416–17.

16. [Affidavit of Andrew Lewis], *Unis v. Charlton*, 416–17.

17. Rockbridge County Law Order Book, 1846–52:280 and 428, Rockbridge; [affidavit of John Mc. Taylor], *Unis v. Charlton*, 389–90.

18. Wicker, "Transportation"; federal censuses 1830, 1840, and 1850.

19. Noe, *Southwest Virginia's Railroad*, 11–30.

20. Ibid.; federal censuses 1850 and 1860 (agricultural schedules).

21. Craven, *Soil Exhaustion as a Factor in the Agricultural History of Virginia and Maryland*, 118–126; Beeman, *The Evolution of the Southern Backcountry*, 170–71; federal censuses 1850 and 1860 (slave schedules); Dickenson, *"Entitled": Free Papers in Appalachia Concerning Antebellum Freeborn Negroes*, xiii–xiv.

22. MC Cohabitation.
23. Noe, *Southwest Virginia's Railroad.*
24. Montgomery County Com. Law Orders No. 3:472 and 497–502, MCCH.
25. Virginia Court of Appeals, Ms 79–83, West Virginia State Archives 07-010; Charlton v. Unis, 4 Gratt, 58–63 (published in Michie, *Virginia Reports,* 14:37–39).
26. [Depositions of James Simpkins, Samuel Pearce, and Jane Burke], *Unis v. Charlton,* 246–49, 418–20, and 423–24.
27. [Depositions of Samuel Pearce and Jane Burke], *Unis v. Charlton,* 418–20 and 423–24; Abraham and others v. Matthews, 6 Munf. 159, published in Michie, *Virginia Reports,* 6:670; Higginbotham and Higginbotham, "Yearning to Breathe Free," 1250.
28. [Interrogatory order], *Unis v. Charlton,* 421–22.
29. Records of the Supreme Court of Appeals include a partial draft of the published report but nothing else (Virginia Court of Appeals, Ms 79–83, West Virginia State Archives 04-079, Charleston).
30. Unis & als. v. Charlton's Adm'r & als. 12 Gratt 484–98 (published in Michie, *Virginia Reports,* 17:673–77); "Highly Interesting Slave Case in Virginia," *Charter Oak,* June 11, 1846; [verdict of the jury], *Unis v. Charlton,* 13.
31. Unis & als. v. Charlton's Adm'r & als. 12 Gratt 484–98 (published in Michie, *Virginia Reports,* 17:673–77).

7. THE COURT SPEAKS

1. Nevins, *Ordeal of the Union: Fruits of Manifest Destiny, 1847–1852;* Nevins, *Ordeal of the Union: A House Dividing, 1852–1857,* 78–159 and 301–46; Freehling, *Road to Disunion,* 455–565; McPherson, *Battle Cry of Freedom,* 6–169.
2. Unis & als. v. Charlton's Adm'r & als. 12 Gratt 484–98 (published in Michie, *Virginia Reports,* 17:673–77). The published decision incorrectly identifies the relevant Supreme Court case as "Conrad v. Guffey"; it is actually Conrad v. Griffey, 57 U.S. 38, 14 L. Ed. 835, 16 How. 38, which was decided in February 1854.
3. Copies of three of the Supreme Court's final orders are included in *Unis v. Charlton,* 164–66. No copy has been found of that for the case of *Phillis v. Charlton's Adm'r,* but it was, presumably, issued when the others were, on August 20 or August 24, 1855. Montgomery County Order Book, Cir. Court, No. 4: 56–57, MCCH; [commissioner's report of Matilda L. Miller's estate], July 3, 1857, Montgomery County Will Book 9: 11, MCCH.

4. MC Cohabitation; *Jno Dooley and Wife v. Jane Johnson's Heirs,* Montgomery County Chancery, 1896002, MCCH; Montgomery County Court Order Book 10: 130, MCCH; "Book of Free Negroes," MCCH; federal censuses of 1850 and 1860; [deposition of Fleming Gardner], *Amiss v. Robinson,* Montgomery County Chancery 1857-022: 24–25, MCCH; [settlement of Matilda L. Miller's estate], Montgomery County Will Book 9:116–18, MCCH; Pulaski County Marriages to 1900, 1868-6 and 1874-48, Pulaski.

5. Federal censuses of 1820, 1840, and 1850; Pulaski County Will Book 1:377, 387, and 434, Pulaski.

6. Montgomery County Superior Court Order Book, 1822–1830:170, MCCH.

7. "Wm. Currin's Appraisement," Montgomery County Will Book 4: 438, MCCH; [will of Rhoda Currin], Montgomery County Will Book 7:454, MCCH.

8. Montgomery County Order Book 23: 48, MCCH; "Mrs. H. Charlton dower," Montgomery County Will Book 4:143, MCCH; [will of Hannah Charlton], Montgomery County Will Book 4:308, MCCH; [inventory of Hannah Charlton], Montgomery County Will Book 4:446, MCCH.

9. Montgomery County Order Book 26:117 and 346, MCCH; "James Charlton division of lands," Montgomery County Will Book 5:262, MCCH; [deposition of John McCandless Taylor], Sept. 27, 1844, *Matilda L. Miller etc. v. Robert Gardner etc.* and *Robert Gardner v. Matilda L. Miller etc.,* Montgomery County Chancery 1846-010:25–27, MCCH.

10. Montgomery County Deed Books K:411, 497, 531, 645; L:242; and M:187, MCCH; federal census of 1860 (population and slave schedules).

11. [Report of William C. Hagan, commissioner], July 3, 1857, Montgomery County Will Book, 9:118, MCCH.

12. [Promissory note to Joseph S. Edie], Oct. 10, 1854, folder 14—Receipts, 1850–59, Rev. Charles Alexander Miller Family Papers, Ms 1983-001, Virginia Tech.

13. [Interview with] "Janie Milton, Spring 1982, by John Nicolay," box 1, folder 38, John Nicolay Papers, Ms 87-027, Virginia Tech; [interview with Eunice Brown], Perdue and Barden, *Weevils in the Wheat,* 60.

14. Barbara Luck, "Lewis Miller's Virginia Slavery Drawings," Encyclopedia Virginia, Virginia Humanities (Dec. 7, 2020), accessed at https://encyclopediavirginia.org/entries/lewis-millers-virginia-slavery-drawings/.

15. "Miss Fillis and child, and Bill, Sold at publick Sale in May 12th, Christiansburg, Montgomery County," *Sketchbook of Landscapes in the State of Virginia,* Abby Aldrich Rockefeller Folk Art Museum, the Colonial Williamsburg, Foundation, Williamsburg, VA; [deposition of Fleming Gardner], *Amiss*

v. Robinson, Montgomery County Chancery 1857-022:24–25, MCCH; [marriage license of Phillis Johnson and Johnathan Bramblett], Montgomery County Marriages, 1872:6, MCCH.

16. MC Cohabitation; "Montgomery County Deaths, 1853–1868," 11, MCCH; [list of members], Records of the Church Session [1827–1869], Christiansburg Presbyterian Church, Christiansburg, VA; [interview with] "Janie Milton, Spring 1982, by John Nicolay," box 1, folder 38, John Nicolay Papers, Ms 87-027, Virginia Tech.

17. [Interview with] "Janie Milton, Spring 1982, by John Nicolay," box 1, folder 38, John Nicolay Papers, Ms 87-027, Virginia Tech.

18. Thorp, *Facing Freedom*, 9–17.

19. Federal census of 1870; [marriage record of Peter Lewis and Laura Keys], 1868–6 and [marriage record of William Stovall and Laura Lewis], 1874–48, Pulaski County Marriages to 1900, Pulaski.

20. 1865 Census; 1867 Census.

21. [Settlement of Matilda L. Miller's estate], Montgomery County Will Book 9: 116–18, MCCH; Montgomery County Court Order Book 33: 24, MCCH; 1865 Census; 1867 Census; federal censuses of 1870 and 1880; "They Are Getting Scarce Now," [loose newspaper article, n.d.], folder 20, Rev. Charles Alexander Miller Family Papers, Ms 1983-001, Virginia Tech.

22. MC Cohabitation; 1867 Census; [Sarah Johnson and Thomas Burks], MC Marriage Licenses, 1871: 35, MCCH; federal censuses of 1870 and 1880.

23. 1867 Census; federal census of 1880; [Helen Beverly and Charles Hunter], Montgomery County Marriage Licenses, 1887:42, MCCH; [deposition of Fleming Gardner], *Amiss v. Robinson*, Montgomery County Chancery 1857-022:24–25, MCCH.

24. [Deposition of Fleming Gardner], *Amiss v. Robinson*, Montgomery County Chancery 1857-022:24–25, MCCH; federal census 1870; MC Marriage License 1872:6.

25. MC Cohabitation; [entry for Mary Brown on list of members], "Records of the Church Session, 1827," Christiansburg Presbyterian Church, Christiansburg, VA; [deposition of Fleming Gardner], *Amiss v. Robinson*, Montgomery County Chancery 1857-022: 24–25, MCCH; [interview with] "Janie Milton, Spring 1982, by John Nicolay," box 1, folder 38, John Nicolay Papers, Ms 870-27, Virginia Tech; 1865 Census; 1867 Census; federal census 1870; [death record of Mary Brown], accessed at Ancestry.com.

26. 1865 Census; 1867 Census; federal censuses 1870, 1880, 1900, 1910, 1920, 1930, 1940, and 1950; [death certificates of Eunice Brown, John

Wyatt Lynch, and Ellen Brown Lynch], accessed at Ancestry.com; [Ellen Brown and John Wyatt Lynch], Montgomery County Marriage Licenses, 1878: 56, MCCH; personal communication with family members, July 2, 2023.

27. MC Cohabitation; federal censuses of 1860 [slave schedule], 1870, 1880, 1900, 1910, 1920, 1930, 1940, and 1950; 1867 Census; personal communication with family members, June 5, 2023.

❖ BIBLIOGRAPHY ❖

Archival Sources

Christiansburg Presbyterian Church, Christiansburg, Virginia
"Records of the Session of the Blacksburg Church"

Duke University Archives and Manuscripts
John Hook Papers

Giles County Courthouse
Chancery Order Book, 1831–43

Kent Memorial Library, Suffield, Connecticut
IX Slaves

Library of Virginia
Dictionary of Virginia Biography
Personal Property Tax Lists

Massachusetts Historical Society
William Cushing Judicial Notebook

Massachusetts State Archives
Suffolk Court Files Collection

Montgomery County Courthouse
Chancery
Court Order Books

Criminal
Deaths, 1853–1868
Deeds
Superior Court Order Books
Wills

Montgomery Museum of Art and History
Map of Christiansburg, 1826

National Archives
Records of the Field Offices for the State of Virginia, Bureau of
    Refugees, Freedmen, and Abandoned Lands, 1865–1872

Roanoke County Courthouse
Common Law Orders No. 1

Rockbridge County Courthouse
Law Order Books, 1841–45 and 1846–52
Record at Large, 1836

Smyth County Courthouse
Common Law Order Book No. 1

St. Paul Methodist Church, Christiansburg, Virginia
"List of Official Members and Records of Quarterly Meetings,
    June 2, 1827 to Dec. 23, 1854"
"Register of Christiansburg Station, Roanoke District, Baltimore
    Conf., M.E. Church, South," [1861–85]

University of Virginia—Albert and Shirley Small
Special Collections Library
Anderson Papers

Virginia Tech—Special Collections and University Archives
Charlton Family Papers
Rev. Charles Alexander Miller Family Papers
John Nicolay Papers
Whisner Memorial Methodist Church Records

West Virginia State Archives
Virginia Court of Appeals

ONLINE SOURCES

American Abolitionists and Antislavery Activists: Conscience of a Nation: http://americanabolitionists.com

Ancestry: https://www.ancestry.com

Atlas of Historical County Boundaries: https://digital.newberry.org/ahcb/

Citing Slavery Project: https://www.citingslavery.org

Encyclopedia Virginia: https://encyclopediavirginia.org

MHS Collections Online: https://www.masshist.org/mhs-collections

New River Notes: https://www.newrivernotes.com

Slavery in the North: http://slavenorth.com

"Suffield History": https://www.suffieldhistoricalsociety.org/suffield-history

Virginia Department of Historic Resources: https://www.dhr.virginia.gov

Virginia Memory: https://www.virginiamemory.com

"Virginia Military Institute Historical Rosters Database": https://archivesweb .vmi.edu/rosters/record.php?ID=142

SECONDARY SOURCES

Abstract of the Fifth Census of the United States, 1830. Washington, DC: F. P. Blair, 1832.

Adams, Catherine, and Elizabeth H. Pleck. *Love of Freedom: Black Women in Colonial and Revolutionary New England.* New York: Oxford University Press, 2010.

Allen, Emily. *James Charlton, Sr. Home: Survey Report, 1937 Oct. 10.* N.p.: Virginia Historical Inventory Project, Works Progress Administration, 1937.

The American Almanac and Repository of Useful Knowledge for the Year 1847. Boston: James Munroe, 1846.

Banks, Taunya Lovell. "Dangerous Woman: Elizabeth Key's Freedom Suit—Subjecthood and Racialized Identity in Seventeenth Century Colonial Virginia." *Akron Law Review* 41 (2008): 799–837.

Beeman, Richard R. *The Evolution of the Southern Backcountry: A Case Study of Lunenburg County, Virginia, 1746–1832.* Philadelphia: University of Pennsylvania Press, 1984.

Berlin, Ira. *Many Thousands Gone: The First Two Centuries of Slavery in North America.* Cambridge, MA: Harvard University Press, 1998.

Billings, Warren M. "The Law of Servants and Slaves in Seventeenth-Century Virginia." *Virginia Magazine of History and Biography* 99 (1991): 45–62.

Blanck, Emily. "Seventeen Eighty-Three: The Turning Point in the Law of Slavery and Freedom in Massachusetts." *New England Quarterly* 75 (2002): 24–51.

———. *Tyrannicide: Forging an American Law of Slavery in Revolutionary South Carolina and Massachusetts.* Athens: University of Georgia Press, 2014.

Breen, Patrick H. *The Land Shall Be Deluged in Blood: A New History of the Nat Turner Revolt.* New York: Oxford University Press, 2016.

Breen, T. H., and Stephen Innes. *"Myne Owne Grounde": Race and Freedom on Virginia's Eastern Shore, 1640–1676.* New York: Oxford University Press, 1980.

Carvalho, Joseph, III. *Black Families in Hampden County, Massachusetts 1650–1865.* 2nd ed. Boston: New England Historic and Genealogical Society, 2011.

Clark, Emily Jeannine. "'Their Negro Nanny Was with Child by a White Man': Gossip, Sex, and Slavery in an Eighteenth-Century New England Town." *William and Mary Quarterly* 79 (2022): 533–62.

Compendium of the Enumeration of the Inhabitants and Statistics of the United States: As Obtained at the Department of State, from the Returns of the Sixth Census. Washington, DC: T. Allen, 1841.

Cooper, Jean L. "Students of the University of Virginia, 1825–1874." https://uvastudents.wordpress.com/about/.

Corré, Jacob I. "Thinking Property at Memphis: An Application of Watson." In *Slavery & the Law,* edited by Paul Finkelman. Madison, WI: Madison House, 1997.

Craven, Avery Odelle. *Soil Exhaustion as a Factor in the Agricultural History of Virginia and Maryland, 1606–1860.* With a new introduction by Louis A. Ferleger. Columbia: University of South Carolina Press, 2006.

Delaney, Lucy A. *From the Darkness Cometh the Light, or Struggles for Freedom.* St. Louis, MO: J. T. Smith, [189?].

Deyle, Steven. *Carry Me Back: The Domestic Slave Trade in American Life.* New York: Oxford University Press, 2005.

di Bonaventura, Allegra. *For Adam's Sake: A Family Saga in Colonial New England.* New York: Liveright, 2013.

Dickenson, Richard B. *"Entitled": Free Papers in Appalachia Concerning Antebellum Freeborn Negroes and Emancipated Blacks of Montgomery County, Virginia.* Washington, DC: National Genealogical Society, 1981.

Dodge, Edward R. "The Southwick Jog." *Southwick, Massachusetts Bicentennial, 1770–1970.* Southwick Bicentennial Committee, 1970.

Dutchess County Historical Society. *The Year Book of the Dutchess County Historical Society: 1926.* N.p., n.d.

Escott, Paul D. *Slavery Remembered: A Record of Twentieth-Century Slave Narratives.* Chapel Hill: University of North Carolina Press, 1979.

Featherstonaugh, George. *Excursion through the Slave States, from Washington on the Potomac to the Frontier of Mexico; with Sketches of Popular Manners and Geological Notices.* New York: Harper & Brothers, 1844.

Fede, Andrew. *Roadblocks to Freedom: Slavery and Manumission in the United States South.* New Orleans: Quid Pro Books, 2011.

Ferguson, Isabel. "County Court in Virginia, 1700–1830." *North Carolina Historical Review* 8 (1931): 14–40.

Finkelman, Paul. "The American Suppression of the American Slave Trade: Lessons on Legal Change, Social Policy, and Legislation." *Akron Law Review* 42 (2009): 431–67.

Fischer, David Hackett, and James C. Kelly. *Bound Away: Virginia and the Westward Movement.* Charlottesville: University Press of Virginia, 2000.

Forbes, Robert P. "Grating the Nutmeg: Slavery and Racism in Connecticut from the Colonial Era to the Civil War." *Connecticut History* 52 (2013): 170–204.

Freehling, William W. *The Road to Disunion: Secessionists at Bay, 1776–1854.* New York: Oxford University Press, 1990.

Gellman, David N. *Emancipating New York: The Politics of Slavery and Freedom, 1777–1827.* Baton Rouge: Louisiana State University Press, 2006.

Genovese, Eugene D. *Roll, Jordan, Roll: The World Slaves Made.* New York: Pantheon, 1972.

Gillmer, Jason A. "Suing for Freedom: Interracial Sex, Slave Law, and Racial Identity in the Post-Revolutionary South." *North Carolina Law Review* 82 (2004): 535–619.

[Green, Samuel]. *Green's Connecticut Annual Register and United States Calendar for 1845.* Hartford: Samuel Green, 1845.

Greene, Lorenzo Johnston. *The Negro in Colonial New England.* 1942. New York: Atheneum, 1974.

Gross, Ariela J. *Double Character: Slavery and Mastery in the Antebellum Southern Court.* Princeton, NJ: Princeton University Press, 2000.

Groth, Michael E. *Slavery and Freedom in the Mid-Hudson Valley.* Albany: State University of New York Press, 2017.

Gutman, Herbert G. *The Black Family in Slavery and Freedom, 1750–1925.* New York: Pantheon, 1976.

Hanchett, Leland. *In Defense of Captain Oliver Hanchett.* Falmouth, ME: Pine Rim, 2018.

Hardesty, Jared Ross. *Unfreedom: Slavery and Dependence in Eighteenth-Century Boston.* New York: New York University Press, 2017.

Harper, Douglas. "Slavery in Connecticut." http://slavenorth.com/connecticut.htm.

Harwood, Douglas L. "A Twisted Road to Freedom." *Rockbridge Advocate,* May 2011, 49–54; June 2011, 45–50; July 2011, 41–46; and September 2011, 41–46.

Headlee, Thomas Jefferson, Jr. "The Virginia State Court System 1776—A Preliminary Survey of the Superior Courts of the Commonwealth with Notes Concerning the Present Location of the Original Court Records and Published Decisions." [Richmond]: Virginia State Library, 1969.

Heinegg, Paul. *Free African Americans of North Carolina, Virginia, and South Carolina from the Colonial Period to about 1820.* Baltimore, MD: Clearfield, 2001.

Hening, William Waller, ed. *The Statutes at Large; Being a Collection of All the Laws of Virginia from the First Session of the Legislature, in the Year 1619.* 13 vols. New York: R. & W. & G. Bartow, 1809–23.

Higginbotham A. Leon, Jr. *In the Matter of Color: Race and the American Legal Process.* New York: Oxford University Press, 1978.

Higginbotham, A. Leon, Jr., and F. Michael Higginbotham. "Yearning to Breathe Free: Legal Barriers Against and Options in Favor of Liberty in Antebellum Virginia." *New York University Law Review* 68 (1993): 1213–71.

Higginbotham, A. Leon, Jr., and Barbara K. Kopytoff. "Property First, Humanity Second: The Recognition of the Slave's Human Nature in Virginia Civil Law." *Ohio State Law Journal* 50 (1989): 511–40.

"A History of the House of Delegates." https://history.house.virginia.gov.

Hooker, John. *Some Reminiscences of a Long Life with a Few Articles on Moral and Social Subjects of Present Interest.* Hartford, CT: Belknap & Warfield, 1899.

Jordan, Winthrop. *White Over Black: American Attitudes toward the Negro, 1550–1812.* Chapel Hill: University of North Carolina Press, 1968.

Kanode, Roy W. *Christiansburg Virginia: Small Town America at Its Finest.* 2nd ed. Charlotte, NC: Jostens, 2008.

Karmazinas, Lucas. *Historic and Architectural Resources Inventory for the Town of Suffield, Connecticut.* [Hartford]: Connecticut State Historic Preservation Office, 2016.

Kegley, Mary B. "Indian Slavery and Freedom Suits: The Cases of Rachel Viney and Rachel Findlay." *Smithfield Review* 12 (2008): 87–92.

Kennington, Kelly. *In the Shadow of Dred Scott: St. Louis Freedom Suits and the Legal Culture of Slavery in Antebellum America.* Athens: University of Georgia Press, 2017.

———. "Law, Geography, and Mobility: Suing for Freedom in Antebellum St. Louis." *Journal of Southern History* 80 (2014): 575–604.

Kim, Sun Bok. *Landlord and Tenant in Colonial New York: Manorial Society, 1664–1775.* Chapel Hill: University of North Carolina Press, 1978.

Lawrence, Edward A. *The Life of the Rev. Joel Hawes, D.D., Tenth Pastor of the First Church, Hartford, Conn.* Hartford: Hamersley, 1871.

"The Ledger." Litchfield Historical Society. https://ledger.litchfieldhistorical society.org/ledger/students/2945.

Leigh, B. W., ed. *The Revised Code of the Laws of Virginia.* Richmond: Thomas Ritchie, 1819.

Leitch, Monty S. *Baptized into One Body: The First 165 Years of Christiansburg Presbyterian Church.* Roanoke, VA: Gurtner Graphics & Printing, 1993.

Lindon, Mary Elizabeth, ed. *Virginia's Montgomery County.* Christiansburg, VA: Montgomery Museum and Lewis Miller Regional Art Center, 2009.

Loveland, Anne C. *Southern Evangelicals and the Social Order, 1800–1860.* Baton Rouge: Louisiana State University Press, 1980.

Luck, Barbara. "Lewis Miller's Virginia Slavery Drawings." In *Encyclopedia Virginia.* Virginia Humanities. https://encyclopediavirginia.org.

Lussana, Sergio A. *My Brother Slaves: Friendship, Masculinity, and Resistance in the Antebellum South.* Lexington: University Press of Kentucky, 2016.

McColley, Robert. *Slavery and Jeffersonian Virginia.* 2nd ed. Urbana: University of Illinois Press, 1973.

McColman, Ora. *Descendants of Elder John Lawrence of Southwest Virginia and New England.* Roanoke, VA: O. B. M. McColman, 1995.

McDonald, Adrian Francis, and Tercentenary Commission of the State of Connecticut, Committee on Historical Publications. *The History of Tobacco Production in Connecticut.* New Haven, CT: Yale University Press, 1936.

McIlwaine, H. R., ed. *Minutes of the Council and General Court of Virginia.* 2nd ed. Richmond: Virginia State Library, 1979.

McPherson, James M. *Battle Cry of Freedom: The Civil War Era.* New York: Oxford University Press, 1988.

Melish, Joannne Pope. *Disowning Slavery: Gradual; Emancipation and "Race" in New England, 1780–1860.* Ithaca, NY: Cornell University Press, 1998.

Michie, Thomas Johnson, ed. *Virginia Reports, Jefferson—33 Grattan. 1730–1880.* 24 vols. Charlottesville, VA: Michie Company, 1900–1904.

Milewski, Melissa. *Litigating across the Color Line: Civil Cases between Black and White Southerners from the End of Slavery to Civil Rights.* New York: Oxford University Press, 2018.

Miller, William Davis. "The Narragansett Planters." *Proceedings of the American Antiquarian Society,* n.s., 43 (1933): 49–115.

Morgan, Edmund S. *American Slavery, American Freedom: The Ordeal of Colonial Virginia.* New York: Norton, 1975.

Nevins, Allan. *Ordeal of the Union: Fruits of Manifest Destiny: 1847–1852.* New York: Charles Scribner's Sons, 1974.

———. *Ordeal of the Union: A House Dividing, 1852–1857.* New York: Charles Scribner's Sons, 1974.

Nicholls, Michael L. "'The Squint of Freedom': African-American Freedom Suits in Post-Revolutionary Virginia." *Slavery and Abolition* 20 (1999): 47–62.

Noe, Kenneth W. *Southwest Virginia's Railroad: Modernization and the Sectional Crisis.* Urbana: University of Illinois Press, 1994.

Northeastern Friends of the Pleistocene. *A Drainage History for Glacial Lake Hitchcock: Varves, Landforms, and Stratigraphy: North Eastern Friends of the Pleistocene Field Guidebook.* Department of Geosciences Contribution No. 73. Amherst: University of Massachusetts, 2000.

Oates, Stephen B. *The Fires of Jubilee: Nat Turner's Fierce Rebellion.* New York: Harper and Row, 1975.

Paige, Jim, and Sherry Joines Wyatt. "'The Nigh and Best Way': The Early Development of Roads in Montgomery County." *Smithfield Review* 21 (2017): 65–79.

Parent, Anthony S. *Foul Means: The Formation of Slave Society in Virginia, 1660–1740.* Chapel Hill: University of North Carolina Press, 2003.

Penningroth, Dylan. *Before the Movement: The Hidden History of Black Civil Rights.* New York: Liveright, 2023.

Perdue, Charles L., and Thomas E. Barden, eds. *Weevils in the Wheat: Interviews with Virginia Ex-Slaves.* Charlottesville: University of Virginia Press, 1991.

Piersen, William D. *Black Yankees: The Development of an Afro-American Subculture in Eighteenth-Century New England.* Amherst: University of Massachusetts Press, 1988.

Richey, Russell E., Kenneth E. Rowe, and Jeanne Miller Schmidt. *The Methodist Experience in America: A History.* 2 vols. Nashville, TN: Abingdon, 2000–2010.

Romer, Robert H. *Slavery in the Connecticut Valley of Massachusetts.* Florence, MA: Levellers Press, 2009.

Root, Erik S., ed. *Sons of the Fathers: The Virginia Slavery Debates of 1831–1832.* Plymouth, UK: Lexington, 2010.

Russell, John Henderson. *The Free Negro in Virginia, 1619–1865.* Baltimore, MD: Johns Hopkins University Press, 1913.

Schafer, Judith Kelleher. *Becoming Free, Remaining Free: Manumission and Enslavement in New Orleans, 1846–1862.* Baton Rouge: Louisiana State University Press, 2003.

Schwarz, Philip J. *Twice Condemned: Slaves and the Criminal Laws of Virginia, 1705–1865.* Baton Rouge: Louisiana State University Press, 1988.

Schweninger, Loren. *Appealing for Liberty: Freedom Suits in the South.* New York: Oxford University Press, 2018.

———. "Freedom Suits, African American Women, and the Genealogy of Slavery." *William and Mary Quarterly*, 3rd ser., 71 (2014): 35–62.

———. "The Vass Slaves: County Courts, State Laws, and Slavery in Virginia, 1831–1861." *Virginia Magazine of History and Biography* 114 (2006): 464–97.

The Seventh Census of the United States. Washington, DC: Robert Armstrong, 1853.

Sheldon, Hezekiah Spencer. *Documentary History of Suffield in the Colony and Province of the Massachusetts Bay in New England, 1660–1749*. Springfield, MA: Clark W. Bryan, 1879.

Shelton, Regan. "Flora's Plight: A Montgomery County Freedom Suit." The Uncommonwealth: Voices from the Library of Virginia. April 22, 2015. https://uncommonwealth.virginiamemory.com/blog/2015/04/22/floras-plight-a-montgomery-county-freedom-suit/.

———. "The Long Wait for Freedom: A Montgomery County Freedom Suit." The Uncommonwealth: Voices from the Library of Virginia. April 29, 2015. https://uncommonwealth.virginiamemory.com/blog/2015/04/29/the-long-wait-for-freedom-a-montgomery-county-freedom-suit/.

Shepherd, Samuel, ed. *The Statutes at Large of Virginia, from October Session 1792, to December Session 1806, Inclusive, in Three Volumes, (New Series,) Being a Continuation of Hening*. Richmond: Samuel Shepherd, 1835.

"A Short History of the Supreme Court of Virginia." https://scvahistory.org/scv/supreme-court-of-virginia/.

Snodgrass, Mary Ellen. *The Underground Railroad: An Encyclopedia of People, Places, and Operations*. 2008. London: Routledge, 2015.

Steiner, Bernard C. *History of Slavery in Connecticut*. Johns Hopkins University Studies in Historical and Political Science, 11th ser., no. 9–10. Baltimore, MD: Johns Hopkins University Press, 1893.

Sutelan, David K., and Wayne R. Spencer. "The Virginia Supreme Court of Appeals: Constitutional Relief for an Overburdened Court." *William & Mary Law Review* 8 (1966–67): 244–76.

Sweet, John Wood. *Bodies Politic: Negotiating Race in the American North, 1730–1830*. Baltimore, MD: Johns Hopkins University Press, 2003.

Sword, Kirsten. *Wives Not Slaves: Patriarchy and Modernity in the Age of Revolutions*. Chicago: University of Chicago Press, 2021.

Tarter, Brent. "Elizabeth Key (fl. 1655–1660)." In *Encyclopedia Virginia*. https://encyclopediavirginia.org/entries/key-elizabeth-fl-1655-1660/.

Taylor, Alan. *The Internal Enemy: Slavery and War in Virginia, 1772–1832*. New York: Norton, 2013.

Thomas, William G., III. *A Question of Freedom: The Families Who Challenged Slavery from the Nation's Founding to the Civil War.* New Haven, CT: Yale University Press, 2020.

Thorp, Daniel B. *Facing Freedom: An African American Community in Virginia from Reconstruction to Jim Crow.* Charlottesville: University of Virginia Press, 2017.

Touchstone, Blake. "Planters and Slave Religion in the Deep South." In *Masters and Slaves in the House of the Lord: Race and Religion in the American South,* edited by John B. Boles. Lexington: University Press of Kentucky, 1988.

Troutman, Philip D. "Slave Trade and Sentiment in Antebellum Virginia." Ph.D. diss., University of Virginia, 2000.

———. "A 'Sorrowful Cavalcade': Enslaved Migration through Appalachian Virginia." *Smithfield Review* 5 (2001): 23–45.

Twitty, Anne. *Before Dred Scott: Slavery and Legal Culture in the American Confluence, 1787–1857.* New York: Cambridge University Press, 2016.

Van Cleve, George William. *A Slaveholder's Union: Slavery, Politics, and the Constitution in the Early American Republic.* Chicago: University of Chicago Press, 2010.

VanderVelde, Lea. *Redemption Songs: Suing for Freedom before Dred Scott.* New York: Oxford University Press, 2014.

von Moschzisker, Robert. *Trial by Jury: A Brief Review of Its Origin, Development and Merits and Practical Discussions on Actual Conduct of Jury Trials.* Philadelphia: Geo. T. Bisel, 1922.

Washington, Booker T. *Up from Slavery: An Autobiography.* 1901. Williamstown, MA: Corner House, 1971.

Welch, Kimberly M. *Black Litigants in the Antebellum South.* Chapel Hill: University of North Carolina Press, 2018.

Whitt, R. Michael "'Free Indeed!': Trials and Triumphs of Enslaved and Freedmen in Antebellum Virginia." *Virginia Baptist Register* 50 (2011): 2783–937.

Whittico, Gloria. "The Rule of Law and the Genesis of Freedom: A Survey of Selected Virginia County Court Freedom Suits (1723–1800)." *Alabama Civil Rights & Civil Liberties Law Review* 9 (2018): 407–72.

Wicker, Su Clauson. "Transportation: The Train Age to the Technology Age." In *Virginia's Montgomery County,* edited by Mary Elizabeth Lindon. Christiansburg, VA: Montgomery Museum and Lewis Miller Regional Art Center, 2009.

Wiethoff, William E. *A Peculiar Humanism: The Judicial Advocacy of Slavery in High Courts of the Old South, 1820–1850.* Athens: University of Georgia Press, 1996.

Wong, Edlie L. *Neither Fugitive nor Free: Atlantic Slavery, Freedom Suits, and the Legal Culture of Travel.* New York: New York University Press, 2009.

Wyatt, Sherry Joines. "'There Are Few More Favored Sections': A History of Agriculture in Montgomery County." In *Virginia's Montgomery County,* edited by Mary Elizabeth Lindon. Christiansburg, VA: Montgomery Museum and Lewis Miller Regional Art Center, 2009.

Zilversmit, Arthur. *The First Emancipation: The Abolition of Slavery in the North.* Chicago: University of Chicago Press, 1967.

❖ INDEX ❖

Recent books in

THE AMERICAN SOUTH SERIES